SEP 2008
WI

Grzimek's

Student Animal Life Resource

••••

grzimek's
Student Animal Life Resource

• • • •

Mammals
volume 2

Hedgehogs to Bats

THOMSON

GALE

Detroit • New York • San Francisco • San Diego • New Haven, Conn. • Waterville, Maine • London • Munich

Grzimek's Student Animal Life Resource
Mammals

Project Editor
Melissa C. McDade

Editorial
Julie L. Carnagie, Madeline Harris,
Elizabeth Manar, Heather Price

Indexing Services
Synapse, the Knowledge Link
Corporation

Rights and Acquisitions
Sheila Spencer, Mari Masalin-Cooper

Imaging and Multimedia
Randy Bassett, Michael Logusz, Dan
Newell, Chris O'Bryan, Robyn Young

Product Design
Tracey Rowens, Jennifer Wahi

Composition
Evi Seoud, Mary Beth Trimper

Manufacturing
Wendy Blurton, Dorothy Maki

LIBRARY OF CONGRESS CATALOGING-IN-PUBLICATION DATA

Grzimek's student animal life resource. Mammals / Melissa C. McDade, project
editor.
    p. cm.
  Includes bibliographical references and index.
  ISBN 0-7876-9183-6 (set hardcover : alk. paper) — ISBN 0-7876-9184-4
(volume 1) — ISBN 0-7876-9185-2 (volume 2) — ISBN 0-7876-9187-9 (volume 3)
— ISBN 0-7876-9188-7 (volume 4) — ISBN 0-7876-9234-4 (volume 5)
  1. Mammals—Juvenile literature. I. Grzimek, Bernhard. II. McDade, Melissa C.
QL703.G79 2005
599—dc22   2004015604

ISBN 0-7876-9402-9 (21-vol set), ISBN 0-7876-9183-6 (Mammals set),
ISBN 0-7876-9184-4 (v.1), ISBN 0-7876-9185-2 (v.2), ISBN 0-7876-9187-9 (v.3),
ISBN 0-7876-9188-7 (v.4), ISBN 0-7876-9234-4 (v.5)

This title is also available as an e-book
Contact your Thomson Gale sales representative for ordering information.

Printed in Canada
10 9 8 7 6 5 4 3 2 1

Contents

MAMMALS: VOLUME 3

Reader's Guide

Grzimek's Student Animal Life Resource: Mammals offers readers comprehensive and easy-to-use information on Earth's mammals. Entries are arranged by taxonomy, the science through which living things are classified into related groups. Order entries provide an overview of a group of families, and family entries provide an overview of a particular family. Each entry includes sections on physical characteristics; geographic range; habitat; diet; behavior and reproduction; animals and people; and conservation status. Family entries are followed by one or more species accounts with the same information as well as a range map and photo or illustration for each species. Entries conclude with a list of books, periodicals, and Web sites that may be used for further research.

ADDITIONAL FEATURES

Each volume of *Grzimek's Student Animal Life Resource: Mammals* includes a pronunciation guide for scientific names, a glossary, an overview of Mammals, a list of species in the set by biome, a list of species by geographic location, and an index. The set has 540 full-color maps, photos, and illustrations to enliven the text, and sidebars provide additional facts and related information.

NOTES

The classification of animals into orders, families, and even species is not a completed exercise. As researchers learn more about animals and their relationships, classifications may change. In some cases, researchers do not agree on how or whether to make a change. For this reason, the heading "Number of species" in the introduction of an entry may read "About 36 species" or "34 to 37 species." It is not a question of whether some animals exist or not, but a question of how they are classified. Some researchers are more likely to "lump" animals into the same species classification, while others may "split" animals into separate species.

Grzimek's Student Animal Life Resource: Mammals has standardized information in the Conservation Status section. The IUCN Red List provides the world's most comprehensive inventory of the global conservation status of plants and animals. Using a set of criteria to evaluate extinction risk, the IUCN recognizes the following categories: Extinct, Extinct in the Wild, Critically Endangered, Endangered, Vulnerable, Conservation Dependent, Near Threatened, Least Concern, and Data Deficient. These terms are defined where they are used in the text, but for a complete explanation of each category, visit the IUCN web page at http://www.iucn.org/themes/ssc/redlists/RLcats2001booklet.html.

ACKNOWLEDGEMENTS

Special thanks are due for the invaluable comments and suggestions provided by the *Grzimek's Student Animal Life Resource: Mammals* advisors:

- Mary Alice Anderson, Media Specialist, Winona Middle School, Winona, Minnesota
- Thane Johnson, Librarian, Oklahoma City Zoo, Oklahoma City, Oklahoma
- Debra Kachel, Media Specialist, Ephrata Senior High School, Ephrata, Pennsylvania
- Nina Levine, Media Specialist, Blue Mountain Middle School, Courtlandt Manor, New York
- Ruth Mormon, Media Specialist, The Meadows School, Las Vegas, Nevada

COMMENTS AND SUGGESTIONS

We welcome your comments on *Grzimek's Student Animal Life Resource: Mammals* and suggestions for future editions of this work. Please write: Editors, *Grzimek's Student Animal Life Resource: Mammals*, U•X•L, 27500 Drake Rd., Farmington Hills, Michigan 48331-3535; call toll free: 1-800-877-4253; fax: 248-699-8097; or send e-mail via www.gale.com.

Pronunciation Guide for Scientific Names

Abrocoma cinerea AB-ruh-KOH-muh sin-EAR-ee-uh

Abrocomidae ab-ruh-KOH-muh-dee

Acomys cahirinus ak-OH-meez kay-hih-RYE-nuhs

Acrobates pygmaeus ak-CROW-bah-teez pig-MEE-uhs

Acrobatidae ak-crow-BAH-tuh-dee

Agouti paca ah-GOO-tee PAY-cuh

Agoutidae ah-GOO-tuh-dee

Ailuropoda melanoleuca AYE-lur-uh-POD-uh MEL-uh-noh-LYOO-kuh

Ailurus fulgens AYE-lur-uhs FULL-jens

Alces alces AL-ceez AL-ceez

Alouatta seniculus ah-loo-AH-tuh se-NIH-kul-uhs

Anomaluridae ah-nuh-mah-LOOR-uh-dee

Anomalurus derbianus ah-nuh-MAH-loor-uhs der-BEE-an-uhs

Antilocapra americana AN-til-uh-KAP-ruh uh-mer-uh-KAN-uh

Antilocapridae an-til-uh-KAP-ruh-dee

Antrozous pallidus an-tro-ZOH-uhs PAL-uh-duhs

Aotidae ay-OH-tuh-dee

Aotus trivirgatus ay-OH-tuhs try-VER-gah-tuhs

Aplodontia rufa ap-loh-DON-shuh ROO-fah

Aplodontidae ap-loh-DON-tuh-dee

Arctocephalus gazella ARK-tuh-SEFF-uh-luhs guh-ZELL-uh

Artiodactyla AR-tee-uh-DAK-til-uh

Asellia tridens ah-SELL-ee-uh TRY-denz

Ateles geoffroyi ah-TELL-eez JEFF-roy-eye

Atelidae ah-TELL-uh-dee

Babyrousa babyrussa bah-bee-ROO-suh bah-bee-ROO-suh

Balaena mysticetus bah-LEE-nuh mis-tuh-SEE-tuhs

Balaenidae bah-LEE-nuh-dee

Balaenoptera acutorostrata bah-lee-NOP-teh-ruh uh-KYOOT-uh-ROS-trah-tuh

Balaenoptera musculus bah-lee-NOP-teh-ruh muhs-KU-luhs

Balaenopteridae bah-lee-nop-TEH-ruh-dee

Barbastella barbastellus bar-buh-STELL-uh bar-buh-STELL-uhs

Bathyergidae bath-ih-ER-juh-dee

Bettongia tropica bee-ton-JEE-uh TROP-ik-uh

Bison bison BI-sun BI-sun

Bovidae BOH-vuh-dee

Bradypodidae brad-ih-POD-uh-dee

Bradypus variegatus BRAD-ih-puhs vair-ee-uh-GAH-tuhs

Bubalus bubalis BYOO-bal-uhs BYOO-bal-is

Burramyidae bur-ruh-MY-uh-dee

Cacajao calvus KA-ka-jah-oh KAL-vuhs

Caenolestes fuliginosus kee-NOH-less-teez fyoo-li-JEH-noh-suhs

Caenolestidae kee-noh-LESS-tuh-dee

Callicebus personatus kal-luh-SEE-buhs per-SON-ah-tuhs

Callimico goeldii kal-luh-MEE-koh geel-DEE-eye

Callitrichidae kal-luh-TRIK-uh-dee

Camelidae kam-EL-uh-dee

Camelus dromedarius KAM-el-uhs drom-uh-DARE-ee-uhs

Canidae KAN-uh-dee

Canis lupus KAN-is LYOO-puhs

Caperea marginata kay-per-EE-uh mar-JIN-ah-tuh

Capricornis sumatraensis kap-rih-KOR-nis soo-mah-TREN-sis

Capromyidae kap-roh-MY-uh-dee

Capromys pilorides KAP-roh-meez pi-LOH-ruh-deez

Carnivora kar-NIH-voh-ruh

Castor canadensis KAS-tor kan-uh-DEN-sis

Castoridae kas-TOR-uh-dee

Caviidae kave-EYE-uh-dee

Cebidae SEE-buh-dee

Cebuella pygmaea see-boo-ELL-uh pig-MEE-uh

Cebus capucinus SEE-buhs kap-oo-CHIN-uhs

Cebus olivaceus SEE-buhs ah-luh-VAY-see-uhs

Ceratotherium simum suh-rah-tuh-THER-ee-um SIM-um

Cercartetus nanus ser-kar-TEE-tuhs NAN-uhs

Cercopithecidae ser-koh-pith-EEK-uh-dee

Cervidae SER-vuh-dee

Cervus elaphus SER-vuhs EL-laff-uhs

Cetacea sih-TAY-she-uh

Cheirogaleidae KY-roh-GAL-uh-dee

Cheiromeles torquatus ky-ROH-mel-eez TOR-kwah-tuhs

Chinchilla lanigera chin-CHILL-uh la-NIJ-er-uh

Chinchillidae chin-CHILL-uh-dee

Chironectes minimus ky-roh-NECK-teez MIN-ih-muhs

Chiroptera ky-ROP-ter-uh

Chlamyphorus truncatus klam-EE-for-uhs TRUN-kah-tuhs

Choloepus hoffmanni koh-LEE-puhs HOFF-man-eye

Chrysochloridae krih-soh-KLOR-uh-dee

Chrysocyon brachyurus krih-SOH-sigh-on bra-kee-YOOR-uhs

Civettictis civetta sih-VET-tick-tis SIH-vet-uh

Coendou prehensilis SEEN-doo prih-HEN-sil-is

Condylura cristata KON-dih-LUR-uh KRIS-tah-tuh

Connochaetes gnou koh-nuh-KEE-teez NEW

Craseonycteridae kras-ee-oh-nick-TER-uh-dee

Craseonycteris thonglongyai kras-ee-oh-NICK-ter-is thong-LONG-ee-aye

Cricetomys gambianus kry-see-TOH-meez GAM-bee-an-uhs

Cricetus cricetus kry-SEE-tuhs kry-SEE-tuhs

Crocuta crocuta kroh-CUE-tuh kroh-CUE-tuh

Cryptomys damarensis krip-TOH-meez DAM-are-en-sis

Cryptoprocta ferox krip-TOH-prok-tuh FAIR-oks

Cryptotis parva krip-TOH-tis PAR-vuh

Ctenodactylidae ten-oh-dak-TIL-uh-dee

Ctenomyidae ten-oh-MY-uh-dee

Ctenomys pearsoni TEN-oh-meez PEAR-son-eye

Cyclopes didactylus SIGH-kluh-peez die-DAK-til-uhs

Cynocephalidae sigh-nuh-seff-UH-luh-dee

Cynocephalus variegatus sigh-nuh-SEFF-uh-luhs VAIR-ee-uh-GAH-tus

Cynomys ludovicianus SIGH-no-mees LOO-doh-vih-SHE-an-uhs

Dasypodidae das-ih-POD-uh-dee

Dasyprocta punctata das-IH-prok-tuh PUNK-tah-tuh

Dasyproctidae das-ih-PROK-tuh-dee

Dasypus novemcinctus DAS-ih-puhs noh-VEM-sink-tuhs

Dasyuridae das-ih-YOOR-uh-dee

Dasyuromorphia das-ih-yoor-oh-MOR-fee-uh

Daubentoniidae daw-ben-tone-EYE-uh-dee

Daubentonia madagascariensis daw-ben-TONE-ee-uh mad-uh-GAS-kar-EE-en-sis

Delphinapterus leucas del-fin-AP-ter-uhs LYOO-kuhs

Delphinidae del-FIN-uh-dee

Dendrohyrax arboreus den-droh-HI-raks are-BOHR-ee-uhs

Dendrolagus bennettianus den-droh-LAG-uhs BEN-net-EE-an-uhs

Dermoptera der-MOP-ter-uh

Desmodus rotundus dez-MOH-duhs ROH-tun-duhs

Dicerorhinus sumatrensis die-ser-uh-RHY-nuhs soo-mah-TREN-sis

Didelphidae die-DELF-uh-dee

Didelphimorphia die-delf-uh-MOR-fee-uh

Didelphis virginiana DIE-delf-is ver-JIN-ee-an-uh

Dinomyidae die-noh-MY-uh-dee

Dinomys branickii DIE-noh-meez BRAN-ick-ee-eye

Dipodidae dih-POD-uh-dee

Dipodomys ingens dih-puh-DOH-meez IN-jenz

Diprotodontia dih-pro-toh-DON-she-uh

Dipus sagitta DIH-puhs SAJ-it-tuh

Dolichotis patagonum doll-ih-KOH-tis pat-uh-GOH-num

Dromiciops gliroides droh-MISS-ee-ops gli-ROY-deez

Dugong dugon DOO-gong DOO-gon

Dugongidae doo-GONG-uh-dee

Echimyidae ek-ih-MY-uh-dee

Echinosorex gymnura EH-ky-noh-SORE-eks JIM-nyoor-uh

Echymipera rufescens ek-ee-MIH-per-uh ROO-fehs-sens

Ectophylla alba ek-toh-FILE-luh AHL-buh

Elephantidae el-uh-FAN-tuh-dee

Elephas maximus EL-uh-fuhs MAX-im-uhs

Emballonuridae em-bal-lun-YOOR-uh-dee

Equidae EK-wuh-dee

Equus caballus przewalskii EK-wuhs CAB-uh-luhs prez-VAL-skee-eye

Equus grevyi EK-wuhs GREH-vee-eye

Equus kiang EK-wuhs KY-an

Eremitalpa granti er-uh-MIT-ahl-puh GRAN-tie

Erethizon dorsatum er-uh-THY-zun DOR-sah-tum

Erethizontidae er-uh-thy-ZUN-tuh-dee

Erinaceidae er-ih-nay-SIGH-dee

Erinaceus europaeus er-ih-NAY-shuhs yoor-uh-PEE-uhs

Eschrichtiidae ess-rick-TIE-uh-dee

Eschrichtius robustus ess-RICK-shuhs roh-BUHS-tuhs

Eubalaena glacialis yoo-bah-LEE-nuh glay-SHE-al-is

Felidae FEE-luh-dee

Furipteridae fur-ip-TER-uh-dee

Galagidae gal-AG-uh-dee

Galago senegalensis GAL-ag-oh sen-ih-GAHL-en-sis

Galidia elegans ga-LID-ee-uh EL-uh-ganz

Gazella thomsonii guh-ZELL-uh TOM-son-ee-eye

Genetta genetta JIN-eh-tuh JIN-eh-tuh

Geomyidae gee-oh-MY-uh-dee

Giraffa camelopardalis JIH-raf-uh KAM-el-uh-PAR-dal-is

Giraffidae jih-RAF-uh-dee

Glaucomys volans glo-KOH-meez VOH-lans

Glossophaga soricina glos-SUH-fag-uh sore-ih-SEE-nuh

Gorilla gorilla guh-RILL-uh guh-RILL-uh

Hemicentetes semispinosus hemi-sen-TEE-teez semi-PINE-oh-suhs

Herpestidae her-PES-tuh-dee

Heterocephalus glaber HEH-tuh-roh-SEFF-uh-luhs GLAH-ber

Heteromyidae HEH-tuh-roh-MY-uh-dee

Hexaprotodon liberiensis hek-suh-PRO-tuh-don lye-BEER-ee-en-sis

Hippopotamidae HIP-poh-pot-UH-muh-dee

Hippopotamus amphibius HIP-poh-POT-uh-muhs am-FIB-ee-uhs

Hipposideridae HIP-poh-si-DER-uh-dee

Hominidae hom-IN-uh-dee

Homo sapiens HOH-moh SAY-pee-enz

Hyaenidae hi-EE-nuh-dee

Hydrochaeridae hi-droh-KEE-ruh-dee

Hydrochaeris hydrochaeris hi-droh-KEE-ris hi-droh-KEE-ris

Hydrodamalis gigas hi-droh-DAM-uhl-is JEE-guhs

Hylobates lar hi-loh-BAY-teez lahr

Hylobates pileatus hi-loh-BAY-teez pie-LEE-ah-tuhs

Hylobatidae hi-loh-BAY-tuh-dee

Hylochoerus meinertzhageni hi-loh-KEE-ruhs MINE-ertz-hah-gen-eye

Hyperoodon ampullatus hi-per-OH-uh-don am-PUH-lah-tuhs

Hypsiprymnodontidae HIP-see-PRIM-nuh-DON-shuh-dee

Hypsiprymnodon moschatus hip-see-PRIM-nuh-don MOS-kah-tuhs

Hyracoidea HI-rah-koy-DEE-uh

Hystricidae hiss-TRIK-uh-dee

Hystrix africaeaustralis HISS-triks AF-rik-ee-au-STRA-lis

Hystrix indica HISS-triks IN-dik-uh

Indri indri IN-dri IN-dri

Indriidae in-DRY-uh-dee

Inia geoffrensis in-EE-uh JEFF-ren-sis

Iniidae in-EYE-uh-dee

Insectivora IN-sek-TIV-uh-ruh

Kerodon rupestris KER-uh-don ROO-pes-tris

Kogia breviceps koh-JEE-uh BREV-ih-seps

Lagomorpha LAG-uh-MOR-fuh

Lagothrix lugens LAG-uh-thriks LU-jens

Lama glama LAH-muh GLAH-muh

Lama pacos LAH-muh PAY-kuhs

Lemmus lemmus LEM-muhs LEM-muhs

Lemur catta LEE-mer KAT-tuh

Lemur coronatus LEE-mer KOR-roh-nah-tuhs

Lemuridae lee-MYOOR-uh-dee

Lepilemur leucopus lep-uh-LEE-mer LYOO-koh-puhs

Lepilemur ruficaudatus lep-uh-LEE-mer ROO-fee-KAW-dah-tuhs

Lepilemuridae LEP-uh-lee-MOOR-uh-dee

Leporidae lep-OR-uh-dee

Lepus americanus LEP-uhs uh-mer-uh-KAN-uhs

Lepus timidus LEP-uhs TIM-id-uhs

Lipotes vexillifer lip-OH-teez veks-ILL-uh-fer

Lipotidae lip-OH-tuh-dee

Lorisidae lor-IS-uh-dee

Loxodonta africana LOK-suh-DON-tuh AF-rih-kan-uh

Loxodonta cyclotis LOK-suh-DON-tuh SIGH-klo-tis

Lutra lutra LOO-truh LOO-truh

Lynx rufus LINKS ROO-fuhs

Macaca mulatta muh-KAY-kuh MYOO-lah-tuh

Macroderma gigas ma-CROW-der-muh JEE-guhs

Macropodidae ma-crow-POD-uh-dee

Macropus giganteus ma-CROW-puhs jy-GAN-tee-uhs

Macropus rufus ma-CROW-puhs ROO-fuhs

Macroscelidea MA-crow-sel-uh-DEE-uh

Macroscelididae MA-crow-sel-UH-duh-dee

Macrotis lagotis ma-CROW-tis la-GO-tis

Macrotus californicus ma-CROW-tuhs kal-uh-FORN-uh-kuhs

Madoqua kirkii ma-DOH-kwah KIRK-ee-eye

Mandrillus sphinx man-DRILL-uhs SFINKS

Manidae MAN-uh-dee

Manis temminckii MAN-is TEM-ink-ee-eye

Marmota marmota MAR-mah-tuh MAR-mah-tuh

Massoutiera mzabi mas-soo-TEE-er-uh ZA-bye

Megadermatidae meg-uh-der-MUH-tuh-dee

Megalonychidae meg-uh-loh-NICK-uh-dee

Megaptera novaeangliae meg-uh-TER-uh NOH-vee-ANG-lee-dee

Meles meles MEL-eez MEL-eez

Mephitis mephitis MEF-it-is MEF-it-is

Microbiotheria my-crow-bio-THER-ee-uh

Microbiotheriidae my-crow-bio-ther-EYE-uh-dee

Microcebus rufus my-crow-SEE-buhs ROO-fuhs

Micropteropus pusillus my-crop-TER-oh-puhs pyoo-SILL-uhs

Miniopterus schreibersi min-ee-OP-ter-uhs shry-BER-seye

Mirounga angustirostris MIR-oon-guh an-GUHS-tih-ROS-tris

Molossidae mol-OS-suh-dee

Monachus schauinslandi MON-ak-uhs SHOU-inz-land-eye

Monodon monoceros MON-uh-don mon-UH-ser-uhs

Monodontidae mon-uh-DON-shuh-dee

Monotremata mon-uh-TREEM-ah-tuh

Mormoopidae mor-moh-UP-uh-dee

Moschus moschiferus MOS-kuhs mos-KIF-er-uhs

Muntiacus muntjak mun-SHE-uh-kuhs MUNT-jak

Muridae MUR-uh-dee

Mustela erminea MUS-tuh-luh er-MIN-ee-uh

Mustelidae mus-TUH-luh-dee

Myocastor coypus MY-oh-KAS-tor COI-puhs

Myocastoridae MY-oh-kas-TOR-uh-dee

Myotis lucifugus my-OH-tis loo-SIFF-ah-guhs

Myoxidae my-OKS-uh-dee

Myoxus glis MY-oks-uhs GLIS

Myrmecobiidae mur-mih-koh-BYE-uh-dee

Myrmecobius fasciatus mur-mih-KOH-bee-uhs fah-SHE-ah-tuhs

Myrmecophaga tridactyla mur-mih-KOH-fag-uh try-DAK-til-uh

Myrmecophagidae mur-mih-koh-FAJ-uh-dee

Mystacina tuberculata miss-tih-SEE-nuh too-ber-KYOO-lah-tuh

Mystacinidae miss-tih-SEE-nuh-dee

Myzopoda aurita my-zoh-POD-uh OR-it-uh

Myzopodidae my-zoh-POD-uh-dee

Nasalis larvatus NAY-zal-is LAR-vah-tuhs

Natalidae nay-TAL-uh-dee

Natalus stramineus NAY-tal-uhs struh-MIN-ee-uhs

Neobalaenidae nee-oh-bah-LEE-nuh-dee

Noctilio leporinus nok-TIHL-ee-oh leh-por-RYE-nuhs

Noctilionidae nok-tihl-ee-ON-uh-dee

Notomys alexis noh-TOH-meez ah-LEK-sis

Notoryctemorphia noh-toh-rik-teh-MOR-fee-uh

Notoryctes typhlops noh-TOH-rik-teez TIE-flopz

Notoryctidae noh-toh-RIK-tuh-dee

Nycteridae nik-TER-uh-dee

Nycteris thebaica NIK-ter-is the-BAH-ik-uh

Nycticebus pygmaeus nik-tih-SEE-buhs pig-MEE-uhs

Nyctimene robinsoni nik-TIM-en-ee ROB-in-son-eye

Ochotona hyperborea oh-koh-TOH-nuh hi-per-BOHR-ee-uh

Ochotona princeps oh-koh-TOH-nuh PRIN-seps

Ochotonidae oh-koh-TOH-nuh-dee

Octodon degus OK-tuh-don DAY-gooz

Octodontidae ok-tuh-DON-tuh-dee

Odobenidae oh-duh-BEN-uh-dee

Odobenus rosmarus oh-DUH-ben-uhs ROS-mahr-uhs

Odocoileus virginianus oh-duh-KOI-lee-uhs ver-JIN-ee-an-nuhs

Okapia johnstoni oh-KAH-pee-uh JOHNS-ton-eye

Ondatra zibethicus ON-dat-ruh ZIB-eth-ih-kuhs

Onychogalea fraenata oh-nik-uh-GAL-ee-uh FREE-nah-tuh

Orcinus orca OR-sigh-nuhs OR-kuh

Ornithorhynchidae OR-nith-oh-RIN-kuh-dee

Ornithorynchus anatinus OR-nith-oh-RIN-kuhs an-AH-tin-uhs

Orycteropodidae or-ik-ter-uh-POD-uh-dee

Orycteropus afer or-ik-TER-uh-puhs AF-er

Otariidae oh-tar-EYE-uh-dee

Otolemur garnettii oh-tuh-LEE-mer GAR-net-ee-eye

Ovis canadensis OH-vis kan-uh-DEN-sis

Pagophilus groenlandicus pa-GO-fil-luhs GREEN-land-ih-cuhs

Pan troglodytes PAN trog-luh-DIE-teez

Panthera leo PAN-ther-uh LEE-oh

Panthera tigris PAN-ther-uh TIE-gris

Paucituberculata paw-see-too-ber-KYOO-lah-tuh

Pedetidae ped-ET-uh-dee

Peramelemorphia per-uh-mel-eh-MOR-fee-uh

Peramelidae per-uh-MEL-uh-dee

Perameles gunnii PER-uh-MEL-eez GUN-ee-eye

Perissodactyla peh-RISS-uh-DAK-til-uh

Perodicticus potto per-uh-DIK-tuh-kuhs POT-toh

Perognathus inornatus PER-ug-NAH-thuhs in-AWR-nah-tuhs

Peropteryx kappleri per-OP-ter-iks KAP-ler-eye

Peroryctidae per-uh-RIK-tuh-dee

Petauridae pet-OR-uh-dee

Petauroides volans pet-or-OY-deez VOH-lanz

Petaurus breviceps PET-or-uhs BREV-ih-seps

Petrogale penicillata pet-ROH-gah-lee pen-ih-SIL-lah-tuh

Petromuridae pet-roh-MUR-uh-dee

Petromus typicus PET-roh-muhs TIP-ih-kuhs

Phalanger gymnotis FAH-lan-jer jim-NOH-tis

Phalangeridae fah-lan-JER-uh-dee

Phascogale tapoatafa fas-KOH-gah-lee TAP-oh-uh-TAH-fuh

Phascolarctidae fas-koh-LARK-tuh-dee

Phascolarctos cinereus fas-KOH-lark-tuhs sin-EAR-ee-uhs

Phocidae FOE-suh-dee

Phocoena phocoena FOE-see-nuh FOE-see-nuh

Phocoena spinipinnis FOE-see-nuh SPY-nih-PIN-is

Phocoenidae foe-SEE-nuh-dee

Pholidota foe-lih-DOH-tuh

Phyllostomidae fill-uh-STOH-muh-dee

Physeter macrocephalus FY-se-ter ma-crow-SEFF-uh-luhs

Physeteridae fy-se-TER-uh-dee

Piliocolobus badius fill-ee-oh-KOH-loh-buhs BAD-ee-uhs

Pithecia pithecia pith-EEK-ee-uh pith-EEK-ee-uh

Pitheciidae pith-eek-EYE-uh-dee

Plantanista gangetica plan-TAN-is-tuh gan-JET-ik-uh

Platanistidae plan-tan-IS-tuh-dee

Pongo pygmaeus PON-goh pig-MEE-uhs

Pontoporia blainvillei pon-toh-POR-ee-uh BLAIN-vill-ee-eye

Pontoporiidae PON-toh-por-EYE-uh-dee

Potoroidae pot-uh-ROY-dee

Primates PRY-maytes

Proboscidea proh-BOS-see-uh

Procavia capensis proh-CAVE-ee-uh KAP-en-sis

Procaviidae proh-kave-EYE-uh-dee

Procyon lotor proh-SIGH-on LOH-tor

Procyonidae proh-sigh-ON-uh-dee

Proechimys semispinosus proh-EK-ih-meez sem-ih-SPY-noh-suhs

Propithecus edwardsi proh-PITH-eek-uhs ED-werds-eye

Proteles cristatus PROH-tell-eez KRIS-tah-tuhs

Pseudocheiridae soo-doh-KY-ruh-dee

Pseudocheirus peregrinus soo-doh-KY-ruhs PEHR-eh-GRIN-uhs

Pteronotus parnellii ter-uh-NOH-tuhs PAR-nell-ee-eye

Pteropodidae ter-uh-POD-uh-dee

Pteropus giganteus ter-OH-puhs jy-GAN-tee-uhs

Pteropus mariannus ter-OH-puhs MARE-ih-an-uhs

Pudu pudu POO-doo POO-doo

Puma concolor PYOO-muh CON-kuh-luhr

Puripterus horrens PYOOR-ip-TER-uhs HOR-renz

Pygathrix nemaeus PIG-uh-thriks neh-MEE-uhs

Rangifer tarandus RAN-jih-fer TAR-an-duhs

Rhinoceros unicornis rye-NOS-er-uhs YOO-nih-KORN-is

Rhinocerotidae rye-NOS-er-UH-tuh-dee

Rhinolophidae rye-noh-LOH-fuh-dee

Rhinolophus capensis rye-noh-LOH-fuhs KAP-en-sis

Rhinolophus ferrumequinum rye-noh-LOH-fuhs FEHR-rum-EK-wy-num

Rhinopoma hardwickei rye-noh-POH-muh HARD-wik-eye

Rhinopomatidae rye-noh-poh-MAT-uh-dee

Rhynchocyon cirnei rin-koh-SIGH-on SIR-neye

Rodentia roh-DEN-she-uh

Rousettus aegyptiacus ROO-set-tuhs ee-JIP-tih-kuhs

Saccopteryx bilineata sak-OP-ter-iks BY-lin-EE-ah-tuh

Saguinus oedipus SAG-win-uhs ED-uh-puhs

Saimiri sciureus SAY-meer-eye sigh-OOR-ee-uhs

Sarcophilus laniarius SAR-kuh-FIL-uhs lan-ee-AIR-ee-uhs

Scalopus aquaticus SKA-loh-puhs uh-KWAT-ik-uhs

Scandentia skan-DEN-she-uh

Sciuridae sigh-OOR-uh-dee

Sciurus carolinensis SIGH-oor-uhs kar-uh-LINE-en-sis

Sigmodon hispidus SIG-muh-don HISS-pid-uhs

Sirenia sy-REEN-ee-uh

Solenodon paradoxus so-LEN-uh-don PAR-uh-DOCKS-uhs

Solenodontidae so-len-uh-DON-shuh-dee

Sorex palustris SOR-eks PAL-us-tris

Soricidae sor-IS-uh-dee

Stenella longirostris steh-NELL-uh LAWN-juh-ROS-tris

Suidae SOO-uh-dee

Sus scrofa SOOS SKRO-fuh

Sylvilagus audubonii SILL-vih-LAG-uhs AW-duh-BON-ee-eye

Symphalangus syndactylus SIM-fuh-LAN-guhs sin-DAK-til-uhs

Tachyglossidae TAK-ih-GLOS-suh-dee

Tachyglossus aculeatus TAK-ih-GLOS-suhs ak-YOOL-ee-ah-tuhs

Tadarida brasiliensis ta-DARE-ih-dah bra-ZILL-ee-en-sis

Talpidae TAL-puh-dee

Tamias striatus TAM-ee-uhs stry-AH-tuhs

Tapiridae tay-PUR-uh-dee

Tapirus indicus TAY-pur-uhs IN-dih-kuhs

Tapirus terrestris TAY-pur-uhs TER-rehs-tris

Tarsiidae tar-SIGH-uh-dee

Tarsipedidae tar-sih-PED-uh-dee

Tarsipes rostratus TAR-si-peez ROS-trah-tuhs

Tarsius bancanus TAR-see-uhs BAN-kan-uhs

Tarsius syrichta TAR-see-uhs STRIK-tuh

Tasmacetus shepherdi taz-muh-SEE-tuhs SHEP-erd-eye

Tayassu tajacu TAY-yuh-soo TAY-jah-soo

Tayassuidae tay-yuh-SOO-uh-dee

Tenrec ecaudatus TEN-rek ee-KAW-dah-tuhs

Tenrecidae ten-REK-uh-dee

Thomomys bottae TOM-oh-meez BOTT-ee

Thryonomyidae thry-oh-noh-MY-uh-dee

Thryonomys swinderianus THRY-oh-NOH-meez SWIN-der-EE-an-uhs

Thylacinidae thy-luh-SEEN-uh-dee

Thylacinus cynocephalus THY-luh-SEEN-uhs sigh-nuh-SEFF-uh-luhs

Thyroptera tricolor thy-ROP-ter-uh TRY-kuh-luhr
Thyropteridae thy-rop-TER-uh-dee
Tragulidae tray-GOO-luh-dee
Tragulus javanicus TRAY-goo-luhs jah-VAHN-ih-kuhs
Trichechidae trik-EK-uh-dee
Trichechus manatus TRIK-ek-uhs MAN-uh-tuhs
Trichosurus vulpecula TRIK-uh-SOOR-uhs vul-PEK-yoo-luh
Tubulidentata toob-yool-ih-DEN-tah-tuh
Tupaia glis too-PUH-ee-uh GLIS
Tupaiidae too-puh-EYE-uh-dee
Tursiops truncatus tur-SEE-ops TRUN-kah-tuhs
Uncia uncia UN-see-uh UN-see-uh
Ursidae UR-suh-dee
Ursus americanus UR-suhs uh-mer-uh-KAN-uhs
Ursus maritimus UR-suhs mar-ih-TIME-uhs
Vespertilionidae ves-puhr-TEEL-ee-UHN-uh-dee
Viverridae vy-VER-ruh-dee
Vombatidae vom-BAT-uh-dee
Vombatus ursinus VOM-bat-uhs ur-SIGH-nuhs
Vulpes vulpes VUHL-peez VUHL-peez
Xenarthra ZEN-areth-ruh
Yerbua capensis YER-byoo-uh KAP-en-sis
Zalophus californianus ZA-loh-fuhs kal-uh-FORN-uh-kuhs
Zalophus wollebaeki ZA-loh-fuhs VOLL-back-eye
Ziphiidae ziff-EYE-uh-dee

Words to Know

A

Aborigine: Earliest-known inhabitant of an area; often referring to a native person of Australia.

Adaptation: Any structural, physiological, or behavioral trait that aids an organism's survival and ability to reproduce in its existing environment.

Algae: Tiny plants or plantlike organisms that grow in water and in damp places.

Anaconda: A large snake of South America; one of the largest snakes in the world.

Aphrodisiac: Anything that intensifies or arouses sexual desires.

Aquatic: Living in the water.

Arboreal: Living primarily or entirely in trees and bushes.

Arid: Extremely dry climate, with less than 10 inches (25 centimeters) of rain each year.

Arthropod: A member of the largest single animal phylum, consisting of organisms with segmented bodies, jointed legs or wings, and exoskeletons.

B

Baleen: A flexible, horny substance making up two rows of plates that hang from the upper jaws of baleen whales.

Biogeography: The study of the distribution and dispersal of plants and animals throughout the world.

Bipedal: Walking on two feet.

Blowhole: The nostril on a whale, dolphin, or porpoise.

Blubber: A layer of fat under the skin of sea mammals that protects them from heat loss and stores energy.

Brachiation: A type of locomotion in which an animal travels through the forest by swinging below branches using its arms.

Brackish water: Water that is a mix of freshwater and saltwater.

Burrow: Tunnel or hole that an animal digs in the ground to use as a home.

C

Cache: A hidden supply area.

Camouflage: Device used by an animal, such as coloration, allowing it to blend in with the surroundings to avoid being seen by prey and predators.

Canine teeth: The four pointed teeth (two in each jaw) between the incisors and bicuspids in mammals; designed for stabbing and holding prey.

Canopy: The uppermost layer of a forest formed naturally by the leaves and branches of trees and plants.

Carnivore: Meat-eating organism.

Carrion: Dead and decaying animal flesh.

Cecum: A specialized part of the large intestine that acts as a fermentation chamber to aid in digestion of grasses.

Cervical vertebrae: The seven neck bones that make up the top of the spinal column.

Clan: A group of animals of the same species that live together, such as badgers or hyenas.

Cloud forest: A tropical forest where clouds are overhead most of the year.

Colony: A group of animals of the same type living together.

Coniferous: Refers to evergreen trees, such as pines and firs, that bear cones and have needle-like leaves that are not shed all at once.

Coniferous forest: An evergreen forest where plants stay green all year.

Continental shelf: A gently sloping ledge of a continent that is submerged in the ocean.

Convergence: In adaptive evolution, a process by which unrelated or only distantly related living things come to resemble one another in adapting to similar environments.

Coprophagous: Eating dung. Some animals do this to extract nutrients that have passed through their system.

Crepuscular: Most active at dawn and dusk.

Critically Endangered: A term used by the IUCN in reference to a species that is at an extremely high risk of extinction in the wild.

D

Data Deficient: An IUCN category referring to a species that is not assigned another category because there is not enough information about the species' population.

Deciduous: Shedding leaves at the end of the growing season.

Deciduous forest: A forest with four seasons in which trees drop their leaves in the fall.

Deforestation: Those practices or processes that result in the change of forested lands to non-forest uses, such as human settlement or farming. This is often cited as one of the major causes of the enhanced greenhouse effect.

Delayed implantation: A process by which the fertilized egg formed after mating develops for a short time, then remains inactive until later when it attaches to the uterus for further development, so that birth coincides with a better food supply or environmental conditions.

Den: The shelter of an animal, such as an underground hole or a hollow log.

Dentin: A calcareous material harder than bone found in teeth.

Desert: A land area so dry that little or no plant or animal life can survive.

Digit: Division where limbs terminate; in humans this refers to a finger or toe.

Digitigrade: A manner of walking on the toes, as cats and dogs do, as opposed to walking on the ball of the feet, as humans do.

Dingo: A wild Australian dog.

Diurnal: Refers to animals that are active during the day.

Domesticated: Tamed.

Dominant: The top male or female of a social group, sometimes called the alpha male or alpha female.

Dorsal: Located in the back.

Dung: Feces, or solid waste from an animal.

E

Echolocation: A method of detecting objects by using sound waves.

Ecotourist: A person who visits a place in order to observe the plants and animals in the area while making minimal human impact on the natural environment.

Electroreception: The sensory detection of small amounts of natural electricity by an animal (usually underwater), by means of specialized nerve endings.

Elevation: The height of land when measured from sea level.

Endangered: A term used by the U. S. Endangered Species Act of 1973 and by the IUCN in reference to a species that is facing a very high risk of extinction from all or a significant portion of its natural home.

Endangered Species Act: A U. S. law that grants legal protection to listed endangered and threatened species.

Endemic: Native to or occurring only in a particular place.

Erupt: In teeth, to break through the skin and become visible.

Estivation: State of inactivity during the hot, dry months of summer.

Estuary: Lower end of a river where ocean tides meet the river's current.

Eutherian mammal: Mammals that have a well-developed placenta and give birth to fully formed live young.

Evergreen: In botany, bearing green leaves through the winter and/or a plant having foliage that persists throughout the year.

Evolve: To change slowly over time.

Extinct: A species without living members.

Extinction: The total disappearance of a species or the disappearance of a species from a given area.

F

Family: A grouping of genera that share certain characteristics and appear to have evolved from the same ancestors.

Feces: Solid body waste.

Fermentation: Chemical reaction in which enzymes break down complex organic compounds into simpler ones. This can make digestion easier.

Forage: To search for food.

Forb: Any broad-leaved herbaceous plant that is not a grass; one that grows in a prairie or meadow, such as sunflower, goldenrod, or clover.

Fragment: To divide or separate individuals of the same species into small groups that are unable to mingle with each other.

Frugivore: Animal that primarily eats fruit. Many bats and birds are frugivores.

Fuse: To become joined together as one unit.

G

Genera: Plural of genus.

Genus (pl. genera): A category of classification made up of species sharing similar characteristics.

Gestation: The period of carrying young in the uterus before birth.

Gland: A specialized body part that produces, holds, and releases one or more substances (such as scent or sweat) for use by the body.

Gleaning: Gathering food from surfaces.

Grassland: Region in which the climate is dry for long periods of the summer, and freezes in the winter. Grasslands are characterized by grasses and other erect herbs, usually without trees or shrubs, and occur in the dry temperate interiors of continents.

Grooming: An activity during which primates look through each other's fur to remove parasites and dirt.

Guano: The droppings of birds or bats, sometimes used as fertilizer.

Guard hairs: Long, stiff, waterproof hairs that form the outer fur and protect the underfur of certain mammals.

Gum: A substance found in some plants that oozes out in response to a puncture, as plant sap, and generally hardens after exposure to air.

H

Habitat: The area or region where a particular type of plant or animal lives and grows.

Habitat degradation: The diminishment of the quality of a habitat and its ability to support animal and plant communities.

Hallux: The big toe, or first digit, on the part of the foot facing inwards.

Harem: A group of two or more adult females, plus their young, with only one adult male present.

Haul out: To pull one's body out of the water onto land, as when seals come out of the water to go ashore.

Herbivore: Plant-eating organism.

Hibernation: State of rest or inactivity during the cold winter months.

Hierarchy: A structured order of rank or social superiority.

Home range: A specific area that an animal roams while performing its activities.

I

Ice floe: A large sheet of floating ice.

Incisor: One of the chisel-shaped teeth at the front of the mouth (between the canines), used for cutting and tearing food.

Indigenous: Originating in a region or country.

Insectivore: An animal that eats primarily insects.

Insulate: To prevent the escape of heat by surrounding with something; in an animal, a substance such as fur or body fat serves to retain heat in its body.

Invertebrate: Animal lacking a spinal column (backbone).

IUCN: Abbreviation for the International Union for Conservation of Nature and Natural Resources, now the World Conservation Union. A conservation organization of government agencies and nongovernmental organizations best known for its Red Lists of threatened and endangered species.

K

Keratin: Protein found in hair, nails, and skin.

Krill: Tiny shrimp-like animals that are the main food of baleen whales and are also eaten by seals and other marine mammals.

L

Lactate: To produce milk in the female body, an activity associated with mammals.

Larva (pl. larvae): Immature form (wormlike in insects; fishlike in amphibians) of an organism capable of surviving on its own. A larva does not resemble the parent and must go through metamorphosis, or change, to reach its adult stage.

Leprosy: A disease of the skin and flesh characterized by scaly scabs and open sores.

Lichen: A complex of algae and fungi found growing on trees, rocks, or other solid surfaces.

Litter: A group of young animals, such as pigs or kittens, born at the same time from the same mother. Or, a layer of dead vegetation and other material covering the ground.

M

Malaria: A serious disease common in tropical countries, spread by the bites of female mosquitoes, that causes complications affecting the brain, blood, liver, and kidneys and can cause death.

Mammae: Milk-secreting organs of female mammals used to nurse young.

Mammals: Animals that feed their young on breast milk, are warm-blooded, and breathe air through their lungs.

Mangrove: Tropical coastal trees or shrubs that produce many supporting roots and that provide dense vegetation.

Marsupial: A type of mammal that does not have a well-developed placenta and gives birth to immature and underdeveloped young after a short gestation period. It continues to nurture the young, often in a pouch, until they are able to fend for themselves.

Matriarchal: Headed by a dominant female or females; said of animal societies.

Mechanoreceptor: Sensory nerve receptor modified to detect physical changes in the immediate environment, often having to do with touch and change of pressure or turbulence in water or air. In the platypus, mechanoreceptors in its bill may detect prey and obstacles.

Megachiroptera: One of the two groups of bats; these bats are usually larger than the microchiroptera.

Melon: The fatty forehead of a whale or dolphin.

Membrane: A thin, flexible layer of plant or animal tissue that covers, lines, separates or holds together, or connects parts of an organism.

Microchiroptera: One of two categories of bats; these make up most of the bats in the world and are generally smaller than the megachiroptera.

Migrate: To move from one area or climate to another as the seasons change, usually to find food or to mate.

Migratory pattern: The direction or path taken while moving seasonally from one region to another.

Molar: A broad tooth located near the back of the jaw with a flat, rough surface for grinding.

Mollusk: A group of animals without backbones that includes snails, clams, oysters, and similar hard-shelled animals.

Molt: The process by which an organism sheds its outermost layer of feathers, fur, skin, or exoskeleton.

Monogamous: Refers to a breeding system in which a male and a female mate only with each other during a breeding season or lifetime.

Muzzle: The projecting part of the head that includes jaws, chin, mouth, and nose.

Myxomatosis: A highly infectious disease of rabbits caused by a pox virus.

N

Near Threatened: A category defined by the IUCN suggesting that a species could become threatened with extinction in the future.

Nectar: Sweet liquid secreted by the flowers of various plants to attract pollinators (animals that pollinate, or fertilize, the flowers).

Neotropical: Relating to a geographic area of plant and animal life east, south, and west of Mexico's central plateau that includes Central and South America and the West Indies.

New World: Made up of North America, Central America, and South America; the western half of the world.

Nocturnal: Occurring or active at night.

Non-prehensile: Incapable of grasping; used to describe an animal's tail that cannot wrap around tree branches.

Noseleaf: Horseshoe-shaped flap of skin around the nose.

Nurse: To feed on mother's milk.

O

Old World: Australia, Africa, Asia, and Europe; in the eastern half of the world.

Omnivore: Plant- and meat-eating animal.

Opportunistic feeder: An animal that eats whatever food is available, either prey they have killed, other animals' kills, plants, or human food and garbage.

P

Pack ice: Large pieces of ice frozen together.

Patagium: The flap of skin that extends between the front and hind limbs. In bats, it stretches between the hind legs and helps the animal in flight; in colugos this stretches from the side of the neck to the tips of its fingers, toes, and tail.

Phylogenetics: Field of biology that deals with the relationships between organisms. It includes the discovery of these relationships, and the study of the causes behind this pattern.

Pinnipeds: Marine mammals, including three families of the order Carnivora, namely Otariidae (sea lions and fur seals), Phocidae (true seals), and Odobenidae (walrus).

Placenta: An organ that grows in the mother's uterus and lets the mother and developing offspring share food and oxygen through the blood.

Placental mammal: Any species of mammal that carries embryonic and fetal young in the womb through a long gestation period, made possible via the placenta, a filtering organ passing nutrients, wastes, and gases between mother and young.

Plantigrade: Walking on the heel and sole of the foot, instead of on the toes. Plantigrade species include bears and humans.

Plate tectonics: Geological theory holding that Earth's surface is composed of rigid plates or sections that move about the surface in response to internal pressure, creating the major geographical features such as mountains.

Poach: To hunt animals illegally.

Pod: In animal behavioral science (and in some zoology uses) the term pod is used to represent a group of whales, seals, or dolphins.

Pollen: Dust-like grains or particles produced by a plant that contain male sex cells.

Pollination: Transfer of pollen from the male reproductive organs to the female reproductive organs of plants.

Pollinator: Animal which carries pollen from one seed plant to another, unwittingly aiding the plant in its reproduction. Common pollinators include insects, especially bees, butterflies, and moths; birds; and bats.

Polyandry: A mating system in which a single female mates with multiple males.

Polyestrous: A female animal having more than one estrous cycle (mating period) within a year.

Polygamy: A mating system in which males and females mate with multiple partners.

Polygyny: A mating system in which a single male mates with multiple females.

Predator: An animal that eats other animals.

Prehensile: Able to control and use to grasp objects, characteristically associated with tails. Prehensile tails have evolved independently many times, for instance, in marsupials, rodents, primates, porcupines, and chameleons.

Prey: Organism hunted and eaten by a predator.

Primary forest: A forest characterized by a full-ceiling canopy formed by the branches of tall trees and several layers of smaller trees. This type of forest lacks ground vegetation because sunlight cannot penetrate through the canopy.

Promiscuity: Mating in which individuals mate with as many other individuals as they can or want to.

Puberty: The age of sexual maturity.

Q

Quadruped: Walking or running on four limbs.

R

Rabies: A viral infection spread through the bite of certain warm-blooded animals; it attacks the nervous system and can be fatal if untreated.

Rainforest: An evergreen woodland of the tropics distinguished by a continuous leaf canopy and an average rainfall of about 100 inches (250 centimeters) per year.

Regurgitate: Eject the contents of the stomach through the mouth; to vomit.

Rookery: A site on land where seals congregate to mate and raise the young.

Roost: A place where animals, such as bats, sit or rest on a perch, branch, etc.

S

Savanna: A biome characterized by an extensive cover of grasses with scattered trees, usually transitioning between areas dominated by forests and those dominated by grasses and having alternating seasonal climates of precipitation and drought.

Scavenger: An animal that eats carrion, dead animals.

Scent gland: Formed from modified, or changed, sweat glands, these glands produce and/or give off strong-smelling chemicals that give information, such as marking territory, to other animals.

Scent mark: To leave an odor, such as of urine or scent gland secretions, to mark a territory or as a means of communication.

Scrotum: The external pouch containing the testicles.

Scrub forest: A forest with short trees and shrubs.

Scrubland: An area similar to grassland but which includes scrub (low-growing plants and trees) vegetation.

Seamount: An underwater mountain that does not rise above the surface of the ocean.

Seashore: When referring to a biome, formed where the land meets the ocean.

Secondary forest: A forest characterized by a less-developed canopy, smaller trees, and a dense ground vegetation found on the edges of forests and along rivers and streams. The immature vegetation may also result from the removal of trees by logging and/or fires.

Semiaquatic: Partially aquatic; living or growing partly on land and partly in water.

Semiarid: Very little rainfall each year, between 10 and 20 inches (25 to 51 centimeters).

Sexually mature: Capable of reproducing.

Solitary: Living alone or avoiding the company of others.

Species: A group of living things that share certain distinctive characteristics and can breed together in the wild.

Spermaceti: A waxy substance found in the head cavity of some whales.

Steppe: Wide expanse of semiarid relatively level plains, found in cool climates and characterized by shrubs, grasses, and few trees.

Streamline: To smooth out.

Succulent: A plant that has fleshy leaves to conserve moisture.

Suckle: To nurse or suck on a mother's nipple to get milk.

Syndactyly: A condition in which two bones (or digits) fuse together to become a single bone.

T

Tactile: Having to do with the sense of touch.

Talon: A sharp hooked claw.

Taxonomy: The science dealing with the identification, naming, and classification of plants and animals.

Teat: A projection through which milk passes from the mother to the nursing young; a nipple.

Temperate: Areas with moderate temperatures in which the climate undergoes seasonal change in temperature and moisture. Temperate regions of the earth lie primarily between 30 and 60° latitude in both hemispheres.

Terrestrial: Relating to the land or living primarily on land.

Territorial: A pattern of behavior that causes an animal to stay in a limited area and/or to keep certain other animals of the same species (other than its mate, herd, or family group) out of the area.

Thicket: An area represented by a thick, or dense, growth of shrubs, underbrush, or small trees.

Threatened: Describes a species that is threatened with extinction.

Torpor: A short period of inactivity characterized by an energy-saving, deep sleep-like state in which heart rate, respiratory rate and body temperature drop.

Traction: Resistance to a surface to keep from slipping.

Tragus: A flap of skin near the base of the external ear.

Tributary: A small stream that feeds into a larger one.

Tropical: The area between 23.5° north and south of the equator. This region has small daily and seasonal changes in temperature, but great seasonal changes in precipitation. Generally, a hot and humid climate that is completely or almost free of frost.

Tundra: A type of ecosystem dominated by lichens, mosses, grasses, and woody plants. It is found at high latitudes (arctic tundra) and high altitudes (alpine tundra). Arctic tundra is underlain by permafrost and usually very wet.

Turbulent: An irregular, disorderly mode of flow.

U

Underfur: Thick soft fur lying beneath the longer and coarser guard hair.

Understory: The trees and shrubs between the forest canopy and the ground cover.

Ungulates: Hoofed animals, such as deer and elk.

Urine washing: A monkey behavior in which it soaks its hands with urine, then rubs the liquid on its fur and feet so as to leave the scent throughout its forest routes.

Uterus: A pear-shaped, hollow muscular organ in which a fetus develops during pregnancy.

V

Vertebra (pl. vertebrae): A component of the vertebral column, or backbone, found in vertebrates.

Vertebrate: An animal having a spinal column (backbone).

Vertical: Being at a right angle to the horizon. Up and down movements or supports.

Vestigial: A degenerate or imperfectly developed biological structure that once performed a useful function at an earlier stage of the evolution of the species.

Vibrissae: Stiff sensory hairs that can be found near the nostrils or other parts of the face in many mammals and the snouts, tails, ears, and sometimes feet of many insectivores.

Vocalization: Sound made by vibration of the vocal tract.

Vulnerable: An IUCN category referring to a species that faces a high risk of extinction.

W

Wallaby: An Australian marsupial similar to a kangaroo but smaller.

Wean: When a young animal no longer feeds on its mother's milk and instead begins to eat adult food.

Wetlands: Areas that are wet or covered with water for at least part of the year and support aquatic plants, such as marshes, swamps, and bogs.

Woodlands: An area with a lot of trees and shrubs.

Y

Yolk-sac placenta: A thin membrane that develops in the uterus of marsupials that does not fuse with the mother's uterus and results in short pregnancies with the young being born with poorly developed organs.

Getting to Know Mammals

MAMMALS

Mammals are found on all continents and in all seas. It isn't easy to tell that an animal is a mammal. A combination of special features separates mammals from other animals.

Mammal milk

Only mammals can feed their young with milk produced by their body. This milk comes from special glands called mammae. A female may have two mammary glands or as many as a dozen or more. Mammal milk is very healthy for infants and immediately available.

Body temperature

Mammals are warm-blooded, meaning they keep a constant body temperature. To keep their temperature fairly constant, a mammal needs some protective covering. Hair, made of a protein called keratin, serves several functions. One function is insulation, controlling the amount of body heat that escapes into the mammal's environment through the skin.

Mammal hair

All mammals have hair at some time of their life. Some have a lot, such as gorillas, and some have very little, such as the naked mole rats. There are three types of hair: a coarse long topcoat, a fine undercoat, and special sensory hairs, or whiskers.

In some mammals, hair has unusual forms. Porcupines have stiff, sharp, and thickened hairs called quills. Anteaters have

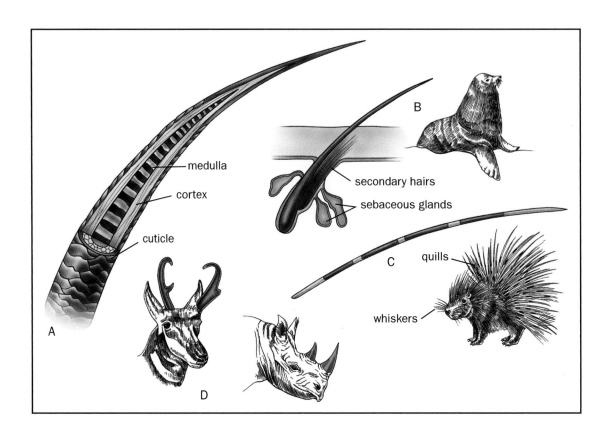

A. Cross section of a hair. B. Hairs may provide insulation and waterproofing. Specialized hair includes quills, whiskers (C), and horns (D). (Illustration by Patricia Ferrer. Reproduced by permission.)

sharp-edged scales made of modified hairs. These modified, or changed, hairs are protective against predators.

Mammals that live all or most of their lives in water, such as sea otters, may have a lot of dense, long hair, or fur. Others have much less hair, but a very thick hide, or skin, plus a thick layer of fat or blubber underneath the hide.

Hair color and pattern may vary. Males and females may have different fur colors. Special color patterns, such as a skunk's black and white fur, act as warnings. Hair color can also serve as camouflage, enabling the mammal to blend into its background.

Some mammals have fur color changes in summer and winter. Colors can be entirely different. Snowshoe rabbits and weasels can be brownish in summer, and almost pure white in winter. But this only happens if there is snow where they live. If it seldom snows, weasels and snowshoe rabbits stay brown.

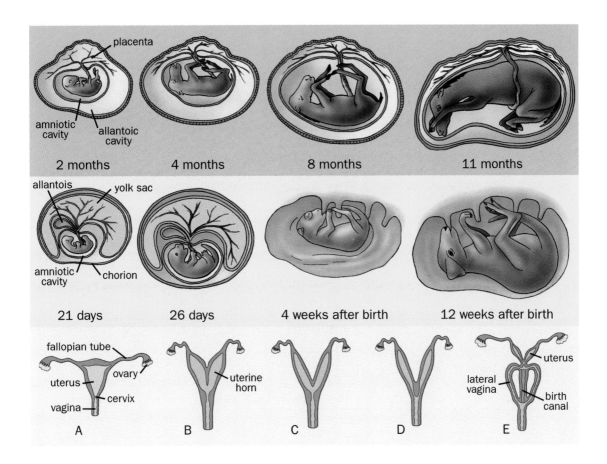

2 months | 4 months | 8 months | 11 months

21 days | 26 days | 4 weeks after birth | 12 weeks after birth

A | B | C | D | E

Reproduction

Mammals have two genetic sexes, male and female. Ninety percent of mammals are placental (pluh-SENT-ul). In placental mammals, the baby develops, or grows, within the mother's body before it enters the world. What about the other 10 percent? These mammals lay eggs. There are only three egg-laying mammals alive today.:

Other mammal features

Other bodily mammal features include their ability to breathe air through their lungs. Water-dwelling mammals, such as the whale and porpoise, do this too. Mammals have jaws, usually with teeth. Mammals usually have four limbs. Mammals have a four-chambered heart. Mammals have vertebrae, or back bones, unlike invertebrates such as insects, in which there is an outside shell or structure called an exoskeleton.

Top: Placental mammal development. Middle row: Marsupial mammal development. Types of uterus: A. Simplex; B. Bipartite; C. Bicornuate; D. Duplex; E. Marsupial. (Illustration by Patricia Ferrer. Reproduced by permission.)

This life-sized woolly mammoth model is kept in the Royal British Columbia Museum. Woolly mammoths were as tall as 10 feet (3 meters). (© Jonathan Blair/Corbis. Reproduced by permission.)

FOSSIL MAMMALS

Fossils are body parts of animals that lived very long ago. Not many long-ago mammals are preserved as fossils. But some entire mammal fossils have been discovered, such as a 10-foot (3-meter) woolly mammoth preserved in Siberian frozen ground, and an Ice Age woolly rhinoceros discovered in Poland, preserved in asphalt.

Many long-ago mammals lived in a warm, wet world. They ate soft, leafy plants. The earliest known mammals were possibly shrew-like creatures living about 190 million years ago. Later larger mammals occurred, then disappeared, or became extinct. These include the mesohippus, a three-toed horse only 24 inches (60 centimeters) high; a giant pig with a head that was 4 feet (1.22 meters) in length; and the smilodon, a huge saber-toothed cat with canine teeth that were 8 inches (20.3

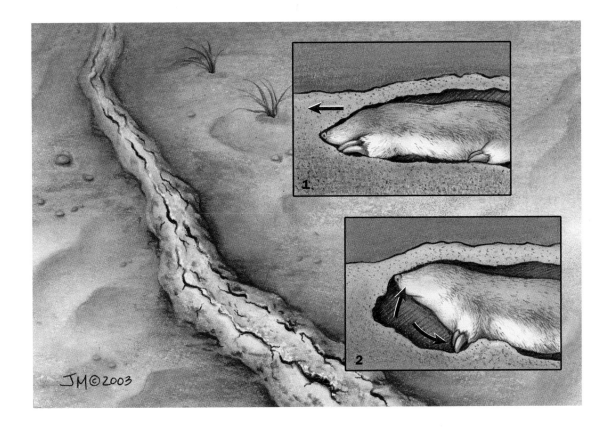

JM©2003

centimeters) in length. By about 15,000 years ago, long-ago people were hunting mammals with stone-pointed spears. Most of the animals they hunted are extinct for various reasons, some known, and some unknown.

WHERE MAMMALS LIVE

Underground mammals

Some small mammals spend all or most of their lives living underground. These include many species of prairie dogs, chipmunks, moles, groundhogs, Greenland collared lemmings, and Peruvian tuco-tucos. Each of these mammals has a special body design enabling it to survive underground.

Moles have large, powerful shoulders and short, very powerful forelimbs. Spade-like feet have claws, enabling quick digging. Hind feet have webbed toes, enabling the mole to kick soil backwards effectively. Velvety-type fur enables a mole to slip easily through its tunnels. And, although moles

The Grant's desert mole uses its powerful forelimbs to burrow through the sands of the Namib Desert in southern Africa. The golden mole moves forward (1), and enlarges the tunnel by pushing dirt up with its head and back with its claws (2). (Illustration by Jacqueline Mahannah. Reproduced by permission.)

A RECENT DISCOVERY

A bright orange, mouse-like mammal, weighing 0.5 ounces (15 grams) and measuring 3.12 inches (8 centimeters) plus a long tail, has recently been discovered in the Philippines. It has whiskers five times longer than its head. It can open and eat very hard tree nuts that no other mammal in the area can eat.

have almost no eyes, they can rely on touch, smell, and sensitivity to vibration to find underground insects and earthworms.

Sea mammals

Some mammals live in the sea, including manatees, whales, seals, and dolphins. While some need air every few minutes, a sperm whale can remain underwater for an hour and a half. How is this possible? Some sea mammals have a very low metabolism. They don't use up the the their oxygen quickly and can store large amounts of oxygen in their bodies.

Tree mammals

Some mammals spend all or most of their lives in trees. Tree-dwelling mammals are often hidden from sight by leaves, vines, and branches. Tree-dwelling mammals include the Eastern pygmy possum, which nests in small tree hollows; the koala; Lumholtz's tree kangaroo, which leaps from branch to branch; the three-toed sloth; and the clouded leopard.

Flying mammals

The only truly flying mammals are bats. The sound of bat wings was first heard about 50 million years ago. Some bats are large, with a wingspan almost 7 feet (21.3 meters) wide. Some are small, as the Philippine bamboo bat, whose body is just 2 inches (5.08 centimeters) long.

Other mammals only appear to fly, such as the southern flying squirrel and the colugo, or Malayan flying lemur. These mammals have gliding membranes, skin folds from body front to legs, that, when spread out, act almost like a parachute. For example, the feathertail glider, a tiny possum, crawls along narrow branches. At branch end, it leaps out and slightly downward. Spreading its gliding membranes, it speeds through the air, landing on a nearby tree.

Mountain mammals

Some mammals spend most of their lives on mountain peaks. These include Asian corkscrew-horned markhor goats, North

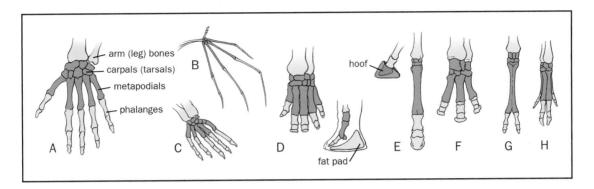

A. arm (leg) bones
carpals (tarsals)
metapodials
phalanges
B
C
D
hoof
fat pad
E
F
G
H

American Rocky Mountain bighorn sheep, and Siberian ibex. Siberian ibex can stand anyplace on any pinnacle with just enough room for its four feet. North American mountain goats can climb up a mountain peak, almost going straight up. Specially shaped hooves help.

Other high mountain dwelling mammals include snow leopards and Asian pikas that can survive at 19,685 feet (6,000 meters). Gunnison's prairie dogs do well up to 11,500 feet (3,505 meters).

Desert mammals

Some mammals spend most of their lives in arid, or very dry areas. Not all deserts are sandy like Death Valley or the Sahara. Some are rocky. Other arid areas are mountainous. Desert dwelling mammals include the North African elephant shrew, white-tailed antelope squirrel, and the desert kangaroo rat. No mammal can live without water. Desert rodents have a way to extract, or get, water from their own body functions. Rodents may also get water by eating plants, seeds, roots, and insects that contain water.

Larger mammals live in arid regions too. The striped hyena can survive in stony desert as long as it is within 6 miles (9.7 kilometers) of water. Fennecs, a very small fox living near sand dunes, can go a long time without drinking. Camels can use body fluids when no water is available.

WHAT DO MAMMALS EAT?

Insect-eaters

Some mammals have mostly insect meals. Insect-eating mammals include the moles, aye-ayes and aardvarks. The aardvark

Mammals' hands and feet differ depending on where the animal lives and how it gets around. A. A hominid hand is used for grasping objects; B. A bat's wing is used for flight; C. A pinniped's flipper helps move it through the water. Hoofed animals move around on all fours: D. Elephant foot; E. Equid (horse family) foot; F. Odd-toed hoofed foot; G. Two-toed hoofed foot; H. Four-toed hoofed foot. (Illustration by Patricia Ferrer. Reproduced by permission.)

has a sticky tongue that can reach out as long as 1 foot (0.3 meters) to capture its ant and termite meals.

Plant eaters

Some mammals eat nothing but plants. Plant eaters include pandas, the West Indian manatee, and the red-bellied wallaby. Some mammals have a single stomach that breaks the plant food down into small pieces. Other mammals, such as cows and camels, have a large stomach made of several parts. Each part does a separate job of breaking down difficult-to-digest plants.

Some mammals eat both plants and fruit. These include the 14-ounce (400-gram) Eurasian harvest mouse, the 100-pound (45-kilogram) South American capybara, and the African elephant. An elephant can eat up to 500 pounds (227 kilograms) of grass, plants, and fruit per day.

Meat eaters

Mammals eating mostly meat or fish are carnivorous. Carnivorous mammals have long, pointed, and very strong incisor teeth. Carnivores include polar bears, hyenas, walruses, and Eu-

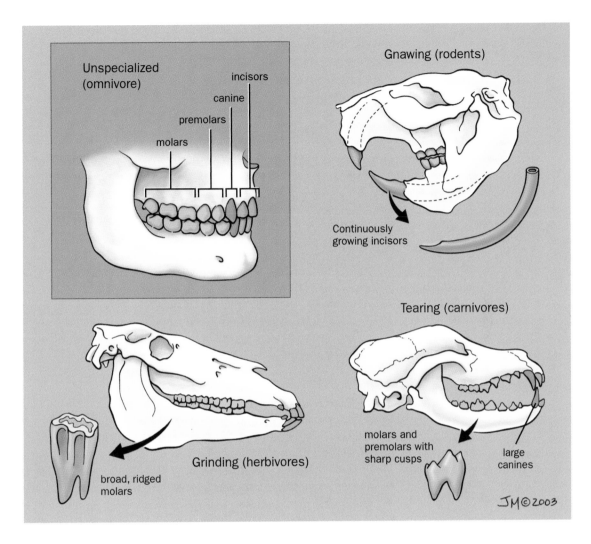

Unspecialized (omnivore)

incisors
canine
premolars
molars

Gnawing (rodents)

Continuously growing incisors

Tearing (carnivores)

molars and premolars with sharp cusps

large canines

Grinding (herbivores)

broad, ridged molars

JM©2003

ropean wild cats. The European wild cat may be an ancestor of our house cats.

Omnivores

Some mammals eat just about anything. They are omnivorous. Omnivorous mammals include wolverines, raccoons, and wild pigs. Wild pigs are the ancestors of our domestic pigs.

MAMMAL SLEEPING HABITS

Day or night

Some mammals sleep during the night, others sleep during the day. The night sleepers are diurnal, active during the day.

Mammals have different tooth shapes for different functions. Herbivores typically have large, flattened teeth for chewing plants. Rodents' ever-growing incisors are used for gnawing. Carnivores have teeth for holding and efficiently dismembering their prey. (Illustration by Jacqueline Mahannah. Reproduced by permission.)

THE BIGGEST, THE TALLEST, AND THE SMALLEST

The largest and heaviest mammal alive today is the blue whale. One adult female measured 110.2 feet (33.6 meters). Blue whale weight can reach 268,400 pounds (121,853 kilograms).

The largest living land animal is the African bush elephant. From trunk tip to tail tip, a male has measured 33 feet (10 meters). Body weight was 24,000 pounds (10,886 kilograms).

The smallest non-flying mammal is the Savi's white-toothed pygmy shrew. An adult's head and body together measure only 2 inches (5.1 centimeters) long. Maximum weight is 0.09 ounces (2.5 grams).

How small is this? This pygmy shrew can travel through tunnels left by large earthworms!

The smallest flying mammal is the rare Kitti's hog-nosed bat, or "bumblebee bat," from Thailand. Head and body length is just 1.14 to 1.29 inches (29 to 33 millimeters). Weight is just 0.06 to 0.07 ounces (1.75 to 2 grams). This tiny bat was only discovered in 1973.

The tallest living animal is the giraffe. The average adult male, or bull, is 16 feet (4.9 meters) high, from front hoof to head horn tip. This size male weighs 2,376 to 2,800 pounds (1,078 to 1,270 kilograms).

The day sleepers are nocturnal, active at night. They may have special night vision. Many desert animals are nocturnal, moving about when it is cooler.

Hibernation

Some bat species hibernate through an entire winter. Hibernation is like a very long deep sleep. When a mammal hibernates, it uses up body fat that has accumulated from food eaten in good weather. Hibernators include the North African jird, groundhogs or woodchucks, and several dormice species. Dormice enter a tree hollow or ground burrow in autumn, and don't come out until springtime.

Bears don't truly hibernate. Their sleep isn't deep. They slow down quite a bit, and nap a lot, but do not sleep through an entire winter.

A new hibernating pattern has just been discovered. Madagascar fat-tailed lemurs hibernate in tree holes when winter daytime temperatures rise above 86° Fahrenheit (30° Celsius). They sleep for seven months. Scientists belief these dwarf lemurs find less food in what is the dry season in Madagascar, so they go to into deep sleep to preserve energy until a better food supply appears.

REPRODUCTION

Mating

Some mammals mate for life, such as wolves and sometimes coyotes. More commonly, a male may mate with several females each breeding period. Or a female may mate with several males.

Some mammals have one litter each year. Others have a litter only every two or three years. But the North American meadow mouse can have seventeen litters per year. That's a group of babies about every three weeks!

There may be one or more infants in a litter. Bats, giraffes, and two-toed sloths have just one baby per year. However, the Madagascar tenrec can produce thirty-two babies in just one litter.

Opossums are marsupial animals. The mother has a pouch in which the young continue to develop after they're born. (© Mary Ann McDonald/Corbis. Reproduced by permission.)

Child care

All mammal infants need protection. They are very small compared to their parents. They may be blind and hairless. Usually females provide care. However, in a few mammal species, such as the golden lion marmoset, the male does most of the care.

Female marsupial mammals, such as opossums, koalas, and kangaroos, have a pouch, like a pocket, on the front or under the body. Their tiny babies are incompletely developed when they are born. At birth, an opossum baby is about the size of a dime. It crawls immediately into its mother's pouch and stays there until ready to survive outside. The pouch contains mammary glands so babies can feed.

SOCIAL LIFE

Solitary mammals

Some mammals are solitary. They keep company with another of the same kind only when mating or when raising young. Solitary mammals include the giant anteaters, European bison, and right whales.

Japanese macaques are social animals, and groom each other regularly. (© Herbert Kehrer/OKAPIA/Photo Researchers, Inc. Reproduced by permission.)

Group living

Many mammals live in groups. In large groups, some eat, some rest, and some keep guard. Baboons, for example, may have from twenty to 300 animals in a group. One or more adult males lead each group. If a predator, such as a leopard, approaches, the males take action against it, while the females and young escape.

Some mammals travel in herds. Musk oxen travel in closely packed herds of fifteen to 100 individuals. These herds include males and females. Bighorn sheep females travel in herds of five to fifteen, with a dominant ewe, or female, as the leader.

Pack mammals get their food by cooperation. They work together to bring down much larger prey. Dingoes, killer whales, and lions hunt in packs.

MAMMALS AND PEOPLE

Domesticated mammals

About 14,000 years ago, humans began controlling, or domesticating, certain animals. This made humans' lives easier.

Horses have been domesticated for practical uses, such as transportation, and for entertainment, such as horse riding and racing. (© Kevin R. Morris/Corbis. Reproduced by permission.)

Rats can spread diseases that affect livestock and people. In addition, they eat and contaminate feed and their gnawing destroys buildings. (Jane Burton/Bruce Coleman, Inc. Reproduced by permission.)

The earliest domesticated mammal was probably the dog. Some scientists think hunters adopted wolf cubs and trained them to smell out game, animals they hunted for food.

People use mammals for many purposes. Cows provide meat, milk, cheese, butter, and hide. Camels, yaks, and Indian elephants carry or pull heavy items. Water buffaloes do hauling and can provide milk. Horses provide transportation and racing activities. Other domesticated animals include rabbits, pigs, goats, sheep, cavies, and capybaras.

People keep animals as pets. Common mammal pets are dogs, cats, guinea pigs, and hamsters.

Pest mammals

Some mammals are considered pests. These include rats, mice, and, depending where they live, gophers, rabbits, and ground squirrels. Rats can transmit disease-carrying fleas. Rabbits and gophers eat garden and food plants.

ENDANGERED MAMMALS

Mammals in danger

Of about 5,000 mammal species currently existing, over 1,000 are seriously endangered. Few wild mammals can live outside their natural habitat. When land is cleared for farming or housing, animals making homes there must leave, if there is any place for them to go. If not, they die from starvation or (because they are easily seen) from predators. Slowly, or quickly, the mammal species disappears.

Many human habits lead to endangerment. Hunting for amusement, killing for fur or body parts, native and commercial killing for food, fishing gear entrapment, land-destructive wars, and the illegal pet trade all take their toll. So do chemicals.

Some mammals are probably on the way to extinction, or total elimination. There are only about sixty Java rhinoceros left in the world. The Seychelles sheath-tailed bat has only about fifty individuals remaining. Yellow-tailed woolly monkeys number no more than 250 individuals. Mediterranean monk seals may be killed by scuba divers, and number only 600 individuals.

Saving endangered animals

Today many people are trying to save endangered animals. Methods include zoo breeding, establishing forest reserves, and training native populations that animals can be an economic benefit. Ecotourism, people visiting a country to see its animals in their natural habitat, is increasing. There are laws against importing and exporting endangered species. And, in some parts of the world, there are laws against land destruction.

Some mammals have possibly been rescued from immediate extinction. The American bison once roamed the North American prairies, numbering about 50 million. After slaughter by soldiers and settlers for food and sport, by 1889 only 541 remained alive. Now, in the United States, there are about 35,000 in protected areas. California northern elephant seals were once reduced to fewer than 100 members due to hunting. Today, protected, there are about 50,000. The ibex was once hunted for supposedly curative body parts and few were left. But in 1922, a National Park was established in the Italian Alps, where several thousand now live. The Mongolian wild horse, once thought to be extinct, now has a special reserve in Mongolia.

Too late to save

Some mammals became extinct only recently. Recently extinct animals include Steller's sea cows, which became extinct in about 1768. The Tasmanian wolf was last seen in 1933, eliminated by bounty hunters. The African bluebuck disappeared from Earth in 1880. The quagga, from southern Asia, was hunted for hides and meat. The last known quagga, a relative of the zebra, died in a Dutch zoo in 1883.

FOR MORE INFORMATION

Books

Boitani, Luigi, and Stefania Bartoli. *Guide to Mammals.* New York: Simon and Schuster, 1982.

Booth, Ernest S. *How to Know the Mammals.* Dubuque, IA: Wm. C. Brown Company Publishers, 1982.

Embery, Joan, and Edward Lucaire. *Joan Embery's Collection of Amazing Animal Facts.* New York: Dell Publishing, 1983.

Jones, J. Knox Jr., and David M. Armstrong. *Guide to Mammals of the Plains States.* Lincoln, NE: University of Nebraska Press, 1985.

Kite, L. Patricia. *Raccoons.* Minneapolis: Lerner Publications Company, 2004.

Kite, L. Patricia. *Blood-Feeding Bugs and Beasts.* Brookfield, CT: Millbrook Press, 1996.

Line, Les, and Edward Ricciuti. *National Audubon Society Book of Wild Animals.* New York: H. L. Abrams, 1996.

Nowak, Ronald M., and John L. Paradiso. *Walker's Mammals of the World.* Baltimore and London: The Johns Hopkins University Press, 1983.

Vogel, Julia, and John F. McGee. *Dolphins (Our Wild World.* Minnetonka, MN: Northword Press, 2001.

Walters, Martin. *Young Readers Book of Animals.* New York, London, Toronto, Sydney, and Tokyo: Simon & Schuster Books for Young Readers, 1990.

Whitaker, John O. Jr. *National Audubon Society Field Guide to North American Mammals.* New York: Alfred A. Knopf, 2000.

Wilson, D. E., and D. M. Reeder. *Mammal Species of the World.* Washington, DC: Smithsonian Institution Press, 1993.

Wood, Gerald L. *Animal Facts and Feats.* New York: Sterling Publishing, 1977.

Woods, Samuel G., and Jeff Cline. *Amazing Book of Mammal Records: The Largest, the Smallest, the Fastest, and Many More!* Woodbridge, CT: Blackbirch Press, 2000.

Periodicals

Allen, Leslie. "Return of the Pandas." *Smithsonian Magazine* (April 2001): 44–55.

Chadwick, Douglas H. "A Mine of Its Own." *Smithsonian Magazine* (May 2004): 26–27.

Cheater, Mark. "Three Decades of the Endangered Species Act." *Defenders* (Fall 2003): 8–13.

Conover, Adele. "The Object at Hand." *Smithsonian Magazine* (October 1996).

Gore, Rick. "The Rise of Mammals." *National Geographic* (April 2003): 2–37.

Mitchell, Meghan. "Securing Madagascar's Rare Wildlife." *Science News* (November 1, 1997): 287.

Pittman, Craig. "Fury Over a Gentle Giant." *Smithsonian Magazine* (February 2004): 54–59.

"Prehistoric Mammals." *Ranger Rick* (October 2000): 16.

Sherwonit, Bill. "Protecting the Wolves of Denali." *National Parks Magazine* (September/October 2003): 21–25.

Sunquist, Fiona. "Discover Rare Mystery Mammals." *National Geographic* (January 1999): 22–29.

Weidensaul, Scott. "The Rarest of the Rare." *Smithsonian Magazine* (November 2000): 118–128.

"Wildlife of Tropical Rain Forests." *National Geographic World* (January 2000): 22–25.

Web sites

Animal Info. http://www.animalinfo.org/ (accessed on June 6, 2004).

"Class Mammalia." Animal Diversity Web. http://animaldiversity. ummz.umich.edu/site/accounts/information/Mammalia004 (accessed on June 5, 2004).

"Hibernating Primate Found in Tropics." CNN Science & Space. http://www.cnn.com/2004/TECH/science/06/24/science .hibernation.reuit/inex.html (accessed on June 24, 2004).

"Ice Age Mammals." National Museum of Natural History. http://www.mnh.si.edu/museum/VirtualTour/Tour/First/ IceAge/index.html (accessed on June 6, 2004).

"Mammary Glands." Animal Diversity Web. http://animaldiversity .ummz.umich.edu/site/topics/mammal_anatomy/mammary_ glands.html (accessed on June 6, 2004).

order

C H A P T E R

PHYSICAL CHARACTERISTICS

Insectivora is the third largest order of mammals after the rodents and bats. Most of the insectivores are smaller than a child's hand, and shrews are some of the smallest mammals known. A few, however, reach a foot long (30 centimeters) or more. The largest insectivore is the moonrat, which stretches 24 inches (60 centimeters) long from the tip of its snout to the end of its tail.

A typical insectivore is covered with smooth fur, although some, like the hedgehogs, have spines. They usually have five clawed fingers or toes at the end of each of its four, short legs, but the tenrecs and golden moles have only four claws. Their skulls are small, long, and flat, however the furry coat may make the head appear larger. They also have tiny, often unnoticeable ears and eyes. Insectivores have an excellent sense of smell that is assisted by their snouts, which may be long and flexible, or short and stout. Many insectivores have rows of stiff sensory hairs, called vibrissae (vuh-BRIS-ee), on their snouts, tails, ears, and sometimes feet. Beyond this general description, these animals vary widely.

GEOGRAPHIC RANGE

Insectivores occur worldwide except Antarctica, Australia, and northern South America.

HABITAT

Insectivores live primarily on land, typically at ground level or beneath it. A few species, like the Asiatic water shrews, are aquatic. Insectivores can survive in a wide range of habitats from tropical rainforests to temperate marshes, from thick forests to open fields, and from sea-level deserts to mountainsides up to 14,760 feet (4,500 meters). Some fossorial, underground, species, like the star-nosed mole, prefer to burrow in the wet soil around freshwater marshes and occasionally venture into somewhat salty, brackish, waters, while others, like the eastern mole, use enlarged, shovel-like forefeet to tunnel through the drier soils of forests and fields. The gymnures prefer hiding places among tree roots or fallen branches, sometimes even inside termite mounds. Shrews, which comprise almost three-quarters of all species in the order, spend much of their time in shallow depressions that they dig beneath some form of shelter, including rocks, logs, and fallen leaves.

DIET

As the name of the order implies, most of these animals primarily eat insects, although many will also eat other invertebrates, animals without a backbone. In addition to insects, many will also eat leaves, tender shoots, seeds, fruits, and other plant materials. Some, like hedgehogs and tenrecs, prefer to dine on invertebrates other than insects, such as snails, clams, and worms, or on vertebrate animals, animals with a backbone, like small snakes or lizards, fish, frogs, and bird eggs.

Many insectivores require a lot of energy, so they must eat frequently. Some, like the long-tailed shrew, spend almost every waking moment eating in order to meet their energy needs.

BEHAVIOR AND REPRODUCTION

These active little mammals prefer to remain out of sight, whether that is underground in tunnels, beneath leaf litter or brush piles, under rocks, or in some species, in the water. Typically nocturnal, active at night, although a few are active during the day. Insectivores have poor eyesight and they must rely on other senses. Sensory hairs, which are located on various parts of their bodies, heighten their sense of touch and make them extremely sensitive to their surroundings. Their hearing is also good, and the animals communicate with others of their own species and with other animals through a variety of squeaks, hisses, whistles, and buzzes. Insectivores have a keen sense of smell, which is important in locating and identifying prey, picking up the scent markings that border the territories of other insectivores, and in finding mates during the reproductive season. The moles and desmans have sensory receptors called Elmer's organs on their snouts, to identify and possibly to locate food items.

Insectivores' best defense against predators, animals that hunt them for food, is to remain hidden, so that predators are more likely to overlook them. Some, however, use other defense tactics. Hedgehogs, for example, can erect their spines to present an intimidating barrier to attacker. Some shrews and solenodons actually produce venom that they transfer with their bites in order to capture prey. Many species, especially shrews, will also attack members of their own species—not for food, but to protect territory. When placed in a confined space, shrews will typically charge one another, sometimes locking together and inflicting tearing bites until one dies.

Insectivores are typically active all year long, even in climates where temperatures in the winter drop below freezing. In colder areas of North America, for example, shrews are sometimes seen scurrying across the snow. A few, like some hedgehogs and tenrecs, hibernate, a dormant state where the animal does not eat or pass wastes, or go into a hibernation-like state when temperatures dip too low or when food becomes scarce.

For many insectivores, details about their reproductive behavior and their early development are unavailable. In general, however, individual insectivores remain alone all year, except during the breeding season. Even then, males and females come together for a very short time, and the male leaves the female well before she has her offspring. Depending on the species, an insectivore may mate once a year with many offspring, as the tenrecs do, or several times a year with fewer offspring per litter, which is common in many moles. Often the young of several nearby females will have the same father. The young of all species are born fully developed, with some becoming independent of their mothers within a few weeks, while others rely on their mother for food and protection for several months. In an unusual display of mother-and-child interplay, the mother in a few shrew species will lead the family in a caravan, with one youngster gripping the tip of her tail with its teeth. A second youngster does the same to the first youngster and on down the line, until the entire three to seven member family is all linked together in a row.

Most insectivores live only about a year, but a few, like the solenodons, may live several years in the wild.

ARE THEY ALL INSECTIVORES?

Scientists are beginning to rethink exactly which animals should be placed in the order Insectivora. Many scientists believe that two of the families traditionally placed under the Insectivora should fall under a separate order known as Afrotheria. Under this arrangement, the tenrecs and golden moles would be classified in Afrotheria with such animals as elephants and aardvarks. While this controversy continues, field biologists are still finding new species, especially in the tropics of Africa where the small, hidden shrews are particularly difficult to find.

INSECTIVORES AND PEOPLE

For the most part, people rarely see insectivores and are not affected by them. A few, like the eastern mole, make above-ground mounds when they tunnel, which are visible and may present a source of frustration to people who want to maintain a perfect lawn. The majority of insectivores are small and inactive during the day, which makes them poor pets. Hedgehogs, however, are larger, easy to keep, and have become quite popular in homes around the world.

CONSERVATION STATUS

Dozens of insectivores around the world are threatened, according to the World Conservation Union (IUCN). Thirty-six are listed as Critically Endangered, facing an extremely high risk of extinction in the wild. Forty-five are Endangered, facing a very high risk of extinction in the wild, and eighty-eight are Vulnerable, facing a high risk of extinction in the wild. In the United States, only the Buena Vista Lake ornate shrew is listed as Endangered by the U.S. Fish and Wildlife Service.

Habitat destruction has proven to be the biggest danger to these species. As humans clear forests, farm more land, and use toxic chemicals to control plants and animals, populations of these small animals can be destroyed.

FOR MORE INFORMATION

Books:

Nowak, R. *Walker's Mammals of the World,* 6th ed. Baltimore: Johns Hopkins University Press, 1999.

Wilson, D., and S. Ruff, eds. *The Smithsonian Book of North American Mammals.* Washington, DC: Smithsonian Institution Press, 1999.

Web sites:

"2003 IUCN Red List of Threatened Species." World Conservation Union. http://www.redlist.org (accessed on July 1, 2004).

Haberl, Werner. *The Shrew-ists Site.* http://members.vienna.at/shrew/index.html (accessed on July 1, 2004).

"Threatened and Endangered Species System (TESS)." *U.S. Listed Vertebrate Animal Species Report.* http://ecos.fws.gov/tess_public/TESSWebpageVipListed?code=V&listings=0#A (accessed on July 1, 2004).

University of Michigan Museum of Zoology. "Order Insectivora." *Animal Diversity Web.* http://animaldiversity.ummz.umich.edu/site/accounts/information/Insectivora.html (accessed on July 1, 2004).

Other sources:

Insectivore Specialist Group (ISG). Hamburgerstrasse 11, A-1050 Vienna, Austria. E-mail: shrewbib@sorex.vienna.at Web site: http://members.vienna.at/shrew/itses.html.

IUCN/SSC Afrotheria Specialist Group. Web site: http://www.calacademy.org/research/bmammals/afrotheria/ASG.html.

European Hedgehog Research Group (EHRG). Phone: +47 370 36 509. Fax: +47 370 35 050. E-mail: bsjohans@stud.hia.no Web site: http://www.ngo.grida.no/ngo/hedgehog/.

Class: Mammalia

Order: Insectivora

Family: Erinaceidae

Number of species: 21 species

family

CHAPTER

phylum

class

subclass

order

monotypic order

suborder

▲ **family**

PHYSICAL CHARACTERISTICS

Gymnures and hedgehogs are generally small, pointy-snouted animals covered with fur, or in the case of hedgehogs, with spines. Each of their four, short legs ends in a flat, walking foot with five toes. In a few African hedgehogs, the big toe is small or nearly nonexistent (not there).

Overall, this group ranges from 4 to 18 inches (10 to 46 centimeters) in body length plus tails from 0.4 to 12 inches (1 to 30 centimeters), and weighs from 0.5 ounces to 4.4 pounds (15 to 2,000 grams). Most members of this group have bodies about 4 to 6 inches (10 to 15 centimeters) long, and short, sometimes barely noticeable tails. A few, however, have longer tails and larger bodies. For example, the Madagascar hedgehog has a grasping tail that can be more than two times the length of its body. The Malayan moonrat is the largest member of this family. With a body that can reach 16 to 18 inches (41 to 46 centimeters) long and a tail that stretches up to 8 to 12 inches (20 to 30 centimeters) long, this animal can measure more than 2 feet (0.6 meters) long from snout to tail tip and weigh up to 4.4 pounds (2 kilograms).

GEOGRAPHIC RANGE

Gymnures and hedgehogs are found in parts of Africa, Eurasia, central Asia, and southeast Asia. New Zealand is also home to a healthy population introduced by humans. Hedgehogs tend toward the cooler climates, while gymnures and moonrats demand tropical and subtropical areas.

HABITAT

Members of this family thrive in a number of varying habitats on land, usually living and feeding at ground level and, in some species, in burrows. A few, like the moonrat, may take an occasional swim in the water. Gymnures prefer humid forests, while hedgehogs can live in a dry and rocky desert, a busy city park, or a mountainside meadow. In fact, hedgehogs can survive almost anywhere they can find food during their night-time hunts and sheltered hideaways for their daytime slumber.

DIET

The diet of hedgehogs and gymnures can include a variety of things, but they mostly eat insects, spiders, worms and other invertebrates, animals without backbones. If they are big enough to kill a reptile, amphibian, or a small mammal, they will do so once in a while. Sometimes they will also eat fungi or fruit. In addition, hedgehogs often prey on birds' eggs. They spend most of their active hours either looking for food or eating it.

BEHAVIOR AND REPRODUCTION

Most members of this family are nocturnal, active only at night. Some species, like the lesser gymnure, may venture out in the daytime if they become hungry enough, but they usually spend their days resting in a sheltered spot. In the winter, many cold-climate species have the ability to slow their body processes, and essentially enter a deep sleep known as hibernation until the weather warms. The European hedgehog sometimes hibernates for six or seven months, surviving on body fat it stored when it was active earlier in the year. Warm-climate species do not have to contend with bitter winters, but they do sometimes face extended dry periods, or droughts, when food can become scarce. During droughts, many will enter a deep sleep, called estivation (est-ih-VAY-shun), which is similar to hibernation.

Adult gymnures and hedgehogs typically live alone. They protect a territory by marking its edges with often-powerful scents and by threatening other adults to stay away with raspy hisses. If a predator approaches, hedgehogs take on a defensive posture by rolling into a ball and standing their spines on end—turning themselves into living pin cushions. Gymnures have no spines for protection and instead try to stay out of sight of predators as often as possible, hiding beneath piles of branches or leaves, among tree roots, or sometimes in burrows dug by other animals.

AN ODD HEDGEHOG BEHAVIOR

A particularly odd behavior among the hedgehogs—and one that is still not fully understood—is called "self-anointing." It happens when a hedgehog comes across a powerful odor. The animal stops what it is doing, and begins licking and sometimes even chewing the source of the odor until it starts to foam at the mouth. Next, it smears the foam over its body spines with small backward jerks of its head and flicks of its tongue. Although many people have seen hedgehogs perform this ritual, scientists still are not sure exactly why animals do it.

Adult gymnures and hedgehogs give up their solitary existence during mating periods, and the females welcome males with the same types of hisses they used earlier in the year to scare them away from their territories. Because of their spines, hedgehog mating can be tricky. To accomplish it, the female smoothes down her spines, so the male can approach without being hurt. After mating, the male leaves and returns to his solitary life. Females, on the other hand, must care for the two to five, blind and helpless babies now living in the nest. The young stay with the mother for five to seven weeks until they are ready to survive on their own.

GYMNURES, HEDGEHOGS, AND PEOPLE

The most intense relationships between people and this family surround the hedgehogs. Gardeners often consider a hedgehog in the yard a helpful addition that will suppress insect and spider numbers. On the other hand, poultry farmers dislike hedgehogs, which are quite fond of eggs and will occasionally eat a chick.

Superstitions in some cultures view a hedgehog as a good omen, and some folk remedies call for the use of blood or some other part of a hedgehog. Historically, hedgehogs have also been killed for their meat, and for their spines to use to comb newly cut sheep wool.

CONSERVATION STATUS

Seven species of this family are at some risk, according to the World Conservation Union (IUCN). The dwarf gymnure is Critically Endangered, facing an extremely high risk of extinction in the wild. In addition, three species are Endangered, facing a very high risk of extinction in the wild, and two species are Vulnerable, facing a high risk of extinction in the wild. In addition, one is considered Near Threatened, not currently threatened, but may become so. Many of these species live in small areas, and human activities like logging and new farms are destroying their limited habitats.

Western European hedgehog *(Erinaceus europaeus)*

WESTERN EUROPEAN HEDGEHOG
Erinaceus europaeus

Physical characteristics: Western European hedgehogs are round-to oval-shaped and mostly brown. Their most recognizable feature is the layer of light-yellow and brown spines on their backs. They have small, but noticeable rounded ears, fairly long snouts, and dark, beady eyes. Their body ranges from 9 to 11 inches (23 to 28 centimeters) long with short tails of 0.5 to 1.2 inches (1.5 to 3 centimeters) long. The adult weight can vary from 14 to 42 ounces (400 to 1,200 grams).

Geographic range: Western European hedgehogs are found in Western and central Europe from Scandinavia, northern European Russia, Britain and Ireland to Italy and the Mediterranean islands. A population introduced by humans in New Zealand is also thriving.

Habitat: People most frequently see western European hedgehogs in farmlands, parks and gardens, but the animals are also quite common in forests and meadows where they are less likely to encounter humans.

Diet: Active at night, these hedgehogs primarily eat insects, worms, spiders and other invertebrates, but they will also prey on eggs and

The western European hedgehog eats mainly insects, spiders, and worms, which makes it a welcome visitor in most yards. (© Hans Reinhard/OKAPIA/ Photo Researchers, Inc. Reproduced by permission.)

fruit. In captivity or when otherwise fed by humans, they will eat just about anything from dog food to bread.

Behavior and reproduction: They do not set up territories like some other insectivores, but adults still live alone. Those in cooler climates survive the winter by hibernating for four to seven months. Mating occurs from spring to summer, and females usually have four to six babies, although they sometimes have as few as two or as many as ten at a time. The babies are blind, naked, and helpless, and remain in the mother's nest for no more than six weeks, then they are pushed out to face the world on their own.

Western European hedgehogs and people: Hedgehogs are becoming increasingly popular as pets. Most human contact with the animals, however, comes from positive encounters in the yard. Homeowners generally welcome the hedgehogs, which have a taste for insects and spiders that homeowners view as pests.

Conservation status: Western European hedgehogs are not threatened. ■

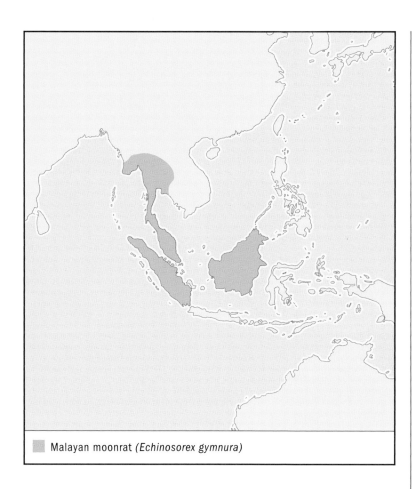

Malayan moonrat *(Echinosorex gymnura)*

MALAYAN MOONRAT
Echinosorex gymnura

Physical characteristics: Malayan moonrats have long and narrow bodies, coarse hair, pointy snouts and long, almost naked tails giving them an appearance that resembles a Virginia opossum. They have mostly black fur toward the back and white fur toward the head, although they may have quite large, black patches on the head. Sometimes they are completely white. Malayan moonrats range from 10 to 18 inches (26 to 46 centimeters) in body length, plus a 6.5- to 12-inch (16.5- to 30-centimeter) tail. Adult weight varies from about 1 to 3 pounds (0.45 to 1.4 kilograms), but can sometimes reach 4.4 pounds (2 kilograms). Males are generally a bit smaller than females.

Malayan moonrats search at night for worms, insects, crabs, and other invertebrates found in moist areas. (© N. Smythe/Photo Researchers, Inc. Reproduced by permission.)

Geographic range: Malayan moonrats are found on the Malay Peninsula, Sumatra, and Borneo.

Habitat: Moist forests, mangrove swamps, and wet farmlands are the typical habitats of Malayan moonrats. Scientists believe the animals spend at least part of their time in the water.

Diet: An animal of the night, Malayan moonrats eat worms, insects, crabs, and other invertebrates found in moist areas. They will also eat fruit, and occasionally frogs or fish.

Behavior and reproduction: When they are not looking for food at night, Malayan moonrats rest in hiding places among tree roots, inside hollow logs, or in other tight spaces. Adults live alone. They release strong odors to mark the edges of their territories and warn other moonrats to stay away with threatening hisses. They also release odors to ward off predators. When they are preparing to have young, they will make nests mostly from leaves. Females usually have two babies at a time, either once or twice a year. Scientists know little more about moonrat adults or young.

Malayan moonrats and people: Generally speaking, Malayan moonrats leave people alone, and people leave them alone.

Conservation status: Malayan moonrats are not threatened. ■

FOR MORE INFORMATION

Books:

McDonald, D. *Collins Field Guide: Mammals of Britain and Europe.* London: Harper Collins, 1993.

Nowak, Ronald M. *Walker's Mammals of the World Online.* Baltimore: John Hopkins University Press, 1995. http://www.press.jhu.edu/books/walkers_mammals_of_the_world/insectivora/insectivora.erinaceidae.echinosorex.html (accessed on July 1, 2004).

Reeve, N. *Hedgehogs.* London: Poyser Natural History, 1994.

Web sites:

"European hedgehog." BBC. http://www.bbc.co.uk/nature/wildfacts/factfiles/193.shtml (accessed on July 1, 2004).

"European Hedgehog." Boreal Forests of the World Mammal Species. http://www.borealforest.org/world/mammals/hedgehog.htm (accessed on July 1, 2004).

IUCN Red List of Threatened Species—Species Information. http://www.redlist.org (accessed on July 1, 2004).

GOLDEN MOLES
Chrysochloridae

Class: Mammalia
Order: Insectivora
Family: Chrysochloridae
Number of species: 21 species

PHYSICAL CHARACTERISTICS

Generally, a golden mole looks like little more than a round to oblong lump of fur with a tiny, naked nose poking out at one end. Adults range from 2.7 to 9 inches (7 to 23.5 centimeters) long, and 0.5 to 17.6 ounces (16 to 500 grams). The fur is generally brown to gray, but it shines golden, bronze, and even purple and blue when the light hits it just right. Their small ears and tails are typically buried under their silky, thick fur, and their eyes are covered with skin beneath the fur. They have four short legs, the front two of which often have enlarged claws they use for digging. Their back legs are more slender than their powerful forelimbs and their back feet have webbing between the toes—a big help when kicking away the soil they've just dug. One species, the yellow golden mole, can tunnel through the soil so quickly and efficiently that it is sometimes called a "sand swimmer." Many of the other species, like the Grant's desert golden mole, also almost appear to be swimming when they travel through the loose sand in dunes.

GEOGRAPHIC RANGE

The southern half of Africa.

HABITAT

Golden moles typically live much of their lives underground in shallow burrows they dig themselves. The burrows are often visible above ground as slight ridges in the soil. Many golden moles prefer loose soil that is easily moved by their hollow claws. Some species, such as the rough-haired golden mole, make tunnels to connect chambers within mounds of soil.

DIET

Because their eyes are buried beneath the skin, golden moles are blind and they must rely on other senses, like touch and smell, to get around and to find prey. Food items include ants, termites, beetles, earthworms, and other invertebrates (animals without backbones) that they hunt at night. Sometimes, they will feel above-ground vibrations, then burst out of their shallow tunnels to grab an insect on a blade of grass or a lizard moving along the ground. De Winton's golden mole is noted for its ability to kill a lizard with its enlarged front claws. The typical golden mole will alternate between periods of activity and rest throughout the night, spending a considerably greater amount of time resting. Most remain active only at night, but a few, like Sclater's golden moles, stay busy digging through the soil and looking for food both day and night.

NOT ALWAYS LONERS

Although adult golden moles are typically described as loners that live a solitary life all year, except for mating season, the adults of one species are a little more friendly to one another. Among the species known as large golden moles, several adults may share a single burrow system in the winter months. This species, which is Endangered, lives in South Africa.

When golden moles are confronted with a span of extreme temperatures, lengthy dry periods, and/or a lack of prey, golden moles can become inactive for a few days—a state called torpor—to conserve their energy until conditions become more favorable.

BEHAVIOR AND REPRODUCTION

Like most other insectivores, golden moles live alone as adults. During the spring breeding season, males and females will come together, but only briefly. Although much of their behavior is still unknown, some mating rituals have been observed in which the male nods its head, stomps its feet, and chases the female. The two also communicate through scents that ooze out of body glands, and by making chirping and squeaking noises at one another. Females give birth to their young in a grassy nest built within a tunnel that may be several feet (a few meters) below ground. Each brood commonly has one or two, sometimes three young. The mother recognizes her offspring by their scent. She raises them only until they are able to survive on their own, and then she kicks them out and lives alone again until the next mating season.

GOLDEN MOLES AND PEOPLE

Golden moles are sometimes seen as beneficial, and other times as pests. Because they eat insects that may be destructive to vegetation, many people welcome their presence. At the same time, farmers, gardeners and homeowners may prefer that the moles and their noticeable burrows stay out of the crops and the lawn. In some cases, people kill and skin the moles for their shiny fur.

CONSERVATION STATUS

Eleven species of golden mole are at some risk, according to the World Conservation Union (IUCN). The Red List describes four as Critically Endangered, facing an extremely high risk of extinction, dying out; one as Endangered, facing a very high risk of extinction; and six as Vulnerable, facing a high risk of extinction. These golden moles exist in limited areas and those areas are becoming ever smaller through habitat destruction due to human activities, like farming, mining, and lumbering.

Grant's desert golden mole (*Eremitalpa granti*)

GRANT'S DESERT GOLDEN MOLE
Eremitalpa granti

Physical characteristics: One of the smallest golden moles, this species reaches only about 3.0 to 3.3 inches (7.6 to 8.8 centimeters) in body length and weighs 0.5 to 1.0 ounces (15 to 32 grams). On its back, it has long, shiny, light-gray fur that is sometimes tinged with yellow. Its underside fur is lighter and yellowish. Grant's desert golden mole has three long claws on each forelimb, although they aren't as hefty as the claws in some other golden mole species.

Geographic range: South Africa and the Namib Desert in extreme southwestern Africa.

Habitat: Coastal sand dunes, typically areas with some dune grass, are its preferred habitat.

Grant's desert golden mole prefers to live in coastal sand dunes, where it searches for food at night and spends the days in shallow burrows. (Illustration by Jacqueline Mahannah. Reproduced by permission.)

Diet: Its diet consists of various invertebrates, such as spiders, termites, beetles, and ants, that it hunts at night. When the opportunity presents itself, these moles will also eat kill and eat lizards, some of which may be as long as the mole.

Behavior and reproduction: Active at night, it will venture above ground in search of prey, sometimes covering as much as 3.6 miles (5.8 kilometers) in a single twenty-four-hour period. It spends its days in shallow burrows. Interestingly, this species doesn't maintain a constant body temperature during the day. Instead, its body becomes cooler or warmer with the temperature of the sand around it. In breeding season, the females will crawl into deeper tunnels that may lie 6 feet (1.8 meters) or more beneath the surface, where it gives birth to and raises typically one or two offspring. As soon as the youngsters are old enough to survive alone, the mother forces them out of her nest. Although details about behavior are lacking, scientists believe that males may mate with more than one female, and therefore father numerous young with different females. Outside of breeding season, adult moles live alone and have little contact with other adults.

Grant's desert golden moles and people: Since this is a desert species that lives in sand dunes away from most people, it has little impact on humans.

Conservation status: The IUCN lists the Grant's golden mole as Vulnerable. Dune removal and diamond mining are destroying the habitat within the limited range of this animal, but efforts are under way to create a national park, which will protect at least part of the mole's range. ■

FOR MORE INFORMATION

Books:

Apps, P. *Smithers' Mammals of Southern Africa.* Cape Town, South Africa: Struik Publishers, 2000.

Kingdon, J. *The Kingdon Field Guide to African Mammals.* San Diego, CA: Academic Press, 1997.

Nowak, R. M. *Walker's Mammals of the World Online.* Baltimore: Johns Hopkins University Press, 1997. http://www.press. jhu.edu/books/walkers _mammals_of_the_world/insectivora/insectivora.chrysochloridae. eremitalpa.html (accessed on July 1, 2004).

Smithers, R. H. N. *The Mammals of the Southern African Subregion.* Pretoria, South Africa: University of Pretoria, 1983.

Web sites:

"Insectivore Specialist Group 1996, *Eremitalpa granti.*" 2003 IUCN Red List of Threatened Species. http://www.redlist.org (accessed on July 1, 2004).

"A Mammal that Imitates Reptiles." *Clive Cowley's Journey into Namibia: Namibia Guidebook #12.* http://www.orusovo.com/guidebook/ content8.htm (accessed on July 1, 2004).

family

CHAPTER

phylum

class

subclass

order

monotypic order

suborder

▲ **family**

PHYSICAL CHARACTERISTICS

Rat- or shrew-like in general appearance, tenrecs vary greatly in body size, tail length, and color. One of the most consistent features is the long, pointy snout that is typically adorned with long whiskers. The smallest tenrecs have head and body lengths of just 2 inches (5.5 centimeters) and weights of 0.14 ounces (4 grams), while the largest can reach 14 inches (35.7 centimeters) and weigh up to 44 pounds (2 kilograms). Tails vary from tiny, unnoticeable stubs to long and very obvious structures stretching up to three times the length of the body. Some species have soft yellow to brown fur, and a few have vivid black-and-white or yellow-and-black fur patterns. Adults in several species have sharp spines that are quite effective in thwarting attacks by would-be predators. Some youngsters, like the common tenrec, have blunt spines that produce a sound when rubbed together.

GEOGRAPHIC RANGE

Tenrecs live in Madagascar and western central Africa. Introduced to Comoros, Mascarenes, and Seychelles, which are islands in the Indian Ocean.

HABITAT

Most species live in humid forests or in grasslands. A few species can survive well in marshy areas, drier forests, or agricultural fields. Aquatic tenrecs and otter shrews spend much of their time in or near freshwater streams.

DIET

The tenrec diet varies considerably among species. For the most part, the land-living tenrecs eat insects, worms, and other invertebrates (animals without backbones). A few will also devour baby mice and other small vertebrates (animals with backbones), and some will even munch on dead animals they come across. The tenrecs that live in marshes, near streams, or in the water dine on other water-loving creatures, like aquatic insects, frogs, fishes, mollusks, and crabs.

BEHAVIOR AND REPRODUCTION

Scientists have few details about many species of tenrecs, partly because the animals are relatively small and are typically only active at night. They rest during the daytime, often in tunnels that they construct. Some, like the Ruwenzori otter shrew, sleep on beds of grass in the tunnels. During their daily rest, several species are known to enter a state of deep sleep, called torpor, which allows them to conserve their energy. One species, known as the large-eared tenrec, is particularly tuned in to the outdoor temperature, and its internal body temperature quite closely matches the outdoor temperature. When weather becomes cool, its body temperature takes a similar dip, and the animal may enter torpor. In long, dry periods, some species take an extended deep sleep, called estivation (est-ih-VAY-shun), during which the heart rate and body temperature fall and the animal needs to burn far less energy to stay alive. Estivation may last days or even weeks. Tenrecs that estivate for longer periods will frequently plug the openings of their burrows in preparation for the extended sleep.

Adults likely spend most of their lives alone, coming together only for mating. Sometime, males will remain with the female while she's pregnant, a span that typically lasts about two months. A few reports suggest that some male-female pairs may remain together during other times of the year, too. Overall, scientists know little about mating rituals in most species, but they have observed some behaviors. In the hedgehog tenrec, for example, the females give off an odor during mating season that causes a milky substance to flow from glands near the eyes

TOGETHERNESS AMONG TENRECS

Usually, less than a handful of different mammals from the same group live together within a small area. With tenrecs, it is different. In one small, forested area in Madagascar, sixteen different species of tenrecs share the same space. This type of high diversity among one type of animal is extremely rare, and may, in fact, represent the greatest concentration of such similar animals found anywhere in the world.

of males. Each year, females have one litter of one to thirty-two babies, depending on the species. The young, most of which are born blind and naked, apparently stay with the mother for at least four or five weeks, and possibly more.

TENRECS AND PEOPLE

Of all the tenrecs, the most popular is perhaps the greater hedgehog tenrec, which has become quite a popular pet. In Madagascar, which has a thriving tenrec community, humans have traditionally viewed the animals as a source of prime meat, and enthusiastically hunted them. Humans also hunt the giant otter shrew for its pelt.

CONSERVATION STATUS

Ten species are at risk, according to the Red List of the World Conservation Union (IUCN). One, the tree shrew tenrec, is listed as Critically Endangered, facing an extremely high risk of extinction, or dying out; six are Endangered, facing a very high risk of extinction; and three are listed as Vulnerable, facing a high risk of extinction. Many of these species exist in small areas and are threatened by human activities that are changing their habitat. For example, the aquatic tenrec is an Endangered species that is found in only a few spots in Madagascar. It needs clean rivers to survive, but agriculture and deforestation are either eliminating the rivers or allowing silt to muddy up the waters.

Common tenrec (*Tenrec ecaudatus*)

COMMON TENREC
Tenrec ecaudatus

Physical characteristics: A grayish brown to reddish brown animal with long, coarse hairs and a lighter-colored belly. It has small, beady eyes, small ears, a long and pointed snout with lengthy whiskers, a short and unnoticeable tail, and front legs that are a bit longer than the hind legs. Youngsters have streaked fur and two rows of blunt spines down their backs, but the stripes disappear when they get older, and the spines are covered with longer fur. Adults weigh about 42 to 70 ounces (1.2 to 2 kilograms), and are about 10.5 to 15.3 inches (26 to 39 centimeters) from nose to rump.

Geographic range: Common tenrecs live in Madagascar. Introduced populations also live on the islands of Comoros, Mascarenes, and Seychelles in the Indian Ocean.

Habitat: Common tenrecs usually live in forested areas with a nearby water source such as a river or paddy field.

Common tenrec adults live alone for most of the year, but males and females come together in the spring to mate. (Illustration by Gillian Harris. Reproduced by permission.)

Diet: Insects, earthworms, and other invertebrates are their primary food, but they will also eat small vertebrate animals, fruit, and plant roots on occasion.

Behavior and reproduction: Adults live alone for most of the year, spending days sleeping in the burrows they make, and nights on the prowl for food. In the dry winter months, food can become quite scarce, triggering the tenrecs to enter a state of deep sleep, called estivation, for up to several months. They mate in the spring, and females give birth to a single litter of twelve to thirty-two babies in the summer, which falls in December and January for these creatures of the Southern Hemisphere. The mother nurses her young for almost a month, then takes them out with her to search for insects and other food items. By the time they are two to two-and-a-half-months old, the youngsters leave the mother to live on their own.

Common tenrecs and people: Humans in Madagascar hunt this species for meat, which is considered a delicacy.

Conservation status: The common tenrec is not considered to be threatened.   ■

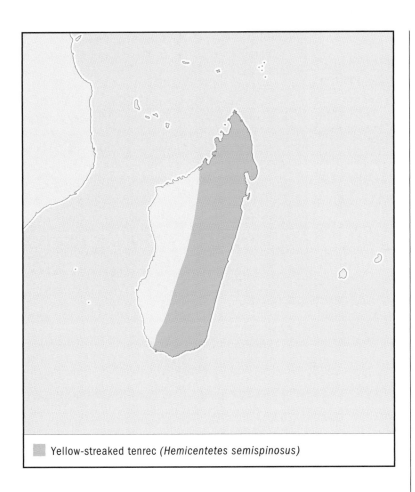

Yellow-streaked tenrec *(Hemicentetes semispinosus)*

YELLOW-STREAKED TENREC
Hemicentetes semispinosus

Physical characteristics: A small, black tenrec with a mane of longer golden-yellow to whitish hairs as well as yellow to whitish stripes down the center and on either side of its face. It has a lighter-colored belly, and its back sports scattered, long, yellowish spines. This species has small eyes, black ears, and a long, pink snout, but no noticeable tail. The yellow-streaked tenrec is about 6 to 7.5 inches (15 to 19 centimeters) long, and weighs 3 to 7 ounces (90 to 220 grams).

Geographic range: Madagascar.

Yellow-streaked tenrecs may live alone (like most other tenrecs), or they may share their burrows with up to twenty-four family members. (© H. Uible/Photo Researchers, Inc. Reproduced by permission.)

Habitat: This is a burrowing species that lives in humid forests, as well as shrubby areas, frequently near a water source.

Diet: The yellow-streaked tenrec prefers earthworms but will also eat other invertebrates.

Behavior and reproduction: Unlike most other tenrecs, which are loners much of the year, yellow-streaked tenrecs can either live alone or share their burrows with up to two dozen members of their families, including parents, grandparents, cousins, and siblings. Females may have more than one litter per year, usually with five to eight babies at a time. The babies quickly mature, becoming old enough to mate at just five weeks old. Yellow-streaked tenrecs survive the dry winter months by estivating in their burrows.

This tenrec's spines come in two types: barbed and stridulating (STRIH-juh-late-ing). A barbed spine is sharp with tiny barbs, or hook-like structures, at the end. These spines detach easily from the animal. When a predator is foolish enough to nip at this tenrec, it gets a mouthful of spines that fall off the tenrec and stick in the predator. Stridulating spines aren't barbed, and don't fall off the tenrec's body so easily, but they do have their own unusual characteristic: they produce a sound when rubbed against one another.

Yellow-streaked tenrecs and people: This species has little contact with humans. Humans do not consider them pets, pests, or a source of meat.

Conservation status: The yellow-streaked tenrec is not considered to be threatened. ■

FOR MORE INFORMATION

Books:

Garbutt, N. *Mammals of Madagascar.* New Haven, CT: Yale University Press, 1999.

Goodman, S. M., and J. P. Benstead, eds. *The Natural History of Madagascar.* Chicago: The University of Chicago Press, 2003.

Periodicals:

Eisenberg, J. F., and E. Gould. "The Tenrecs: A Study in Mammalian Behavior and Evolution." *Smithsonian Contributions to Zoology* 27 (1970): 78–89.

Web sites:

Gorog, A. *"Tenrec ecaudatus."* Animal Diversity Web. http://animaldiversity .ummz.umich.edu/site/accounts/information/ Tenrec_ecaudatus.html (accessed on July 1, 2004).

"Hemicentetes semispinosus: Lowland Streaked Tenrec." http://info. bio.sunysb.edu/rano.biodiv/Mammals/Hemicentetes-semispinosus/ (accessed on July 1, 2004).

IUCN 2003. 2003 IUCN Red List of Threatened Species. http://www. redlist.org (accessed on July 1, 2004).

Shefferly, N. *"Hemicentetes semispinosus."* Animal Diversity Web. http://animaldiversity.ummz.umich.edu/site/accounts/information/ Hemicentetes_semispinosus.html (accessed on July 1, 2004).

"Tenrec ecaudatus: Common Tenrec." http://info.bio.sunysb.edu/ rano.biodiv/Mammals/Tenrec-ecaudatus/ (accessed on July 1, 2004).

"Tenrecidae—Tenrecs—Borstelegels." http://www.animalsonline.be/ insectivora/borstelegels/common_tenrec.html (accessed on July 1, 2004).

SOLENODONS

Solenodontidae

Class: Mammalia

Order: Insectivora

Family: Solenodontidae

Number of species: 2 species

phylum

class

subclass

order

monotypic order

suborder

▲ **family**

PHYSICAL CHARACTERISTICS

The two living species in this family are the Cuban solenodon (suh-LEN-uh-dun), which is also known as the almiqui (ahl-mee-KEE), and the Hispaniolan solenodon, which is sometimes called the Haitian solenodon. Both have extremely long snouts that extend beyond the end of their lower jaw. Their four relatively tall legs, clawed feet, and long tails are nearly hairless. Most are brown on the back, or sometimes black in the Cuban solenodon, and have lighter-colored fur on their undersides. Cuban solenodons have longer, coarser, back hair, giving it a shaggier appearance. They are also slightly smaller than Hispaniolan solenodons. Overall, adult solenodons range from about 10 to 15 inches (25 to 38 centimeters) in length, and their tail adds another 6 to 10 inches (15 to 25 centimeters). Adults weigh 1.3 to 2.4 pounds (0.6 to 1.1 kilograms).

Both species have glands under their front teeth that produce poison. When they bite into a prey animal, the poison flows from the glands down grooves in their teeth and into the prey.

GEOGRAPHIC RANGE

Solenodons live in Haiti, Dominican Republic, and Cuba. In the past they were also found in Puerto Rico.

HABITAT

Solenodons occupy tropical forests on the sides of mountains, and also can be found in plantations and other flat, brushy areas.

DIET

Solenodons spend most of their nighttime hours above ground, poking their long snouts into the dirt and any other little opening they can find to search for insects, spiders, earthworms, and other invertebrates, animals without backbones. They will also claw apart old, rotten logs where many of their prey live.

BEHAVIOR AND REPRODUCTION

Like most other insectivores, solenodons rest during the day and become active at night. They usually spend their days in small groups within burrows or shallow hollows in the ground, but may also rest in small hiding places. They spread out at night to look for food alone, and will attack fellow solenodons that get too close, often inflicting nasty bites. If a predator approaches, the solenodon has the option of charging and biting, or running off. Unless it is startled or has nowhere to flee, it will usually choose running over fighting.

A FIGHT FOR MILK

Like other mammals, solenodon mothers nurse their babies with milk delivered through their nipples. A mother may have up to three babies in each litter, but she has only two nipples. All three of her young cannot feed at once. As a result, one of the three babies typically gets less of the nourishing milk than the other two, becomes weaker and weaker, and eventually dies.

Solenodons make a number of noises, including shrieks, grunts, and clicks. Some scientists believe the clicks may help them find prey. Just as bats make high-pitched noises and listen as the noises bounce off objects and back to them, solenodons may listen for the bounced clicks to detect objects, like prey, in their surroundings. This ability to "see" objects with reflected sound waves is called echolocation (eck-oh-loh-KAY-shun).

Males and females can breed at any time of year, and females usually have two litters (young born at the same time) every year. A mother may have one, two, or three babies at a time. Mothers nurse their young with two nipples located toward the rear of the animal, which are farther back than on a typical mammal. The babies continue nursing for about seventy-five days, but often stay with their mother until well after the next litter is born.

SOLENODONS AND PEOPLE

Solenodons and people usually do not see one another, unless the solenodon makes its home in a plantation or garden. Homeowners and farmers sometimes view them as pests because they occasionally damage crops while rooting around in the dirt for insects and other prey that live near plants.

CONSERVATION STATUS

According to the World Conservation Union (IUCN) both species are Endangered, facing a very high risk of extinction in the wild. The U.S. Fish and Wildlife Service also list these two species as Endangered. The causes for their decline include hunting by dogs and cats, and the removal of the forests where the solenodons live. The IUCN lists a third species, Marcano's solenodon, as extinct.

Hispaniolan solenodon *(Solenodon paradoxus)*

HISPANIOLAN SOLENODON
Solenodon paradoxus

Physical characteristics: This large insectivore's long tail, long snout, and rather lengthy legs are nearly naked. From the tip of the snout to the end of the tail, an adult can reach 22 inches (56 centimeters) long. Adults range from 11 to 12 inches (28 to 32.5 centimeters) in body length with tails of 7 to 10 inches (17.5 to 25.5 centimeters), and weigh 1.3 to 2.4 pounds (0.6 to 1.1 kilograms). Color varies somewhat, but individuals usually have a brownish coat on the back and a lighter-colored underside. The forelimbs are stronger and have larger paws than the hind limbs. All four paws have five toes.

Geographic range: Dominican Republic and Haiti.

Habitat: Hispaniolan solenodons typically live in forests, but sometimes make their homes in plantations or gardens.

The Hispaniolan solenodon is considered Endangered. Dogs and cats prey on the animal, and humans have cleared many of the forests where it lives. (© N. Smythe/photo Researchers, Inc. Reproduced by permission.)

Diet: The Hispaniolan solenodon's diet includes insects and other invertebrates, small reptiles, some fruit and vegetables, and possibly an occasional young chicken.

Behavior and reproduction: During the day, Hispaniolan solenodons rest in various hiding places, including hollow trees or logs, tight places in caves or slender cracks in rocks, or in the burrows they make. Several solenodons may rest together in a burrow. When they become active at night, they scout around on the surface looking for food. Adults are loners during this period, even fighting with one another.

Males and females produce an oily, greenish fluid, which tells members of the opposite sex that they are ready to mate. Females can have one or two litters each year, and may have them in any season. Each litter typically has one to three babies, which the mother feeds from two nipples located near the mother's rump. The young can latch onto the nipples and remain attached even if the mother decides to go for a walk. The young simply drag along the ground underneath her. The babies stop nursing after about two-and-a-half months, but may stay with the family for several months, even after the mother has another litter.

Hispaniolan solenodons and people: Other than an occasional run-in in a farm field or garden, solenodons and humans rarely see one another.

Conservation status: Both the IUCN and the U.S. Fish and Wildlife Service list this species as Endangered. Threats come in the form of dogs and cats that prey on the animal, and the human destruction of the forests where it lives. ∎

FOR MORE INFORMATION

Books:

Eisenberg, John F. "Tenrecs and Solenodons in Captivity." In *International Zoo Yearbook 15.* London: Zoological Society of London, 1975.

Nowak, Ronald M. *Walker's Mammals of the World,* 6th ed. Baltimore: Johns Hopkins University Press, 1999.

Periodicals:

Eisenberg, John F., and Edwin Gould. "The Behavior of *Solenodon para-doxus* in Captivity with Comments on the Behavior of other Insectivora." *Zoologica* 51 (1966): 49–57.

Wood, Charles A. "The Last Endemic Mammals in Hispaniola." *Oryx* 16 (1981): 146–152.

Web sites:

Baillie, J. "*Solenodon cubanus.*" 2003 IUCN Red List of Threatened Species. http://www.redlist.org (accessed on July 1, 2004).

Baillie, J. "*Solenodon marcanoi.*" 2003 IUCN Red List of Threatened Species. http://www.redlist.org (accessed on July 1, 2004).

Baillie, J. "*Solenodon paradoxus.*" 2003 IUCN Red List of Threatened Species. http://www.redlist.org (accessed on July 1, 2004).

Eatroff, A. "*Solenodon paradoxus.*" Animal Diversity Web. http://animaldiversity.ummz.umich.edu/site/accounts/information/Soleondon_paradoxus.html (accessed on July 1, 2004).

"The Haitian Solenodon." Dominican Fauna. http://www.geocities.com/cuyaya/solenen.html (accessed on July 1, 2004).

Massicot, P. "Haitian Solenodon." Animal Info. http://www.animalinfo.org/species/solepara.htm (accessed on July 1, 2004).

family

CHAPTER

PHYSICAL CHARACTERISTICS

Sometimes confused with mice, the typical shrew has a long, pointy snout with sensitive whiskers, a long and thin tail, tiny eyes that are sometimes hidden under their fur, noticeable ears, and fairly short legs with five clawed toes on each foot. Most have short, brown or gray fur, and many of them have red-tinged teeth. The vast majority of shrews are no bigger than a house mouse, but a few species, like the water shrews, can top 5 inches (12.5 centimeters) in head and body length. Overall, shrews range from 1.4 to 5.3 inches (3.6 to 13.5 centimeters) in head and body length and 0.06 to 1.5 ounces (2 to 40 grams) in body weight. Tails are typically from half the length to the same length as the head and body measurement. The smallest shrew, and indeed one of the tiniest living mammals, is Savi's pygmy shrew with a body that is just 1.4 to 2.1 inches (3.6 to 5.3 centimeters) long. The tail is about half that size. The tiny shrew weighs 0.4 to 0.1 ounces (1.2 to 2.7 grams).

GEOGRAPHIC RANGE

Shrews can be found nearly worldwide, including North America, Central America, northern South America, Africa, Europe, and Asia.

HABITAT

This is a very wide-ranging family, but most species tend to prefer areas with at least some moisture. Many scuttle along the damp earth under leaf litter, but a few will climb trees in search of food. The aquatic species naturally seek out water sources that may range from bogs and swamps to streams and rivers. A few species survive well in the desert.

DIET

Shrews are not picky eaters. While insects and other invertebrates (animals without backbones) make up the bulk of their diet, they will also eat fruit and seeds, as well as small mammals, lizards, frogs, and even other shrews if food is scarce. They burn energy very quickly, so many shrews spend just about every waking moment either eating or looking for their next meal. Many species eat at least their body weight, and sometimes up to four times that amount in food every day.

SCARED TO DEATH

Shrews are very active little animals, dashing from place to place with noses almost always twitching. A typical heart rate for a shrew is in the hundreds, five or more times higher than a human heart rate, and can nearly double if the animal is frightened. In fact, a shrew can actually die of fright if it is startled by a loud noise, like a clap of thunder.

BEHAVIOR AND REPRODUCTION

Most shrews are active at night and rest during the day. A few, however, like the long-tailed shrew, stay awake for much of the day trying to feed their hefty appetites. When they can't find enough food, some species may spend a few hours in an inactive state called torpor that decreases their energy needs. Unlike most other mammals, some shrews actually produce venom to immobilize their prey, and then either kill the prey immediately or save it for a later meal. European water shrews, for instance, have a deep groove in the lower front tooth to help direct the venom from a duct at the base of the tooth into the prey.

Shrews are well-known for being aggressive toward members of their own species and sometimes other species. By making and marking small territories with scents, they typically avoid one another and thus sidestep fights. However, when two shrews, like the short-tailed shrews of North America, encounter one another in a confined space, they will commonly attack quickly and continuously, often until one dies. Despite their reputation as fighters, a few species tolerate other shrews quite well. Adult small-eared shrews will even share a nest.

Most shrews spend their whole lives on land, usually running from place to place. A few species are good swimmers. These aquatic shrews typically have stiff, fringed hairs on their feet that serve to enlarge the surface area of their feet and help them paddle through the water. The elegant water shrew has actual webbing on its feet to aid in swimming.

Shrews generally breed two or more times a year, giving off specific odors or making characteristic movements, such as tail-wagging in house musk shrews, to announce that they are ready to give up fighting long enough to mate. Females may mate with several males during each breeding period, so the offspring in one female's litter may have several different fathers. Many species build nests. The short-tailed shrew, for example, makes a small nest of leaves and grass in a hidden spot, often under a rock or inside a tunnel. Pregnancies last only three to four weeks for most species, and the babies are small and quite helpless. The number of offspring varies, but three to seven is a common litter (young born at the same time) size for shrews. Babies grow very rapidly and are ready to face the world on their own at just three to four weeks old. Before they do so, however, some species of the group, known as white-toothed shrews because they lack the reddish tinge seen in other shrews, take part in an odd behavior. The mother leads them around in a row, with each shrew using its teeth to grasp the hair on the rump of the one in front of it. This line-up of shrews is called a caravan, or chain behavior. Scientists now believe that families of some red-toothed shrews may use this peculiar but effective method of travel, as well.

As noted, shrews develop quickly and they begin having young of their own before they reach their first birthday. Shrews rarely live much past fourteen to eighteen months of age.

SHREWS AND PEOPLE

Since they are small, usually active only at night, and like to hide, shrews avoid human attention most of the time. They do, however, play an important role for farmers and gardeners, who have fewer destructive insects in the crops, thanks to the shrews' appetites. Shrews have cultural significance, as well. For example, Shakespeare's *The Taming of the Shrew* is a classic tale, and people in Taiwan consider a shrew to be a symbol of good luck. On very rare occasions, shrews have bitten people. If the shrew is venomous, this can be quite painful.

CONSERVATION STATUS

According to the Red List of the World Conservation Union (IUCN), twenty-eight species are Critically Endangered, facing an extremely high risk of extinction; twenty-eight are Endangered, facing a very high risk of extinction; fifty-five are Vulnerable, facing a high risk of extinction; and four are Near Threatened, not currently threatened, but could become so. In other words, more than one-third of all shrew species are at some risk. The U.S. Fish and Wildlife Service names one species, the Buena Vista Lake ornate shrew, as Endangered. Many of the at-risk shrews live in limited areas and have very small known populations. This combination puts them in danger, because a single natural disaster, like a flood or one human disruption of their habitat, such as a mining operation, could destroy the entire population.

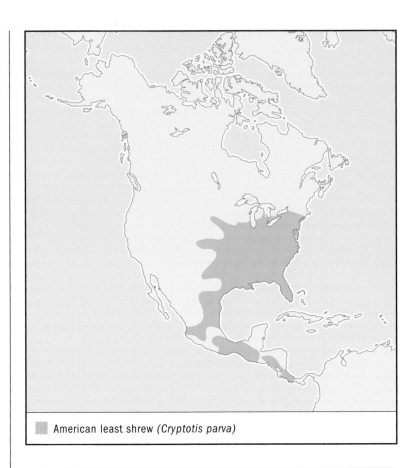

American least shrew (*Cryptotis parva*)

AMERICAN LEAST SHREW
Cryptotis parva

Physical characteristics: Just 2.2 to 3.1 inches (5.5 to 7.8 cm) in head to body length, this small shrew has a brownish gray back and whitish belly, a long snout, red-tinged teeth, and a tail that is no more than a third of the length of its head and body. It weighs from 0.1 to 0.3 ounces (4 to 8 grams). Its eyes are small and its ears are unnoticeable.

Geographic range: United States, extreme southeastern Canada, Mexico, and much of Central American to Panama.

Habitat: American least shrews are common in open, grassy fields, sometimes near a stream, but may also live in damp forests. This species spends much of its time in shallow tunnels it either makes itself or borrows from other animals.

Diet: Active day and night, year-round, they spend most of their time running about in search of food, which can include caterpillars, worms and other invertebrates (animals without backbones), small frogs and lizards, or bits of already-dead animals they find.

Behavior and reproduction: Least shrews are skittish animals that are mainly active at night, although they will also warily venture about during the day. Their brownish gray coloration, small size, and tendency to hide among grasses or underground helps them avoid their numerous predators, animals that hunt them for food, which include owls, skunks, snakes, and a variety of other animals. They make a variety of sounds, some of which may be used to help them find their next meal. Just as bats make high-pitched noises and listen as the noises bounce off objects and back to them, American least shrews may make clicking noises, and then listen for the bounced clicks to detect objects, like prey, in their surroundings. This ability to "see" objects with reflected sound waves is called echolocation (eck-oh-loh-KAY-shun).

Most shrews prefer to live alone, but two dozen or more adult American least shrews may share a burrow, where they click at one another to communicate. (Illustration by Emily Damstra. Reproduced by permission.)

Unlike most other shrews that like to live alone, several to sometimes even more than two dozen adult American least shrews may share a burrow, where they click at one another to communicate. They mate all year long in warmer areas of their range, but limit mating to spring, summer, and fall in cooler areas. The female has her young after a pregnancy of about three weeks in grassy and/or leafy nests built in the burrow. The litter size is usually three to seven, but may be as small as one or as large as nine. The babies stay with the mother for almost three weeks.

American least shrews and people: This shrew usually remains out of sight, but it can assist gardeners and farmers by eating crop-destroying insects.

Conservation status: Neither the IUCN nor the U.S. Fish and Wildlife Service lists them as endangered, but some states consider them to be threatened. Connecticut, for example, lists American least shrews as endangered because their habitat is rapidly disappearing. ■

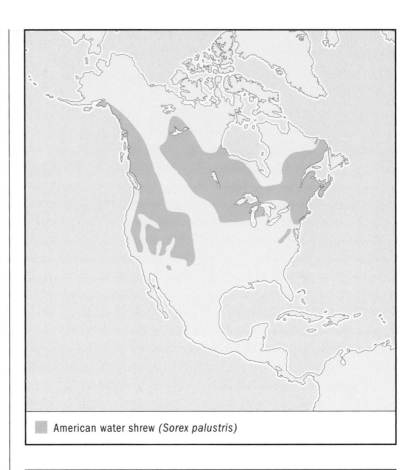

American water shrew *(Sorex palustris)*

AMERICAN WATER SHREW
Sorex palustris

Physical characteristics: The American water shrew ranges from 2.5 to 3.2 inches (6.3 to 8.1 centimeters) in head and body length with a similar-sized tail, and weighs 0.3 to 0.6 ounces (8 to 18 grams). They have dark brownish gray backs and whitish bellies, a likewise two-toned tail, red-tinged front teeth, and hind feet that are larger than the forefeet. Like many other water-loving shrews, they have stiff, fringed hairs on their feet that aid in swimming.

Geographic range: United States and Canada.

Habitat: Usually found in or near water, these shrews prefer damp, forested areas with many places on land where they can hide, such as fallen logs, a thick understory, and/or rock piles. They readily take to the water, where they can make good use of their specially designed feet and swim underwater or run across the water surface like some water insects do.

Diet: Active mainly at night, they eat caterpillars, grubs, worms, and an occasional fish. Unlike many shrews that have to eat their body weight in food every day, this species can survive on just a tenth of its body weight or less in food per day. Compared to humans, however, that is still a considerable amount.

The American water shrew has stiff, fringed hairs on its feet that aid in swimming underwater or running across the surface of the water. (Illustration by Emily Damstra. Reproduced by permission.)

Behavior and reproduction: A variety of land animals find the American water shrew to be a tasty treat, but the shrews are quite adept at escaping into the water. Unfortunately, they must also be wary of several fish species, including trout, which also eat shrews. The shrews float well, so they must paddle with their hindfeet furiously to stay underwater. This species also makes chirping noises that may be used to find food through echolocation. Adults keep to themselves most of the time and will fight other adults that come too close. Mating occurs in the spring and summer. Pregnancies last about three weeks, and mothers retreat to tunnel nests to have their young. She may have two or three litters each year with three to ten babies at a time. Although the babies are helpless when they are born, they grow quickly and leave their mothers in about a month. The young can start their own families a few months later. Those that survive to adulthood usually only live to be about eighteen months old.

American water shrews and people: Other than a fleeting glimpse, people rarely have any contact with this shrew.

Conservation status: American water shrews are not considered threatened. ■

FOR MORE INFORMATION

Books:

Nowak, Ronald M. *Walker's Mammals of the World,* 6th ed. Baltimore: Johns Hopkins University Press, 1999.

Stone, David, and the IUCN/SSC Insectivore, Tree Shrew and Elephant Shrew Specialist Group. *Eurasian Insectivores and Tree Shrews-Status Survey and Conservation Action Plan.* Gland, Switzerland: IUCN, 1995.

Wilson, D. E., and S. Ruff, eds. *The Smithsonian Book of North American Mammals.* Washington, DC: Smithsonian Institution Press, 1999.

Periodicals:

Matsuzaki O. "The Force Driving Mating Behavior in the House Musk Shrew (*Suncus murinus*)." *Zoological Sciences* 19, no. 8 (2002): 851–69.

Web sites:

"American Water Shrew." BBC. http://www.bbc.co.uk/nature/wildfacts/factfiles/642.shtml (accessed July 1, 2004).

Endangered Species Program, U.S. Fish & Wildlife Service. http://endangered.fws.gov/ (accessed on July 1, 2004).

IUCN Red List of Threatened Species—Species Information. http://www.redlist.org (accessed on July 1, 2004).

"Least Shrew." All Taxa Biodiversity Inventory. http://www.dlia.org/atbi/species/animals/vertebrates/mammals/soricidae/Cryptotis_parva.html (accessed July 1, 2004).

"Savi's pygmy shrew, Etruscan shrew." America Zoo. http://www.americazoo.com/goto/index/mammals/48.htm (accessed July 1, 2004).

"Soricidae—Shrews." All Taxa Biodiversity Inventory. http://www.dlia.org/atbi/species/animals/vertebrates/mammals/soricidae/ (accessed July 1, 2004).

"Water Shrew." All Taxa Biodiversity Inventory. http://www.dlia.org/atbi/species/animals/vertebrates/mammals/soricidae/Sorex_palustris.html (accessed July 1, 2004).

MOLES, SHREW MOLES, AND DESMANS

Talpidae

Class: Mammalia

Order: Insectivora

Family: Talpidae

Number of species: 42 species

PHYSICAL CHARACTERISTICS

Moles are small, short-legged, smooth-furred animals with tiny, sometimes hidden eyes, and long, nearly naked snouts. Many land-living moles have large, wide, shovel-like front feet adapted for digging through the soil. Some moles, including the desmans, are swimmers and have slender, webbed forefeet. Shrew moles, which live on land but dig little, if at all, have feet that are neither shovel-like nor webbed. Overall, adult moles range from about 2.4 to 17.0 inches (6 to 43 centimeters) in body length and another 0.6 to 8.3 inches (1.5 to 21.5 centimeters) in tail length. They weigh from 0.4 ounces (12 grams) in the smallest species to 7.8 ounces (220 grams) in the largest.

GEOGRAPHIC RANGE

Moles, shrew moles, and desmans are found in the United States, Canada, Mexico, and much of Europe and Asia.

HABITAT

About three-quarters of the species in this family live much of their lives underground. A few live above ground on land, and others spend a good deal of their time in or near the water. Those that prefer the water usually make their homes near fresh water, but a few will also enter brackish water, water that is somewhat salty.

DIET

The primary diet among the moles is insects, earthworms, centipedes, and other invertebrates, animals without backbones,

IS IT A SHREW OR A MOLE?

At first glance, an observer might think that the smallest mole in North America is actually a shrew. Its size of just 3.5 to 5.2 inches (8.9 to 13.2 centimeters) is similar to shrews, and it does not have the large front feet that are common in many moles. Most of its activity occurs above ground, where it runs beneath the leaf litter in a manner similar to shrews. Land-living moles, on the other hand, are mainly tunneling animals. Even its name can be confusing. This small animal is called the American shrew-mole.

but many will also eat roots and other parts of plants. Water-living species may also include frogs and fish in their diet.

BEHAVIOR AND REPRODUCTION

Most moles have long and narrow snouts that they are able to wiggle and bend. The snout tip has tiny Elmer's organs that the mole uses to sense its environment and to find prey. Desmans that spend a good amount of time underwater use their snouts for several purposes. In one common behavior, a desman will stick just its snout tip out of the water to sniff the air for prey as well as predators, animals that hunt them for food. They will also dig through the water bottom with their snouts looking for food.

Some moles are active mainly at night, but others move around both day and night. The land-living, digging species are capable of making tunnels quickly for such a small animal. The eastern mole, which is less than 12 inches (30 centimeters) long from the tip of its nose to the end of its tail, can tunnel up to 15 feet (4.6 meters) in a single hour, and more than 100 feet (30 meters) in a day. Their tunnels are often visible from above ground, and look like long, sometimes-branching strings of broken ground. These are called mole runs. A molehill is a circular mound of dirt that is created when the mole pops above ground from the tunnel. Both the land-living and the water-loving species also dig deeper chambers for breeding and to escape the winter cold. Moles usually spend their lives alone, although some are more social. Reports suggest that Russian desmans may share their dens on occasion.

After mating one or two months earlier, most moles have one set, or litter, of about three to five babies in early to mid-summer. A few species have one or more additional litters later in the year. The young are helpless and naked at birth, but after approximately four to six weeks, they are ready to leave the mother. The young can have babies of their own within a year.

MOLES, SHREW MOLES, DESMANS, AND PEOPLE

The land-living, tunneling moles have the greatest contact with humans. Their tunneling activity is beneficial in that it loosens the soil and actually helps plants to grow, but their plant-eating habits and the visible mole runs frequently make them an unwelcome guest in yards, gardens, and farm fields. At one time, people also hunted moles for their silky fur, which was used for collars and cuffs on women's clothing. People even hunted some species, like the Russian desman, for their scent, which was used in perfumes.

CONSERVATION STATUS

According to the World Conservation Union (IUCN), two species are Critically Endangered, facing an extremely high risk of extinction in the wild. Five species are Endangered, facing a very high risk of extinction in the wild, and three are Vulnerable, facing a high risk of extinction in the wild. That means that nearly one quarter of all mole species are at some risk. The U.S. Fish and Wildlife Service lists no species as endangered. Many of the at-risk moles have small populations and/or live in habitats that are disappearing due to human activity. In addition, some species are facing threats from hunting or from introduced species that are invading their habitat. The Vulnerable Russian desman, for example, is now competing for food and shelter with the introduced muskrat and coypu (KOY-poo).

Eastern mole (*Scalopus aquaticus*)

EASTERN MOLE
Scalopus aquaticus

Physical characteristics: Eastern moles are shiny grayish, occasionally black, moles with very large, clawed, shovel-like front feet that are well-suited for digging. A typical adult, which has a short tail, may be 5.9 to 7.9 inches (15 to 20 centimeters) long and weigh 3.2 to 5.0 ounces (90 to 143 grams).

Geographic range: Eastern moles are found in the eastern United States, far southern Canada, and far northern Mexico.

Habitat: Eastern moles live much of their lives underground in good soils in forests or grasslands.

Diet: Eastern moles eat mostly grubs and earthworms, but also centipedes and slugs. If they come across a root or seed during their tunneling, they will also eat those.

Behavior and reproduction: Eastern moles spend much of their time alone, making shallow tunnels in search of food. They also make deeper, living chambers. Their below-ground life protects them from most predators, although dogs, cats and other large digging mammals will sometimes root out a mole. Rarely, when a mole pops out of its tunnel, a nearby owl or snake will attack it. Moles mate once a year in early spring—a bit earlier in warmer areas and later in cooler climates—and build a nest in an underground chamber. About a month and a half afterward, the mother gives birth to a litter of three to five young. They stay with her for four to five weeks, and are ready to become parents themselves by the following spring.

Eastern moles and people: Most people are familiar with eastern moles from their mole runs, which are visible above the ground and often considered unsightly. Moles will also eat some crop roots, so they are sometimes considered pests. Homeowners, gardeners, and farmers frequently try various methods to rid their yards and fields of the moles.

Conservation status: Eastern moles are not threatened. ■

Eastern moles spend much of their time alone, making shallow tunnels in search of food. (E. R. Degginger/Bruce Coleman Inc. Reproduced by permission.)

Star-nosed mole (*Condylura cristata*)

STAR-NOSED MOLE
Condylura cristata

Physical characteristics: This dark-brown mole is best-known for the collection of twenty-two short and pink, fleshy tentacles on the tip of its snout. They have wide, clawed hands, and a tail that is almost as long as their body. Adults range from 6.1 to 8.1 inches (15.5 to 20.5 centimeters) and weigh 1.1 to 3.0 ounces (30 to 85 grams).

Geographic range: Star-nosed moles are found in the eastern United States and eastern Canada.

Habitat: Star-nosed moles prefer wet meadows and forests near water. Occasionally waterside homeowners may find evidence of one in a moist lawn area.

Diet: Star-nosed moles like grubs, earthworms, and other invertebrates, and will occasionally eat a small fish.

Behavior and reproduction: A star-nosed mole's always-wiggling tentacles act like feelers and help the animal to find its food and to make its way through the dark tunnels it digs. Active all year, and both day and night, this mole not only hunts for food inside its tunnels but above ground and in the water. Predators vary depending on the mole's location. When they are in the water, fish pose a threat. On land, meat-eating birds, snakes, and mammals may attack and kill moles. Other moles make long and winding mole runs, but the usual outward sign of the star-nosed mole is its molehills, which are small mounds of dirt at the entrances and exits for their tunnels. Although they are usually loners, two or more individuals may spend the winter together in shared, below-ground chambers. They do not hibernate, and even in the cold of winter, may leave their tunnels to dig through the snow. Females have one litter of two to seven babies each year. The young leave the nest in about a month, and begin having their own families by the following year.

Star-nosed moles and people: People rarely see star-nosed moles or recognize evidence of them, so interactions between these moles and humans are rare.

Conservation status: Star-nosed moles are not threatened. ∎

FOR MORE INFORMATION

Books:

Gorman, M. L., and R. D. Stone. *The Natural History of Moles.* Ithaca, NY: Comstock Publishing Associates, 1990.

Kurta, A. *Mammals of the Great Lakes Region.* Ann Arbor: University of Michigan Press, 1995.

Nevo, Eviatar, and Osvaldo Reig. *Evolution of Subterranean Mammals at the Organismal and Molecular Levels.* New York: Wiley-Liss, 1990.

Nowak, Ronald M. *Walker's Mammals of the World.* Baltimore: Johns Hopkins University Press, 1999.

Wilson, D., and S. Ruff, eds. *The Smithsonian Book of North American Mammals.* Washington, DC: Smithsonian Institution Press, 1999.

Periodicals:

Catania, K. C. "A Comparison of the Elmer's Organs of Three North American Moles: The Hairy-Tailed Mole (*Parascalops breweri*), the Star-Nosed Mole (*Condylura cristata*), and the Eastern Mole (*Scalopus aquaticus*)." *Journal of Comparative Neurology* 354 (1995): 150–160.

Mason, Matthew J., and Peter M. Narins. "Seismic Signal Use by Fossorial Mammals. " *American Zoologist* (November 2001): 1171–1184.

Web sites:

Hebert, P. D. N., ed. "Star-nosed mole, *Condylura cristata.*" Canada's Aquatic Environments. http://www.aquatic.uoguelph.ca/mammals/freshwater/accounts/mole.htm (accessed on July 1, 2004).

Insectivore, Tree Shrew and Elephant Shrew Specialist Group. http://members.vienna.at/shrew/itsesAP95-desmana.html (accessed on July 1, 2004).

"Talpidae." Discover Life. http://www.discoverlife.org/nh/tx/Vertebrata/Mammalia/Talpidae/ (accessed on July 1, 2004).

Class: Mammalia

Order: Scandentia

One family: Tupaiidae

Number of species: 19 species

monotypic order
CHAPTER

PHYSICAL CHARACTERISTICS

In physical appearance, tree shrews resemble a squirrel with a long snout, nose. The scientific family name is from the Malay word *tupai*, which means squirrel. Animals in this family are commonly referred to as tree shrews, ever since they were first mistaken for shrews when they were first spotted in 1780. Shrews are small, insect eating mammals with pointy snouts.

Tree shrews are relatively small, with the head and body length ranging from about 5 to 9.5 inches (13 to 24 centimeters). These animals have a long tail, which is covered with long thick hair in all the species except the pen-tailed tree shrew. The tails of pen-tailed tree shrews are hairless except for a whitish feather-shaped arrangement of hairs near the end. In general, tree shrews have small ears similar to those of a squirrel, and their ears are covered with fur. An exception is the ears of the pen-tailed tree shrews, which are bare and larger than all the other species.

Fur colors of tree shrews range from gray to dark brown on the upper side of their body, and white, yellow-brown, or dark brown on their belly. Their fur is generally soft and thick. Some species have light shoulder stripes and others have facial markings. Their legs are short, with claws on their fingers and toes.

GEOGRAPHIC RANGE

Tree shrews are found in south and Southeast Asia, ranging from India and southwest China eastward through Malaysia, Indonesia, and the Philippines. Out of the nineteen tree shrew species, ten live on the island of Borneo.

HABITAT

Tree shrews live in shrub and forested areas, which are often mountainous. Many of the tree shrews are arboreal, meaning that they live in trees. Some species spend the majority of their time on the ground.

DIET

Tree shrews primarily eat a combination of insects and fruits. They also will occasionally feed on plant material, along with other small animals, including fish and mice. Different tree shrew species have their own feeding method, one species may collect black ants at night while another species digs up earthworms.

BEHAVIOR AND REPRODUCTION

In general, tree shrews are active during the day. The pen-tailed tree shrew is nocturnal, meaning that it is active at night. Researchers do not know a lot about the behavior of tree shrews. One reason is that they are difficult to observe because they are highly active animals that move quickly and constantly.

All tree shrews have the ability to climb trees. They use their sharp claws to dig into the trees and branches as they climb. Many species are arboreal, while others find their food and spend a great deal of time on the ground. Tree shrews commonly use the same paths along the ground or on branches to reach their favorite feeding or resting areas.

They have well-developed senses of vision, hearing, and smell. These animals typically catch food with their snout, and use their hands only when they cannot reach their food. They may grab hold of flying insects with their hands. They eat in a style similar to squirrels, hunching on their hind legs while holding the food in their arms and eating it.

Most species nest in holes in tree trunks or branches. These animals make a nest of dried leaves, twigs, and soft wood. Tree shrews are territorial, meaning they protect their own territory. They release droplets of urine and scent to mark their territory. Tree shrews have specialized glands, located on their chest and belly, which produce the chemical scent. Many of the scents are distinct to a particular animal. They deposit their scent in areas where other animals may smell it to let them know that the area is occupied.

Tree shrews live in monogamous (muh-NAH-guh-mus) pairs, meaning they have one mate. Gestation, or pregnancy, lasts between forty-three and fifty-six days. Females give birth to small litters (young born at the same time) of poorly developed, hairless offspring. The typical litter size ranges from one to three offspring. Baby tree shrews are often born in pairs.

In many of the species studied, researchers found an unusual mothering strategy unlike other mammals. Mother tree shrews visit their babies only once every two days for about two minutes each visit. When the mother visits her young in the nest, she immediately allows the babies to nurse, which they do quickly. Babies take in large amounts of milk and lie back with a bloated stomach. With no mother in the nest, the babies snuggle with each other to keep warm. The babies also groom each other, a task traditionally done by the mother.

Field studies have found that tree shrews breed when fruiting peaks occur in the forest.

A CASE OF MISTAKEN IDENTITY

For years, scientists debated about who was the tree shrews' closest relative. In the 1920s, a scientist proposed that tree shrews were related to primates based on studies of primate and shrew skulls. Many accepted these findings and said the tree shrew belonged in the primate order. Other researchers said it was more similar to animals in the insectivore order, because of its resemblance to animals such as the shrew. In 1984, researchers decided the tree shrew was unique enough to have its own order.

TREE SHREWS AND PEOPLE

With their close relationship to primates, and a well-developed sense of vision and hearing, tree shrews are being used by researchers as animal models for human diseases. An animal model is an animal studied that mimics human biological or psychological disease. Research studies have included hepatitis (hep-uh-TIE-tuhs), a disease of the liver, vision disorders, and psychosocial stress.

CONSERVATION STATUS

The majority of tree shrew species are common, however several are Endangered or Threatened. Long-footed tree shrews and Nicobar tree shrews are Endangered, facing a very high risk of extinction in the wild. Bornean smooth-tailed tree shrews, golden-bellied tree shrews, Palawan tree shrews, and Mindanao tree shrews are Vulnerable, facing a high risk of extinction in the wild. Mindanao tree shrews are listed as Near Threatened, not currently threatened, but could become so.

Common tree shrew (*Tupaia glis*)

COMMON TREE SHREW
Tupaia glis

Physical characteristics: Common tree shrews have a head and body length of about 7.5 inches (19.5 centimeters). They have a long, pointed snout. Their fur is darker on the upper side of their body than on their bellies. Upper side fur can be dark brown, pale brown, blackish gray or it can appear almost black. Their undersides are whitish, orange or rusty red, or a light or dark brown. Common tree shrews that live in northern areas with less rainfall are typically lighter than those in southern areas with greater rainfall.

They often have a pale stripe along their shoulder. Similar to a squirrel, common tree shrews have a long, bushy tail. It can be about as long as the length of the head and body. These animals have relatively small ears, with their lower lobe smaller than the upper one.

Common tree shrews typically live alone or with their mate. This pair is grooming each other. (R. Williams/Bruce Coleman Inc. Reproduced by permission.)

Geographic range: Common tree shrews are found in Thailand, the Malayan Peninsula, and in Sumatra, Java, and surrounding islands.

Habitat: Common tree shrews live in evergreen tropical rainforests.

Diet: Common tree shrews eat a varied diet that they collect primarily from the ground. Their food includes insects, particularly ants, as well as spiders, seeds, buds, leaves, and fruit. They can also eat lizards.

Behavior and reproduction: Active during the day, common tree shrews are extremely energetic. They spend a great deal of their time on the ground, yet they can also easily climb trees. They typically live alone or with a mate. Field studies in Malaysia have shown that breeding may occur at any time of year. Gestation periods last roughly forty-six to fifty days, and families produce one to three offspring. The newborn young are hairless, with closed eyes. The young are ready to leave the nest about thirty-three days after birth. The young are reared in a nest separated from that of the mother and are suckled every other day.

Common tree shrews and people: There is no known connection between common tree shrews and people.

Conservation status: Common tree shrews are not considered threatened. ∎

FOR MORE INFORMATION

Books:

Nowak, Ronald M. *Walker's Mammals of the World Online.* Baltimore: Johns Hopkins University Press, 1997 http://www.press.jhu.edu/books/walkers_mammals_of_the_world/scandentia/scandentia.html (accessed July 1, 2004).

Stone, David, and the IUCN/SSC Insectivore, Tree Shrew and Elephant Shrew Specialist Group. *Eurasian Insectivores and Tree Shrews-Status Survey and Conservation Action Plan.* Gland, Switzerland: IUCN, 1995.

Periodicals:

Bloch, Jonathan I., and Dough M. Boyer. "Grasping Primate Origins." *Science* (June 2001): 1606–1609.

Crosby, Olivia. "Wild Jobs with Wildlife: Jobs in Zoos and Aquariums." *Occupational Outlook Quarterly* (Spring 2001): 2–15.

Eckstrom, Christine. "What is a Tree Shrew?" *International Wildlife* (November/December 1996): 22–27.

Gore, Rick "The Rise of Mammals: Adapting, Evolving, Surviving." *National Geographic* (April 2003): 2–37.

"Tree Shrews Could Model a Number of Chronic and Infectious Human Diseases." *Hepatitis Weekly* (July 14, 2003): 8.

Web sites:

"Common Tree Shrew (*Tupaia glis*)." America Zoo. http://www.america.zoo.com/goto/index/mammals/83.htm (accessed on July 1, 2004).

Meyers Phil. "Order Scandentia." Animal Diversity Web. http://animaldiversity.ummz.umich.edu/site/accounts/information/Scandentia.html (accessed on July 1, 2004).

"Rainforest Animals: Common Tree Shrew." Missouri Botanical Garden. http://mbgnet.mobot.org/sets/rforest/animals/shrew.htm (accessed on July 1, 2004).

COLUGOS
Dermoptera

Class: Mammalia
Order: Dermoptera
One family: Cynocephalidae
Number of species: 2 species

PHYSICAL CHARACTERISTICS

Colugos are commonly referred to as flying lemurs, even though they do not technically fly and they are not lemurs, primate mammals found in Madagascar. Colugos are about the size of a cat, approximately 20 inches (75 centimeters) long. They weigh about 3 pounds (1.35 kilograms).

Their ability to glide—not fly—is due to their most distinctive feature, after which they are named. The order they belong to, Dermoptera, means "skin wings" in Greek, referring to the flap of skin that extends between the front and hind limbs. This thin layer of skin or membrane is called a patagium (pah-TAY-jee-um). The patagium stretches from the side of the neck to the tips of its fingers, toes, and tail. When the front and hind legs are spread out, the patagium allows the colugo to glide like a kite. The patagium also acts as a parachute, catching air inside of it as it jumps. This parachute effect prevents colugos from losing too much height as they move between trees.

Colugos resemble lemurs, with long noses and wide bulging eyes. The shape of their head and snout is similar to a greyhound dog. They have small round ears and sharp claws.

The fur of male colugos is generally brown to red-brown and in females the fur is grayish brown. Malayan colugos have white spots on their fur, but Philippine colugos do not. The underside of the animal is a lighter orange-yellow, orange, or brownish red color.

phylum

class

subclass

order

● **monotypic order**

suborder

family

Colugos | **269**

GEOGRAPHIC RANGE

The Philippine colugo is found only in the Philippines, and the Malayan colugo is found in Borneo, Peninsular Malaysia, Thailand, Indochina, and some of the Indonesian islands.

HABITAT

Colugos live in the rainforest. They are often found in coconut, banana, and rubber plantations. Their habitat must contain many trees with few branches low on the trunk.

DIET

Colugos are herbivores, animals that eat plants. They feed on leaves, buds, flowers, and occasionally fruits. They get their water from food and also by licking wet leaves.

BEHAVIOR AND REPRODUCTION

Relatively little is known about colugos. They are arboreal, meaning they spend most of their time in trees and bushes. They are solitary animals that move from tree to tree by climbing and gliding. These animals are nocturnal, active at night. They spend the day resting inside tree holes or on branches or tree trunks. They rest either with their head up and all four claws clinging to a branch, or they hang upside down with their two rear claws holding onto the branch. In coconut trees, they curl up in a ball among the leaves.

Colugos usually emerge before dusk and climb to the top of trees. They move awkwardly up trees because of their patagium, bringing both their front limbs together and then both back limbs.

In the evening they move to a feeding area, gliding distances up to 230 feet (70 meters) in one leap. Colugos have been known to glide as far as 450 feet (135 meters) in a single glide. Colugos may land near the bottom of trees, and then climb back up trees slowly before they take off on another glide.

Each colugo tends to have a certain feeding area, which the animal returns to every night. When eating, colugos use their front feet to pull a bunch of leaves towards them, and then use their tongues and teeth to pluck off the leaves.

Little is known about the mating of colugos. Females give birth to one or two young following a gestation, or pregnancy, period of sixty days. The offspring is born in an undeveloped state, almost like a marsupial, an animal that carries its young in a pouch. Young are carried on their mother's belly until they are weaned at about six months old. Females can fold the patagium near the tail to form a pouch for their young. When ready to forage, or look for food, females may carry their young with them. Young colugos cry out with duck-like sounds. Young colugos reach maturity when they are about two or three years old.

COLUGOS AND PEOPLE

Deforestation, clearing trees, of the rainforest by people has caused the loss of colugo habitat and thus, a decrease in their population. Some people also hunt colugos for their fur to make caps, and for food. Plantation growers, especially banana, coconut, and rubber growers, may consider these animals pests because they eat the reproductive flowers and fruits of the trees.

CONSERVATION STATUS

The Philippine colugo is considered Vulnerable, facing a high risk of extinction in the wild.

Malayan colugo (*Cynocephalus variegatus*)

MALAYAN COLUGO
Cynocephalus variegatus

Physical characteristics: Malayan colugos are also called Malayan flying lemurs. They resemble lemurs with their dog-like shaped heads. Malayan colugos have large eyes, long limbs, and sharp claws. Their fur is gray or brown with white spots along the back. Their head and body length is about 15 inches (38 centimeters), and they weigh approximately 3.3 pounds (1.5 kilograms). The fur of male colugos is generally brown to red-brown with white spots, and in females it is grayish brown with white spots. The underside of the animal is a lighter orange-yellow to orange color.

Geographic range: Malayan colugos are found in Southeast Asia, including Malaysia, Thailand, Indonesia, Borneo, and some nearby islands.

Habitat: Malayan colugos live in tropical forests and woodlands.

Diet: Malayan colugos are herbivores, eating leaves, buds, pods, flowers, and fruit.

Behavior and reproduction: Malayan colugos are independent and solitary animals. They are nocturnal, resting during the day in tree hollows, against trees, or while clinging to branches. Individual animals have their own feeding area, or even tree, and follow a pattern of returning to the same area every evening.

Malayan colugos generally have one offspring per birthing period. Gestation period is about sixty days. When the offspring is born it is poorly developed, like a marsupial. It stays on the female's belly, enclosed in the patagium, folded into a pouch, until it is weaned at about six months.

Malayan colugos and people: Destruction of the rainforest for timber and agriculture has caused the loss of habitat for Malayan colugos. They are also hunted for their fur and meat.

Conservation status: Malayan colugos are not listed as a threatened species. ■

FOR MORE INFORMATION

Books:

Clutton-Brock, Juliet, and Don E. Wilson. *Smithsonian Handbooks: Mammals.* New York: DK Publishing, 2002.

Macdonald, David, ed. *The Encyclopedia of Mammals.* New York: Facts on File Publications, 1984.

Nowak, Ronald M. *Walker's Mammals of the World,* 5th ed. Baltimore and London: The Johns Hopkins University Press, 1991.

Periodicals:

Bloch, Jonathan I., and Doug M. Boyer. "Grasping Primate Origins." *Science* (June 2001): 1606–1609.

Gore, Rick. "The Rise of Mammals: Adapting, Evolving, Surviving." *National Geographic* (April 2003): 2–37.

Laman, Tim. "Wild Gliders." *National Geographic* (October 2000): 68–85.

Zimmer, Carl. "Into the Night." *Discover* (November, 1998): 110–115.

Web sites:

"Dermoptera—Skin Winged Mammals." America Zoo. http://www.amer icazoo.com/goto/index/mammals/dermoptera.htm (accessed on June 23, 2004).

Ellis, E. *"Cynocephalus variegates."* Animal Diversity Web. http:// animaldiversity.ummz.umich.edu/site/accounts/information/ Cynocephalus_variegatus.html (accessed on June 23, 2004).

"Flying Lemur Called Another Close Relative of Humans." http://www.colugos.com/flying-lemur.html (accessed on June 23, 2004).

Focus on Wildlife. "Colugo (Flying Lemur)." Ecology Asia. http://www .ecologyasia.com/Vertebrates/colugo.htm (accessed on June 23, 2004).

Sarawak National Parks and Wildlife. "Paratroopers Have Landed: Colugo or Flying Lemur." The Sarawak Wildlife Weblet. http://www. mered.org.uk/saraweb/animals/colugo.htm (accessed on June 23, 2004).

order

CHAPTER

PHYSICAL CHARACTERISTICS

Bats are the second largest group of mammals after rodents. Almost one out of every four mammalian species on the planet is a bat species. Living bats are categorized into two main groups, each with its own distinct features. The Megachiroptera (mega-keer-OP-ter-ah), or "large bats" group includes one family. The Microchiroptera (micro-keer-OP-ter-ah), or "small bats" group includes all the rest of the bats.

Bats are the only mammals that can fly. Chiroptera comes from the Greek roots *cheiro* (hand) and *ptera* (wing), named for the similarity of a bat wing to a hand. Bat wings are long arms, hands and extra-long finger bones that are covered with a double layer of thin skin called a membrane. The membrane is thin enough that light can shine through it. The membrane contains blood vessels, nerves, and muscles.

In some bats, a membrane extends between the legs and encloses the tail. Some bats have tails that extend past the membrane and others have no tails. In most bats, the thumbs are free from the membrane. These thumbs have claws and are often used for climbing up trees or other structures.

Bat membranes are tough and flexible, allowing bats to move their wings much like people move their fingers. Changing the shape of their wings allows bats to turn and maneuver quickly. Some bats can hover in the air while others glide. When it is cold, the bats fold their wings around themselves. When it is warm, bats flap their wings to cool themselves.

Bats range widely in size, yet the majority of bats weigh less than 1 ounce (25 grams). The largest bat is the Malayan flying

phylum

class

subclass

● **order**

monotypic order

suborder

family

fox, which can have a wingspan of 6 feet (1.8 meters) and weigh 3.3 pounds (1.5 kilograms). The smallest bats are the Kitti's hog-nosed bats, also called bumblebee bats, of Thailand, with a wingspan of 6 inches (15 centimeters) and a weight of about 0.07 ounces (2 grams), less than a penny.

Like other mammals, bats are warm-blooded and fur covers their body. Megachiroptera are characterized by large eyes, small ears, and dog-like snouts. Most Microchiroptera species are characterized by wide, extended ears and odd shaped noses. Bats have weak legs and do not walk long distances. Their feet are small with sharp claws on each toe. Bats use their claws to hold the weight of their body when they hang upside down, which is their normal resting position.

GEOGRAPHIC RANGE

Bats live on every continent on Earth except Antarctica and some remote islands. Most bats live in the tropics and species are most numerous around the equator.

HABITAT

Bats need a roost, a place to settle or rest, and a place to find food. The type of roost a bat chooses depends upon the type of bat. Bats can roost in hollow trees, cracks in trees, and under bridges. Many bats depend on caves in the cool winter months to survive, and others roost in caves all year long. Some bat species find their roosting site in abandoned mines. The dome shaped ceilings can hide and protect the bats from predators, the animals that hunt them.

A few species of bats make their roost from large leaves, such as palm and banana leaves. These small bats chew across the leaves so that the sides droop down in the form of a tent. Other bats can roost in flowers and animal dens.

Bats often return to the same site at the same time each year. In warm weather, big brown bats commonly roost in buildings and then shift to caves and abandoned mines during the colder months. The Pallas's mastiff bats are found roosting in buildings, hollow trees, rock crevices, caves, and bridges.

DIET

While the most famous bats are the vampire bats, known for eating blood, the majority of bats eat only insects. Microchiroptera are generally carnivores, meat-eaters, that feed on insects, such as moths, flying beetles, and mosquitoes. Bats can capture insects while flying by catching them in their mouths or scooping them into their tails or wing membranes. Some bats pick the insects off leaves or the ground. One gray bat may eat up to 3,000 insects in one night.

Some bats feed on larger prey, animals hunted or caught for food, such as fish, frogs, birds, mice and other bats. A fish-eating bat will swoop down and grab fish with its claws. A bat that eats mice will swoop down, wrap the prey in its wings, bite it and then whisk it away to eat it.

The three species of vampire bats are the only bats that feed on blood, sucking up the blood of cattle, sheep, or other relatively large animals. The bats use their razor-sharp teeth to pierce the animal's skin, often while the animal is sleeping. The bats then lap up about 2 tablespoons (30 milliliters) for their meal.

Most megachiropteran species are herbivores, plant-eaters, eating fruit, seeds, leaves, nectar, and pollen. Whatever it eats, bats eat only the parts of their prey that they want to ingest. When a bat catches an insect, it will generally bite off and drop its wings and legs. When eating another bat or bird it will not ingest its wings. An Old World fruit bat will chew its fruit thoroughly, swallow the juices then spit out the remaining pulp.

Bats drink by flying close to the water and taking up the water while flying. With the exception of three species of nectar-feeding bats that live along the Mexican border of Arizona and Texas, bats in the United States and Canada eat insects.

BEHAVIOR AND REPRODUCTION

Bats as a group are crepuscular (kri-PUS-kyuh-lur), meaning they are active at dawn and dusk, or nocturnal, meaning they are active at night. When they are roosting, bats generally hang upside down by their claws. This allows them to simply let go of whatever they are hanging onto and start flying.

With their large ears and small eyes, microchiropteran bats depend upon a complex sound technique called echolocation (eck-oh-loh-KAY-shun) to help them find prey and move. While flying, these bats send out high-frequency sounds that bounce off of other objects. The bat listens for the bounced sound, and then determines the location, size, distance, and speed of the object—all within a split second. In most bats, the echolocation is at such a high pitch that it is beyond the human hearing range, though humans can hear the sounds of some bats. Researchers are still working to understand exactly how echolocation works. Megachiroptera generally depend upon their eyes to navigate, but some of these bats also use echolocation.

Like all mammals, bats are warm-blooded, meaning they maintain their body temperature. Bats roost in warm places during the cool months to conserve the energy it takes to keep warm. Unlike other mammals, bats can allow their body temperature to drop to the ambient temperature, or surrounding temperature, when they are not active. As their temperature drops, metabolism slows down.

During the winter, some bats will drop their body temperatures for months at a time and go into hibernation, meaning they go into a resting state in a safe place, typically without eating or passing wastes. A bat's body temperature can drop to as low as 35.6°F (2°C). These bats survive the winter by living off their storages of fat and making occasional food trips during warmer weather.

Other bat species follow an annual migration pattern, traveling to warmer climates in the cool months and cooler climates in the warm months.

Bats are generally social animals and gather together in roosts. Bats can roost in colonies of several hundred to tens of millions. The number of bats in a roost depends upon the type of bat. Pipistrelle maternity, or motherhood, roosts usually contain between fifty and two hundred bats. Brown long-eared bats usually live in colonies of twenty-five up to fifty bats. Mexican free-tailed bats are one of the more social bat species and found in huge populations throughout their range. In Bracken Cave, Texas, the population of Mexican free-tailed bats was estimated at twenty million bats!

Like all mammals, female bats give birth to live young and feed their newborns milk. Females often roost in large colonies, with many females giving birth in the same area. Bats usually give birth to only one young per year. During their first weeks of life newborn bats cling to their mothers while in flight. Only the mother cares for the young, and there is no lasting relationship between the mother and father.

Bats grow quickly; the young are often flying at four weeks. Young microchiropterans become independent at approximately six to eight weeks, megachiropterans at about four months old. At the age of two years bats are sexually mature. Bats live about twenty-five years, far longer than most mammals of a comparable size.

BATS AND PEOPLE

Popular folklore and myths have led to many people having a negative reaction to bats. Because most people do not typically see or interact with bats, many misunderstandings about these creatures remain. The Eastern European tale of a vampire, a corpse that came back to life and sucked blood from the neck of its human victim, dates back to the Middle Ages. After Bram Stoker's *Dracula* was published in 1897, the misconception of bats as dangerous and mysterious became more popular. Although there are only three species of vampire bats, all living in South and Central America, all bats still have a reputation for sucking blood.

Bats also have a reputation for carrying rabies, a viral disease that affects the nervous system and can be spread through bite of an affected animal. Yet less than one half of one percent of bats carries the rabies virus. And bats are rarely aggressive, usually attacking only if they are frightened.

Not all people consider bats a bad omen or scary. In China, bats are considered good luck symbols. Fabrics and dishes are often decorated with bat-shapes for good luck. Native Americans considered the bat a protector.

Bats are beneficial to people in many indirect and direct ways. They are one of the few predators of night-flying insects, some of which are pests to crops and people. People have long used the nitrogen-rich bat droppings, called guano (GWAN-oh), as a fertilizer.

Bats also play an important role in plant pollination, the transfer of pollen, the reproductive spores, for fertilization. When nectar-eating bats move from flower the flower to eat, the bats pick up pollen on their fur and disperse it as they move. Bats are the most important pollinators among mammals in the rainforest. They pollinate many plants that humans eat, including bananas, figs, mangos, and peaches. Bats also are integral for seed dispersal, having led to the continued survival of

A WHOLE LOT OF BATS

Bracken Cave in Texas is home to the world's largest bat colony. Each year, some twenty million Mexican free-tailed bats gather at this cave near San Antonio to give birth and rear their young. And each night they emerge to forage for food. The twenty million bats can eat more than two hundred tons of insects in a single summer night!

over 1,000 species of trees. The fruit bat disperses seeds away from the parent tree by either swallowing them and leaving the seeds in their droppings, or carrying off the fruit to eat.

CONSERVATION STATUS

Bat populations are in decline in the United States and throughout the world. In the United States, out of forty-five bat species, six are federally endangered, facing an extremely high risk of extinction, dying out, or threatened, close to facing the risk of extinction. Twenty species are categorized as being of special concern by the U.S. Fish and Wildlife Service.

The World Conservation Union (IUCN) includes 521 bats on its Red List of Threatened Species. Twenty-nine are Critically Endangered, facing an extremely high risk of extinction; thirty-seven are Endangered, facing a very high risk of extinction; 173 are Vulnerable, facing a high risk of extinction. The rest on the list are not currently threatened, but could become so, or there is not enough information about the bats to know how threatened they are.

FINDING DINNER

Bats have an amazing ability to find food. Fishing bats have echolocation so sophisticated that they can detect a minnow's fin as fine as a human hair, which sticks up above a pond's surface only 0.08 inches (2 millimeters); that's about the thickness of about twenty human hairs. African heart-nosed bats can hear the footsteps of a beetle walking on sand from a distance of more than six feet. And when the Central American fringe-lipped bat hears the mating calls of mud-puddle frogs, it switches to the frogs' lower frequency so that it can detect its exact location.

With few natural predators, the primary reason for declining bat populations is directly and indirectly related to humans. Pesticides on plants have reduced insect populations, the food supply for many bats. Occasionally, people hunt bats for food, but far more harmful to bats is the destruction of their natural areas and living spaces. Deforestation, the clearing of trees for agriculture or people, decreases their food supply and habitats.

People have also killed colonies of bats out of fear or ignorance. In Central America, where vampire bats can be a problem for livestock, locals find bat caves and blow them up, killing entire colonies whether they are colonies of vampire bats or not. In the United States, destroying bat habitats such as mines have killed them and any that remain are left without protection.

FOR MORE INFORMATION

Books:

Fenton, Brock M. *Bats*. New York: Checkmark Press, 2001.

Fenton, Brock M. *The Bat: Wings in the Night Sky*. Buffalo, NY: Firefly Books, 1998.

Richardson, Phil. *Bats*. London: Whittet Books, 1985.

Ruff, Sue, and Don E. Wilson. *Bats*. New York: Benchmark Books, 2001.

Schober, Wilfried, and Eckard Grimmberger. *The Bats of Europe and North America*. Neptune City, NJ: T.F.H. Publications, Inc., 1997.

Periodicals:

Gordon, David George. "13 Reasons You Should Love Bats." *National Geographic Kids* (October 2003): S8.

Hicks, Alan. "A Bit about Bats." *New York State Conservationist* (October 1999): 2.

Kerner, Sarah. "In the Bat Cave." *Boys' Life* (June 2003): 18.

Toufexis, Anastasia. "Bats' New Image: Researchers Say They're Benign, Useful and Endangered." *Time* (August 21, 1995): 58.

Web sites:

"Bat Information." The Bat Conservation Trust. http://www.bats.org.uk/bat_info.htm (accessed on June 22, 2004).

"Bats (Chiroptera)." National Parks Conservation Association. http://www.eparks.org/wildlife_protection/wildlife_facts/bats/default.asp (accessed on June 22, 2004).

"Bats in the Desert Southwest." Desert USA. http://www.desertusa.com/jan97/du_bats.html (accessed on June 22, 2004).

Best, Heather. "Bats: Learning to Love Them." Wildwnc.org. http://wildwnc.org/natnotes/bats.html (accessed on June 22, 2004).

"Cave Life." The National Park Service. http://www.nps.gov/ozar/cavelife.html (accessed on June 22, 2004).

"Discover the Secret World of Bats." Bat Conservation International, Inc. http://www.batcon.org (accessed on June 22, 2004).

Harris, Tom. "How Bats Work." How Stuff Works. http://science.howstuffworks.com/bat.htm (accessed on June 22, 2004).

Tyburec, Janet. "Bats." Arizona-Sonora Desert Museum. http://www.desertmuseum.org/books/nhsd_bats.html (accessed on June 22, 2004).

CHAPTER

PHYSICAL CHARACTERISTICS

Bats are broken into two categories: the Microchiroptera (micro-keer-OP-ter-ah) and the Megachiroptera (mega-keer-OP-ter-ah). The vast majority of bats fall under the microchiropterans, which are in general smaller than the megachiropterans. Pteropodidae is the only family in the megachiropteran category. Pteropodids are commonly referred to as Old World fruit bats. The Old World refers to southern Europe, Asia, and Africa, while New World refers to North and South America.

Old World fruit bats have a wide range in size. Pygmy fruit bats are one of the smallest Old World fruit bats, with a head and body length of 2.4 to 2.8 inches (6 to 7 centimeters), smaller than many microchiropterans. Gigantic flying foxes are 15.7 inches (40 centimeters) long and can have a wingspan of 59 inches (150 centimeters).

In general, Old World fruit bats have large eyes that face forward. These bats have claws on the first finger, their thumb, and most also have claws on their second finger. Their faces are typically doglike, with simple and relatively small ears. Their wings are typically broad and mostly furless. The tail is usually short or absent. With so many different species, fur color varies greatly. Most species of the Old World fruit bat are reddish brown, gray, or black. The underside of the bat is usually a pale color, such as a white or yellow.

Teeth are shaped to bite through fruit skin and crush the soft fruit matter. The front incisors, chisel-shaped teeth at the front of the mouth, are small and all have canines, four pointed teeth. Teeth at the sides and back tend to be flat and wide. In some species, especially those that eat nectar, the tongue is long and can stick out far beyond the end of the mouth.

GEOGRAPHIC RANGE

Old World fruit bats can be found in tropical and subtropical regions of Africa, through southern and central Asia to Australia, including the Philippines, a number of islands of the Indian and Pacific Oceans, in Pakistan, and across India.

HABITAT

Old World fruit bats live in a variety of habitats. Many fruit bats live in humid forests in tropical and subtropical areas. Species of flying foxes live in tropical coastal areas.

DIET

As their name suggests, Old World fruit bats eat fruit along with nectar. Some species eat primarily nectar and pollen, powdery grains that contain the male reproductive cells of seed plants. Other bats also add leaves and flower parts to their diet.

BEHAVIOR AND REPRODUCTION

Like all bats, Old World fruit bats are crepuscular (kri-PUS-kyuh-lur), active at dawn and dusk, or nocturnal, active at night. During the day they roost, settle or rest, by hanging from their feet. They may hang with their wings wrapped around their bodies. If it is hot, they may use their wings to fan themselves. Many of the species roost in extremely large groups, called camps. A bat camp may contain anywhere from ten individual bats to over one million. The larger species often roost in large groups, whereas the smaller species tend to be more solitary. Most roost in trees; others roost in caves, deserted mines, or buildings.

When fruit is not available fruit bats will travel to another area. The larger species are slow and powerful fliers. Some of these bats will fly as far as 30 miles (15 kilometers) to reach a new feeding area. Island bats may fly over to a neighboring island.

Old World fruit bats differ from other families of bats in that most use smell and sight, rather than echolocation (eck-oh-loh-KAY-shun), to navigate and find their food. Echolocation is the technique of emitting sounds than detecting the location of objects from the echoes. Rousette bats are the only Old World fruit bats that use echolocation.

DEADLY DELICACY?

The diet of flying fox bats may have helped solve a medical mystery. Researchers have been trying to understand why the Chamorro people of Guam developed neurological, brain, disorders at 50 to 100 times the rates elsewhere. A 2003 study linked this disease to the popular delicacy of the flying fox bat. These bats eat cycad (SYE-kad) seeds, which come from palm-like cycad plants common on Guam and surrounding Pacific islands. Cycad seeds contain chemicals that are poisonous to the human nervous system. Researchers continue to investigate the connection.

After these bats find their food they typically take it to away to a nearby tree. Smaller species are able to eat while hovering. Large Old World fruit bats, such as many of the flying fox species, may have to land or grab hold of a branch in order to eat the fruits. These bats hang upside down by one foot and use the other foot to hold the food. They bite off chunks of the food, swallow the juice, and spit out the pulp and seeds. Occasionally they also eat the pulp.

Within camps of flying foxes, one male fruit bat usually lives with up to eight female bats. This arrangement is called a harem (HARE-um). Females will produce one young per year. In other species the females may mate with two or more males while the males will mate with as many females as possible. At least one species is considered monogamous (muh-NAH-guh-mus), having one mate. Gestation, or pregnancy, is between four and six months.

OLD WORLD FRUIT BATS AND PEOPLE

Because Old World fruit bats spit out seeds as they eat, they are important for spreading seeds for many plant species that people eat, and use for medicine and materials. Fruits that depend on bats for pollination, the transfer of pollen, or seed dispersal include bananas, peaches, dates, avocadoes, mangoes, and cashews. The species that thrive on nectar are also important pollinators. As these bats lap up nectar with their tongues, pollen sticks to their fur and is then rubbed or dropped when the bat visits its next flower. These bats are an important disperser of many rainforest species, which the planet and people depend upon.

Deforestation, clearing the forest, has caused a decline in the population of many Old World fruit bat species as they lose their habitats and food supply. Forests also protect bats from natural storms, such as cyclones. People consider many of these bats pests, as they can destroy crops, and may try to eliminate them. Other people hunt and eat some of the Old World fruit bats, especially the larger ones. People such as the Chamorro of Guam consider flying foxes a delicacy.

CONSERVATION STATUS

Many of the Old World fruit bat species are facing a serious decline in population, extinction (dying out), and the threat of extinction. Eight species are listed as extinct by the World Conservation Union (IUCN). Thirteen species are listed as Critically Endangered, facing an extremely high risk of extinction in the wild; six species are listed as Endangered, facing a very high risk of extinction; and thirty-six species are listed as Vulnerable, facing a high risk of extinction in the wild.

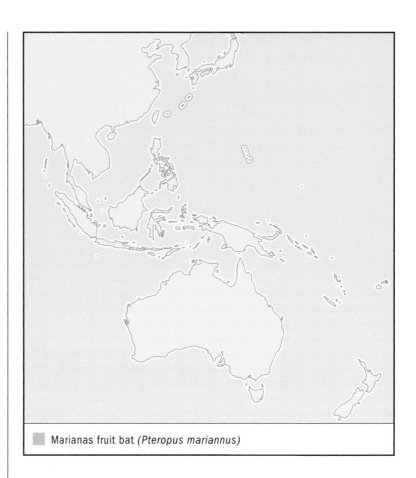

Marianas fruit bat (*Pteropus mariannus*)

MARIANAS FRUIT BAT
Pteropus mariannus

Physical characteristics: Marianas fruit bats are one of the many species commonly called flying foxes. They are medium-sized bats with a body length of 7.5 to 9.9 inches (19 to 25 centimeters). The males are slightly larger than the females. The abdomen and wings are dark brown to black with silver hairs mixed throughout the fur. Around the neck and sides of the neck are yellow to bright gold on most animals. In some bats, this area is pale gold or pale brown. The color of the head varies from brown to dark brown.

Geographic range: The Marianas fruit bats are found in the Mariana Islands, located in the western Pacific Ocean, 1,500 miles

(2,400 kilometers) southeast of Japan. They are also found in Guam, Okinawa, and the Ryuku Islands.

Habitat: Marianas fruit bats live in tropical and subtropical areas. They typically live near a body of water.

Diet: These bats feed primarily on fruit, but they do eat other parts of plant materials, such as the flowers and leaves. Favored foods include the fruits of breadfruit, papaya, and figs, along with the flowers of kapok (KAY-pock), coconut, and gaogao.

Behavior and reproduction: Little is known about the nightly movements and behavior of Marianas fruit bats. Many of these bats live in large colonies that can reach 800 individuals. A smaller portion of these bats roost in smaller colonies of ten to twelve; all-male colonies of ten to fifteen; and some roost independently. During the day these bats primarily sleep. Bats gradually leave the colonies for several hours after sunset to forage, search for food. These bats move from island to island but overall, they do not move about much.

Within larger colonies, some males form harems of several females. The males will defend the females in its group.

Marianas fruit bats and people: Marianas fruit bats are hunted for food and, occasionally, their fur. This is one reason these bats have declined in population. These bats are a delicacy to the native Chamorro culture and are illegally hunted. Habitat destruction is another reason for the decline in population. The introduced species, a species brought from another part of the world, the brown tree snake in Guam has been a major predator on these young fruit bats.

Conservation status: Marianas fruit bats are listed as Endangered by the IUCN. In the Commonwealth of the Northern Mariana Islands (CNMI), the Marianas fruit bat is locally listed as an endangered species due to the decline in population. Under local law it is illegal to hunt the fruit bat anywhere in the CNMI. ■

The Marianas fruit bat may live in colonies of up to 800 bats. Bats leave the colonies after sunset to search for food. (Illustration by Marguette Dongvillo. Reproduced by permission.)

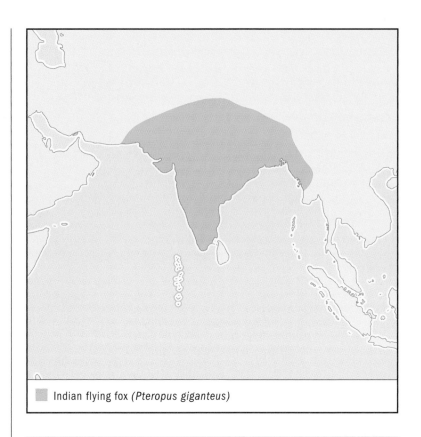

Indian flying fox (*Pteropus giganteus*)

INDIAN FLYING FOX
Pteropus giganteus

Physical characteristics: Named for its physical similarity to a fox, the Indian flying fox has reddish brown fur and the shape of its head is similar to a fox. These bats are one of the largest of all bats and have a wingspan of more than 4 feet (1.2 meters). Its head and body length ranges from 8 to 12 inches (20 to 30 centimeters). These bats have prominent claws that they use to move through trees and branches.

Geographic range: Indian flying foxes are found throughout Bangladesh, Myanmar, India, Pakistan, and Sri Lanka.

Habitat: The Indian flying fox lives in tropical forests and swamps, where there is a large body of water nearby.

Diet: Indian flying foxes feed almost exclusively on a variety of fruit. They chew the fruit to obtain the juice. Very soft fruits such as bananas are swallowed, but usually the bat spits out the fruit pulp and seeds once it has extracted all the juice. The Indian flying fox also feeds on the juice and pollen of various tree flowers.

Behavior and reproduction: During the day Indian flying foxes roost in large camps in trees. These sites are out in the open. Camps may contain several hundred to several thousand flying foxes. Colony size changes with the seasons, becoming smaller during the summer and increasing during the rainy season. These bats typically keep the same roost sites for many years, and the trees become stripped of bark and leaves over time. During the day the bats are noisy and active. At night they can fly great distances to forage for food.

Indian flying foxes fly long distances at night in search of food. (© Stephen Dalton/Photo Researchers, Inc. Reproduced by permission.)

Within the roost there is often a pecking order within the male population. The more dominant males, those that are larger and stronger, take the best roosting sites.

Indian flying foxes breed from July to October. When ready to give birth, the females will gather in upper branches of their roosting trees. Females have one offspring after a gestation period of 140 to 150 days. The baby will cling to its mother for about two months until it is almost full size.

Indian flying foxes and people: While it once fed mainly on wild fruit, the bat now increasingly feeds on cultivated crops of fruit trees, which has caused many people to consider these bats pests. Farmers have used various methods to get rid of these bats. These foxes are also hunted in parts of Pakistan for its fat, which is used for medicine. People have also cleared the trees from many of the islands where these bats live, causing the population to decline.

Conservation status: The Indian flying fox is not considered threatened by the IUCN. In Pakistan, this species is specifically exempted from protection under wildlife regulation. ■

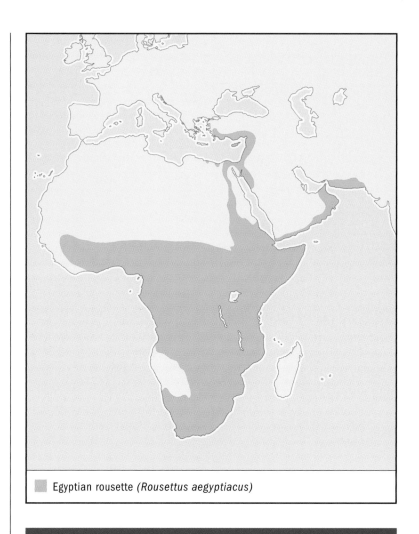

Egyptian rousette *(Rousettus aegyptiacus)*

EGYPTIAN ROUSETTE
Rousettus aegyptiacus

Physical characteristics: Rousettes are relatively small compared to other Old World fruit bats. The head and body are approximately 4.5 to 5 inches long (11.4 to 12.7). These bats have a simple, dog-like face and ears, large eyes, and a very short tail that sticks out. The tail is about 0.4 to 0.9 inches (1 to 2.2 centimeters) long. The fur of these bats is brown, and often tinged with gray.

Geographic range: Egyptian rousettes are found in southern, western, and eastern Africa, Egypt, the Middle East, and Cyprus.

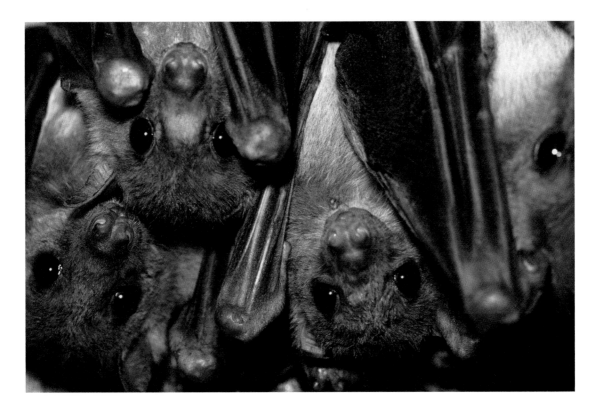

Habitat: Egyptian rousettes roost in humid areas, such as dark caves and abandoned buildings. Most are found roosting in caves. In Cyprus, some colonies may move to open sites in March.

Egyptian rousettes are usually found roosting in caves. (© Clive Druett/Papilio/Corbis. Reproduced by permission.)

Diet: Rousettes feed on many kinds of soft fruits, the juice of hard fruits, and certain leaves. Figs and dates form its main diet in dry regions.

Behavior and reproduction: Egyptian rousettes roost primarily in caves. They also roost in buildings, ancient ruins, trees, and rock crevices. They can form colonies of up to several thousand individuals. In South Africa, camps had an estimated 7,000 to 9,000 bats. In Pakistan, these bats appear to form small roosting colonies of about twenty to forty individuals. The bats use smell to help them locate their food.

While Egyptian rousettes appear to have good vision, these bats also use echolocation. Scientists think they use echolocation to help them navigate in caves and at night. As opposed to the echolocation calls of many other bats, humans can hear the echolocation calls of rousettes. They make a clicking sound with their tongue.

Some populations breed two times during the year. Females have one offspring per year and gestation is about four to six months. In Egypt, a field study found they breed year round.

Egyptian rousettes and people: Fruit farmers are the most important threat to populations. In Turkey and Israel, rousette caves have been fumigated, filled with smoke or fumes in order to kill pests, or the caves have been closed off by walls.

Conservation status: Egyptian rousettes are not listed as threatened by the IUCN. ■

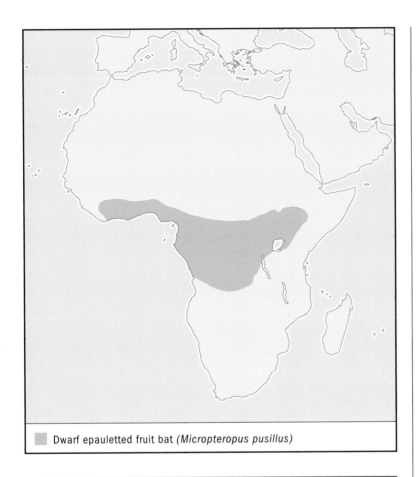

Dwarf epauletted fruit bat (*Micropteropus pusillus*)

DWARF EPAULETTED FRUIT BAT
Micropteropus pusillus

Physical characteristics: Dwarf epauletted fruit bats are relatively small. Their head and body length is approximately 2.6 to 3.7 inches (6.7 to 9.5 centimeters). Males are larger than females. While the tail length varies among individual bats, it is never long, ranging from not having a tail to 0.2 inches (0.4 centimeters). Fur is typically a light brown with a paler color on the underside. The hair is moderately long, thick, and soft. At the base of the ear are small whitish tufts of hair and males have pouches in their shoulder with tufts of white hair.

Geographic range: Dwarf epauletted fruit bats are found in western, southwestern, and central Africa.

Dwarf epauletted fruit bats live in open woodlands and on the edges of forests and feed on small fruits, nectar, and pollen. (Illustration by Brian Cressman. Reproduced by permission.)

Habitat: These bats live in open woodlands and on the edges of forests. Dwarf epauletted bats have also been found between the leaves of dense bushes, usually close to the ground.

Diet: Dwarf epauletted bats feed on small fruits, nectar, and pollen. When eating the fruits, these bats place their mouths around the ripe fruit and slowly suck its juices. They then drop the uneaten fruit pulp when they are finished.

Behavior and reproduction: Little is known about the dwarf epauletted bat's behavior and mating behavior. Dwarf epauletted bats are independent, typically roosting alone, with one other bat, or in small groups of up to ten. These bats move about frequently and do not have a regular roosting spots or feeding areas. These bats may eat two and a half times their body weight in a single night. It digests quickly and disperses, spreads, large quantities of seeds as it flies between feeding sites.

These bats are polygamous (puh-LIH-guh-mus), having more than one mate. There are two breeding seasons. Studies in the Ivory Coast indicate that births peaks from about March to May and from September to November. The gestation period is five to six months. Young females can mate at six months and give birth at twelve months.

Dwarf epauletted fruit bats and people: There is no known relationship between dwarf epauletted bats and people.

Conservation status: Dwarf epauletted bats are not listed as threatened. ■

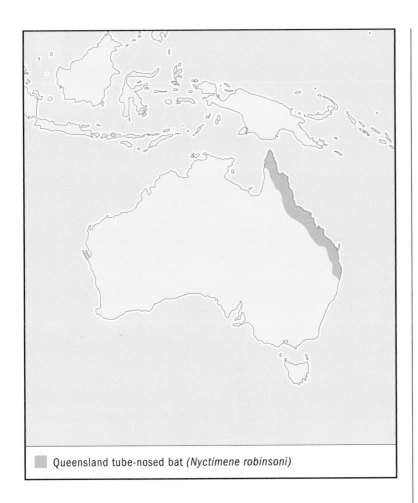

Queensland tube-nosed bat *(Nyctimene robinsoni)*

QUEENSLAND TUBE-NOSED BAT
Nyctimene robinsoni

Physical characteristics: Queensland tube-nosed bats are also called eastern tube-nosed bats. These bats have nostrils shaped like tubes that jut out about 1 inch (2.5 centimeters). Researchers do not yet understand the purpose of these tubes. Their head and body length is 3 to 5.1 inches (7.5 to 13 centimeters) with a tail length of 0.8 to 1 inch (2 to 2.5 centimeters). These bats have light brown fur with a dark stripe down the back. Their wings are brown with yellowish spots.

Geographic range: Queensland tube-nosed bats are found in eastern Australia.

Female Queensland tube-nosed bats typically have one offspring per year. A baby is shown here, hanging on a branch. (© B. G. Thomson/Photo Researchers, Inc. Reproduced by permission.)

Habitat: These bats live in tropical rainforests and subtropical rainforests.

Diet: These bats feed on fruit.

Behavior and reproduction: Queensland tube-nosed bats roost on branches of trees that have thick vegetation. They are solitary and do not appear to roost in groups. The bats often fly very close to the ground as they search for food. Queensland tube-nosed bats are polygamous with one breeding season. Females generally have one offspring per year. Gestation is approximately four to five months.

Queensland tube-nosed bats and people: By clearing these bats' natural habitats, people have caused the population of this bat to decline.

Conservation status: Queensland tube-nosed bats are not listed as threatened by IUCN. They are listed as vulnerable in Australia's New South Wales Threatened Species Conservation Act. ∎

FOR MORE INFORMATION

Books:

Fenton, Brock M. *Bats.* New York: Checkmark Press, 2001.

Fenton, Brock M. *The Bat: Wings in the Night Sky.* Buffalo, NY: Firefly Books, 1998.

Nowak, Ronald M. "Old World Fruit Bats." *Walker's Mammals of the World 5.1 Online.* http://www.press.jhu.edu/books/walkers_mammals_of_the_world/chiroptera/chiroptera.pteropodidae.html (accessed on July 2, 2004).

Richardson, Phil. *Bats.* London: Whittet Books, 1985.

Ruff, Sue, and Don E. Wilson. *Bats.* New York: Benchmark Books, 2001.

Periodicals:

Petersen, David. "Wait Until Dark." *Backpacker* (October, 1993): 24.

"Plants, Bats Magnify Neurotoxin in Guam." *Science News* (December 6, 2003): 366.

Thewissen, J. G. M., and S. K. Babcock. "The Origin of Flight in Bats." *Bioscience* (May 1992): 340–345.

Web sites:

Craig, P., ed. "Flying Foxes (Fruit bats)." *Natural History Guide to American Samoa.* http://www.nps.gov/npsa/book/index.htm (accessed on July 2, 2004).

"Digital Morphology." National Science Foundation Digital Library at the University of Texas. http://www.digimorph.org (accessed on July 2, 2004).

"Discover the Secret World of Bats." Bat Conservation International, Inc. http://www.batcon.org (accessed on July 2, 2004).

"Fruit bats." The Wild Ones. http://www.thewildones.org/Animals/fruitBat.html (accessed on July 2, 2004).

Lemke, Thomas O. "Marianas Fruit Bats Near Extinction." Bat Conservation International, Inc. http://www.batcon.org/batsmag/v3n1-1.html (accessed on July 2, 2004).

"Mammals of the CNMI" Commonwealth of the Northern Mariana Islands. http://www.cnmidfw.org/wildlife/index.html (accessed on July 2, 2004).

Class: Mammalia

Order: Chiroptera

Family: Rhinopomatidae

Number of species: 4 species

family

CHAPTER

phylum

class

subclass

order

monotypic order

suborder

▲ family

PHYSICAL CHARACTERISTICS

Also known as long-tailed bats, the bats in this family have a tail almost as long as their head and body. This slender, long tail is unique among all the bats. These bats are small to medium-sized, about 2 to 3.5 inches (5 to 9 centimeters), not including the tail. Their backs are generally gray-brown to dark brown, and they may be lighter on their underside.

The ears of mouse-tailed bats are rather large and connected by a band of skin across the forehead. The ears extend past the nose when they are laid forward. Their snouts have a small, rounded noseleaf, a horseshoe-shaped flap of skin around the nose.

GEOGRAPHIC RANGE

Mouse-tailed bats are generally found in Africa and Asia, across the Sahara, from western Africa through the Middle East to India and Thailand.

HABITAT

Mouse-tailed bats are usually found in arid, extremely dry, regions. This can range from deserts to extremely dry woodland. They roost, rest or settle, in caves, rock clefts, wells, pyramids, and buildings.

DIET

Mouse-tailed bats eat insects, including flying ants, termites, beetles, and moths.

As the months turn cooler the bat begins store fat, especially in the abdominal, stomach, region. These fat deposits can equal the bat's normal body weight. During the winter months when insects are in short supply some species of mouse-tailed bats go into a type of deep sleep called torpor, and they absorb the fat deposits. During this period the bat is able to survive for several weeks without food and water. In some areas, some species migrate between summer and winter roosts.

BEHAVIOR AND REPRODUCTION

When mouse-tailed bats roost they often hang by the thumbs as well as the feet. They emerge from their roosts at dark and begin their search for food. The small mouse-tailed bat has an unusual flight in that it rises and falls, much like some small birds. This species travels by a series of glides, some of great length, and occasionally it flutters, about 20 to 30 feet (6 to 9 meters) above the ground.

TUNING TO BATS

Bats are difficult to study because they fly and are only active at night. Radio tagging, the marking of bats with a radio transmitter, is one technology that researchers are using to study bats. Transmitters are typically 5 percent of the bat's body weight and can be glued to the bat's back or put on a collar. Results from these studies show that long-tailed bats are highly selective in choosing nest sites and sites are usually used for only one day.

Like all bats, mouse-tailed bats are nocturnal, active at night. They use echolocation (eck-oh-loh-KAY-shun) to pinpoint, identify, and capture their prey, the animals they hunt for food. In echolocation, the bats call out a high-frequency sound in the ultrasonic ranges, which is above the sounds humans can hear. These sound waves bounce off of objects and echoes or bounces back to the bat. The bat can then determines the location, size, distance, and speed of the object.

Mouse-tailed bats generally hunt in the open air high above ground. With small prey distributed throughout a large space, the bats must cover a large search area to find an insect. Mouse-tailed bats can travel up to 12 miles (20 kilometers) from their roost sites in a single night.

Female bats give birth to one young annually. The young are fully grown and weaned in about six weeks. Reproduction periods of these bats depends upon where they live and their species.

MOUSE-TAILED BATS AND PEOPLE

Mouse-tailed bats are indirectly helpful to humans because they eat many insects that humans consider pests.

CONSERVATION STATUS

One species, MacInnes' mouse-tailed bat, is categorized as Vulnerable, facing a high risk of extinction in the wild due to the destruction the bat's natural habitat. The other three species are not listed as threatened with extinction.

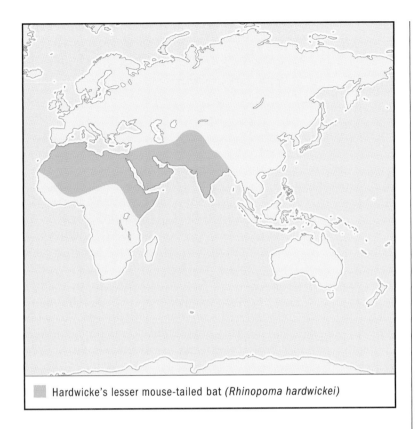

Hardwicke's lesser mouse-tailed bat *(Rhinopoma hardwickei)*

HARDWICKE'S LESSER MOUSE-TAILED BAT
Rhinopoma hardwickei

Physical characteristics: Hardwicke's lesser mouse-tailed bats are also called long-tailed bats, referring to their long, thin mouse-like tail. The tail can be as long to the length of the head and body combined.

These bats are relatively smaller than other species in the family. They have a body length of about 2.5 inches (5.5 centimeters), and their forearms range in length from 2 to 2.5 inches (5.2 to 6.4 centimeters). They weigh about 0.4 to 0.5 ounces (11 to 14 grams).

The fur of lesser mouse-tailed bats is soft. It is generally a gray-brown color on the upper side of and a paler color of the same shade on its underside. These bats appear to be furless on their faces and backsides. These bats feature large ears that are connected by a band of skin across the forehead. The snout has a small, rounded noseleaf. Directly above the nostrils are slits that they can open and close.

Geographic range: Lesser mouse-tailed bats extend from northern Africa to southern Asia. They are found in Morocco, Senegal, Egypt, Israel, Syria, Jordan, Lebanon, Saudi Arabia, Yemen, Afghanistan, India, Socotra Island, and Pakistan.

Habitat: Lesser mouse-tailed bats typically live in extremely dry or arid regions, They are found in mostly treeless areas ranging from deserts to grasslands and dry woodland.

Diet: Lesser mouse-tailed bats feed on flying insects, such as moths and beetles. These bats build up a large fat reserve in their lower abdomen and can go without feeding for two months.

Hardwicke's lesser mouse-tailed bats live in dry regions. To help them survive, they can close valves in their nostrils to keep from breathing in dust, and they can control their kidneys to reduce water loss. (© Merlin D. Tuttle, Bat Conservation International. Reproduced by permission.)

Behavior and reproduction: Lesser mouse-tailed bats have unique adaptations, changes in body structures and functions, for life in dry regions. They can close valves in the nostrils to keep from breathing in dust. They can also control their kidneys to reduce water loss. In extremely hot weather these bats move into a shelter.

Lesser mouse-tailed bats find their food using echolocation. Studies have found that when several of these bats forage for food together, each uses an echolocation call of a different sound frequency.

Lesser mouse-tailed bats roost in caves, rock clefts, wells, pyramids, palaces, and houses. They gather in both large and small colonies. Colonies can number in the thousands, or range from one to ten individuals. They often hang by their thumbs as well as feet. Studies have found that roosting sites are generally used for only one day, and then they will select another site.

Studies indicate that lesser mouse-tailed bats are polygamous (puh-LIH-guh-mus), having more than one mate. Female lesser mouse-tailed bats produce one offspring annually. They gestate, are pregnant, for a period of 90 to 100 days. In a field study of lesser mouse-tailed bats, birth occurred over ten days in mid-December. The young began flying at five to six weeks.

Lesser mouse-tailed bats and people: Lesser mouse-tailed bats eat insects that many humans consider pests. There are indications that these bats may be declining in population, due to human activities. Reasons for the population decline include clearing these bats' forest habitats, disturbing their roosting sites, and introducing animals into an area that are predators of these bats, animals that hunt them for food.

Conservation status: Lesser mouse-tailed bats are not currently in danger of extinction. There is some evidence that long-tailed bats are now rare or absent at many sites where formerly they were common. ■

FOR MORE INFORMATION

Books:

Fenton, Brock M. *Bats.* New York: Checkmark Press, 2001.

Fenton, Brock M. *The Bat: Wings in the Night Sky.* Buffalo, NY: Firefly Books, 1998.

Richardson, Phil. *Bats.* London: Whittet Books, 1985.

Ruff, Sue, and Don E. Wilson. *Bats.* New York: Benchmark Books, 2001.

Schober, Wilfried, and Eckard Grimmberger. *The Bats of Europe and North America.* Neptune City, NJ: T.F.H. Publications, Inc., 1997.

Periodicals:

Schnitzler, Hans-Ulrich and Elisabeth K.V. Kalko. "Echolocation by Insect-Eating Bats." *BioScience* (July, 2001): 557–569.

Web sites:

"Bat Information." The Bat Conservation Trust. http://www.bats.org.uk/bat_info.htm (accessed on July 2, 2004).

Hester, L., and P. Myers. "Rhinopomatidae." Animal Diversity Web. http://animaldiversity.ummz.umich.edu/site/accounts/information/Rhinopomatidae.html (accessed on July 2, 2004).

Simmons, Nancy B. and Tenley Conway. "Rhinopomatoidea." *Tree of Life Web Project.* http://tolweb.org/tree?group=Rhinopomatoidea&contgroup=Microchiroptera (accessed on July 2, 2004).

family

CHAPTER

PHYSICAL CHARACTERISTICS

Emballonurids (bats in the family Emballonuridae) are small to medium in size. Their head and body length is about 1.4 to 6.3 inches (36 to 160 millimeters). They can weigh from 0.1 to 3.5 ounces (3 to 100 grams), about the weight of a first-class letter. These bats have thirty to thirty-four teeth.

For the most part, emballonurids are brown or gray in color, but this family also includes the whitish ghost bats in the genus *Diclidurus,* and bats with a pair of white stripes down their back in the genus *Saccopteryx.* Emballonurids have a smooth face and lips with relatively large eyes. Their ears are usually round and cup-shaped, often joined by a band of skin across the forehead. The ears have a tragus (TRAY-gus), a flap that projects from the inner ear. Researchers theorize the tragus plays some role in echolocation (eck-oh-loh-KAY-shun), the process of sending out high-pitched sounds and identifying objects by interpreting the sound when it bounces back.

Some emballonurids are also known as sheath-tailed bats because of their tail. They have a short tail that juts out from the membrane (double layer of thin skin) between their legs, and when their legs are stretched out their tail appears to be sheathed in the membrane. Another name for some emballonurids is sac-winged bats, referring to the glandular sacs in their wing membranes. Glandular sacs produce and release substances for use in the body. In this case they contain a liquid with a strong odor. In the sac-winged bats these sacs are more pronounced in males. The position and size of these sacs differs depending upon the species.

GEOGRAPHIC RANGE

Emballonurids live in the tropical and subtropical regions of the world, including Mexico, Argentina, Madagascar, and Southeast Asia.

HABITAT

Emballonuridae bats generally live in humid rainforests. These bats tend to roost, rest or settle, in areas that are relatively light compared to what other bat families prefer. Their roosts include the entry areas to caves and other structures, the outside of buildings, hollow trees, and leaves.

DIET

Emballonurids eat primarily insects, although they have been seen eating fruit. They generally eat insects while flying, yet some species are known to look for their food along the ground. These bats start foraging, searching for food, relatively early in the day compared to other bats. Some of these bats such as the ghost bats, capture their meals while flying high in the open air. Other bats, such as the proboscis bat, hunt insects above or close to water surfaces.

BEHAVIOR AND REPRODUCTION

By pulling their hind legs together or apart during flight, the emballonurids can shorten or lengthen their membrane. This gives these bats tremendous control as they steer, maneuver, and turn in flight. Like all bats, they are nocturnal, resting during the day and becoming active at night. During bad weather, some species forage in the afternoon.

Some emballonurids roost in large groups, others gather in smaller groups of about ten to forty, and a few are loners. Colonies of African sheath-tailed bats include up to 50,000 bats, each of which returns to a precise place in a roosting cave along the Kenyan coast. Daytime roosts for the sac-winged bat can reach up to sixty individuals. Proboscis bat females roost apart from the males when the young are born. Different shelters are used by adult male and female gray sac-winged bats during the summer; most of the other forms seem to remain together throughout the year.

Some emballonurids, such as the greater sac-winged bat, live in year-round stable harems (HARE-um; group of females associated with one male), with one to eight females in an area

Emballonurids were first recorded in Europe thirty-eight to fifty-four million years ago.

that is patrolled by a male. Male sac-winged bats in the genus *Saccopteryx* defend their harems with energetic flight maneuvers. Researchers have found that harem males father an average of 30 percent of the offspring within their harem. The majority of offspring is fathered by other harem males or by males from outside the colony.

Some of these bats perform elaborate mating rituals. The social calls they emit are audible to humans. For species in which the males have sacs in the front wing membrane containing a liquid with a strong scent, the males fan the odor towards the females while hovering around them. Each afternoon, male *Saccopteryx* bats store a cocktail of perfume in their wing sacs that consists of urine, saliva and other bodily secretions.

There is a variety of different mating customs among the different species of emballonurids. Most of these bats are polygamous (puh-LIH-guh-mus), meaning that males mate with more than one female during the mating season. Yet the chestnut sac-winged bat, and possibly other species, are monogamous (muh-NAH-guh-mus), meaning a male and female mate and pair only with each other.

Emballonurids generally give birth to a single offspring each year. An exception is the small proboscis bat that reproduces twice a year. Most emballonurid females give birth to their offspring at the beginning of the rainy season.

EMBALLONURIDS AND PEOPLE

Because emballonurids prefer roosting in open areas, these bats are among the more common bats for people to spot. They can be seen in trees, on buildings, and at the edges of caves. The social calls they emit are also within human hearing range. Some emballonurids are declining due to human destruction of their natural habitat.

CONSERVATION STATUS

There are several emballonurid species that are endangered or threatened with becoming endangered. The IUCN lists two species as Critically Endangered, facing an extremely high risk of extinction in the wild; two species as Endangered, facing a very high risk of extinction in the wild; and ten species as Vulnerable, facing a high risk of extinction in the wild.

Greater sac-winged bat *(Saccopteryx bilineata)*

GREATER SAC-WINGED BAT
Saccopteryx bilineata

Physical characteristics: Greater sac-winged bats are relatively small, with a body length of 1.8 to 2.2 inches (47 to 56 millimeters). These bats are also called greater white-lined bats, referring to the two white lines that run down their bodies. Their fur is typically dark brown, while the underside is typically gray. These bats have dark wings, long noses, and the females are slightly larger than the males.

Geographic range: Greater sac-winged bats live in Central and South America; from south Mexico to southeast Brazil.

The greater sac-winged bat is also called the greater white-lined bat, because of the two white lines that run down the back. (Illustration by Barbara Duperron. Reproduced by permission.)

Habitat: Greater sac-winged bats live in lowland evergreen or semi-deciduous forests. They roost in relatively open areas, such as hollow trees and occasionally in buildings.

Diet: Greater sac-winged bats feed on insects.

Behavior and reproduction: Greater sac-winged bats are among the most common bats seen in the rainforest because they often roost on the outer parts of large trees. They use echolocation to locate their prey and then catch the insects while flying. Echolocation is a process by which the bats emit a variety of sounds and use the echoes from the sounds to identify objects around them. These bats are unusual in that males sing songs to females during the day in their colonies. These bats have been found roosting in relatively large colonies of sixty individuals. Within those colonies there can be smaller groupings of one to nine females. As seasons change, colonies move between different areas to forage for food.

Females give birth to a single offspring each year, typically at the beginning of the rainy season in July or August. It is thought these bats are polygamous, meaning that they have more than one mate during the mating season.

Greater sac-winged bats and people: There is no known significant relationship between greater sac-winged bats and people.

Conservation status: Greater sac-winged bats are not listed as threatened. ■

Greater dog-faced bat *(Peropteryx kappleri)*

GREATER DOG-FACED BAT
Peropteryx kappleri

Physical characteristics: Greater dog-faced bats are also referred to as greater dog-like bats. These bats are relatively small, with a head and body length of 2.5 to 2.9 inches (63 to 75 millimeters). Their fur is typically dark or reddish brown and their underside is paler in color. Tufts of hair cover the head. The ears are separated at the base and are usually, along with the wings, black in coloration. Males are generally slightly larger than females.

Geographic range: Greater dog-faced bats live in southern Mexico to Peru and southern Brazil.

Greater dog-faced bats roost in small, shallow caves, holes in trees, and under fallen logs. (Illustration by Barbara Duperron. Reproduced by permission.)

Habitat: Greater dog-faced bats have been found in forests, swamps, and savanna (grassland). They roost in small, shallow caves, holes in trees, and under fallen logs where light can enter. A study in Costa Rica found these bats roost about 39 inches (1 meter) from the ground.

Diet: Greater dog-faced bats eat insects.

Behavior and reproduction: Greater dog-faced bats have been found in Costa Rica to roost in colonies of one to six individuals. Usually there were several adults of each sex in the group. One unique behavior is that males sit on top of females. This implies that the male bat is protecting or guarding the female and that the females and males could be monogamous. At the beginning of the rainy season females give birth to a single offspring.

Greater dog-faced bats and people: There is no known significant relationship between greater dog-faced bats and people.

Conservation status: Greater dog-winged bats are not listed as threatened. ■

FOR MORE INFORMATION

Books:

Fenton, Brock M. *Bats.* New York: Checkmark Press, 2001.

Fenton, Brock M. *The Bat: Wings in the Night Sky.* Buffalo, NY: Firefly Books, 1998.

Richardson, Phil. *Bats.* London: Whittet Books, 1985.

Ruff, Sue, and Don E. Wilson. *Bats.* New York: Benchmark Books, 2001.

Schober, Wilfried, and Eckard Grimmberger. *The Bats of Europe and North America.* Neptune City, NJ: T.F.H. Publications, Inc., 1997.

Periodicals:

Milius, S. "Male Bats Primp Daily for Odor Display." *Science News* (January 1, 2000): 557–557.

Nowak, Ronald M. "Ghost Bats or White Bats." *Walker's Mammals of the World 5.1 Online.* http://www.press.jhu.edu/books/walkers_mammals_of_the_world/chiroptera/chiroptera.emballonuridae.diclidurus.html (accessed on July 2, 2004).

Schnitzer, Hans-Ulrich, and Elisabeth K. V. Kalko. "Echolocation by Insect-Eating Bats." *Bioscience* (July 2001): 557–557.

Web sites:

"Bats in Australia." Australian Museum Online. http://www.austmus.gov.au/bats/records/bat24.htm (accessed on July 2, 2004).

"Ghost Bat—*Macroderma gigas.*" UNEP World Conservation Monitoring Centre. http://www.unep-wcmc.org/index.html?http://www.unep-wcmc.org/species/data/species_sheets/ghostbat.htm~main (accessed on July 2, 2004).

"Monkeying Around! The Mammals of Southeast Asia." Focus on Wildlife. http://www.ecologyasia.com/FOW_Pages/mammals.htm (accessed on July 2, 2004).

Simmons, Nancy. "*Saccopteryx bilineata,* Greater Sac-winged Bat." American Museum of Natural History. http://www.digimorph.org/specimens/Saccopteryx_bilineata/whole/ (accessed on July 2, 2004).

Voigt, Christian C. "The Sac-Winged Bat Project." Institute for Zoo and Wildlife Research. http://www.izw-berlin.de/en/research/fg1/index.html?themen/themen.html~rechts (accessed on July 2, 2004).

family

CHAPTER

PHYSICAL CHARACTERISTICS

The only species in the Craseonycteridae family is Kitti's hog-nosed bat or simply, hog-nosed bat. They are also called bumblebee bats, because they are about the size of a bumblebee. This species was unidentified until 1974.

Kitti's hog-nosed bat is considered the word's smallest mammal. The head and body combined measure only 1.1 to 1.3 inches (29 to 34 millimeters), and they weigh about 0.7 to 0.9 ounces (2.0 to 2.6 grams), which is about the weight of a dime. These bats have a wingspan of about 6 inches (15 centimeters), which is smaller than some butterflies.

The name hog-nosed refers to the bat's facial appearance. Their muzzle is pig-like, with two wide, crescent-shaped nostrils. Their ears are relatively large with rounded tips. They extend beyond the snout when the bat is lying forward. Their eyes are relatively small and partially hidden by fur. Hog-nosed bats have long and broad wings with pointed tips. Fur on the back may be a brown to reddish brown and its belly is typically paler. These bats have twenty-eight teeth.

Kitti's hog-nosed bats have long, slender feet and a short thumb with a well-developed claw. They do not have an external tail. Males have a glandular swelling at the base of the throat. The bumblebee bat also has a web of skin between its hind legs, which is thought to help with flying and catching insects.

GEOGRAPHIC RANGE

Kitti's hog-nosed bats were once found only in Thailand. Most of these bat populations were located in Sai Yok National Park. In 2001 a second population of bumblebee bats was found in a cave in Myanmar.

HABITAT

Bumblebee bats have been found deep inside small, remote limestone caves, caves formed by water dissolving calcium carbonate rock. Hog-nosed bats appear to prefer caves with multiple chambers and domed roofs located near rivers or areas with water.

DIET

Kitti's hog-nosed bats feed on insects, including spiders, beetles, small flies, wasps, and bark lice. They hunt their prey (animals they eat) through echolocation (eck-oh-loh-KAY-shun), a technique in which the bats emit high-pitched sounds that bounce off objects. The bats then detect the objects around them by listening to the sounds' echoes. These sounds are too high pitched for humans to hear.

Kitti's hog-nosed bat is also called the bumblebee bat, because of its very small size (© Merlin D. Tuttle, Bat Conservation International. Reproduced by permission.)

BEHAVIOR AND REPRODUCTION

Hog-nosed bats are crepuscular (kri-PUS-kyuh-lur), meaning that they are active at dawn and dusk. These bats are most active in the evening. A few minutes after the sun sets they leave the cave and fly in a circular pattern above the cave entrance for about one minute before flying away. They then separate into small groups and head off to a foraging area, a place to search for food, which is usually relatively close, within 820 feet (250 meters) of the cave.

Hog-nosed bats eat for about thirty minutes then return to the cave for the night. They are active again during the hours before sunrise. In the early morning they feed and then return to the cave.

The bats roost (settle or rest) together in caves in small numbers of up to fifteen individuals. While they roost together, the bats appear to be independent. They roost alone instead of clustered together with others.

From the shape of their wings and stomach content it appears that they can hover to catch their prey. It is unclear exactly how the hog-nosed bat captures its food. It could snatch small insects

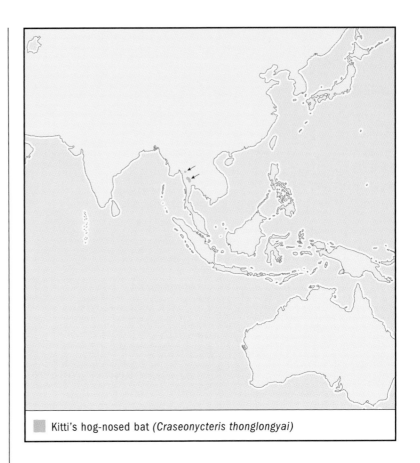

Kitti's hog-nosed bat (*Craseonycteris thonglongyai*)

off surrounding leaves, twigs, or other surfaces. It could hunt near the ground. Other observations conclude that these bats may catch insects on their wings while flying.

Little is known about the hog-nosed bat's mating habits. The species is thought to be polygamous (puh-LIH-guh-mus), meaning that they have more than one mate during the mating season. There is evidence to show that the bats have their young during the beginning of the summer's rainy season.

KITTI'S HOG-NOSED BATS AND PEOPLE

People have caused the population of hog nosed bats to decline by disturbing their habitats and food supplies. Much of the areas around the bats' caves have been cleared for agriculture. Recreation and tourism are also reasons for the disruption of the bat's habitat and the resulting decline in population.

CONSERVATION STATUS

Kitti's hog-nosed bats are listed as Endangered, facing a very high risk of extinction, dying out, by the IUCN; they are one of the rarest bats in the world.

HOLY BAT DISCOVERY!

The discovery of the tiny bumblebee bats set a new record for the smallest bat in the world. The Kitti of Kitti's hog-nosed bats refers to Kitti Thonglongya, who collected the bat in Thailand in 1968. Thonglongya went on to collect and discover other new bat species, such as the extremely rare Salim Ali's fruit bat.

Books:

Fenton, Brock M. *Bats.* New York: Checkmark Press, 2001.

Fenton, Brock M. *The Bat: Wings in the Night Sky.* Buffalo, NY: Firefly Books, 1998.

Nowak, Ronald M. "Kitti's hog-nosed bats." *Walker's Mammals of the World 5.1 Online.* http://www.press.jhu.edu/books/walkers_mammals_ of_the_world/chiroptera/chiroptera.craseonycteridae.craseonycteris.html (accessed on July 2, 2004).

Richardson, Phil. *Bats.* London: Whittet Books, 1985.

Ruff, Sue, and Don E. Wilson. *Bats.* New York: Benchmark Books, 2001.

Schober, Wilfried and Eckard Grimmberger. *The Bats of Europe and North America.* Neptune City, NJ: T.F.H. Publications, Inc., 1997.

Periodicals:

"Bats." *Science Weekly* (September 27, 1995): 1.

Web sites:

"Discover the Secret World of Bats!" Bat Conservation International. http://www.batcon.org (accessed on July 2, 2004).

The Bioproject. http://www.bioproject.info/index.html (accessed on July 2, 2004).

SLIT-FACED BATS

Nycteridae

Class: Mammalia

Order: Chiroptera

Family: Nycteridae

Number of species: 14 species

phylum

class

subclass

order

monotypic order

suborder

▲ **family**

family CHAPTER

PHYSICAL CHARACTERISTICS

Slit-faced bats are small to medium in size. Head and body length is 1.6 to 3.7 inches (4 to 9.3 centimeters), and adults weigh 0.2 to 1.2 ounces (6 to 36 grams). Also called hollow-faced bats, the feature that gives slit-faced bats their name is a deep groove that runs from their nostrils to a pit in the middle of their forehead. The dent is hidden by fur, which makes it hard to see.

Species of slit-faced bats have large, oval ears and their wings are broad. Slit-faced bats range in color from orange, brown, and red to gray. These bats also have a distinctive feature among mammals at the end of their tail. The long tail, completely enclosed within a membrane, ends in a T-shaped tip.

GEOGRAPHIC RANGE

Slit-faced bats are found throughout most of Africa, Southeast Asia, and Madagascar. Most species are found in Africa.

HABITAT

Some species of slit-faced bats live in woodland savanna or dry country, and others live in rainforests in Africa or in Southeast Asia.

DIET

A slit-faced bat's diet depends upon the species. Most species of these bats feed primarily on a variety of arthropods (animals that have jointed bodies and limbs), such as moths, butterflies, beetles, crickets, centipedes, scorpions, and spiders. Some bats, the larger slit-faced bats, will also eat small vertebrates (animals with a backbone), such as frogs, birds, fish, other bats, and mice.

BEHAVIOR AND REPRODUCTION

Like all bats, these bats are nocturnal, meaning they are active at night. Slit-faced bats also use echolocation (eck-oh-loh-KAY-shun), the detection of an object by means of reflected sound. It is not known how much they depend upon echolocation to catch their prey (animals hunted for food). The echolocation calls of these bats are low in intensity, or energy, and brief. Usually the calls last only a millisecond or less.

As well as echolocation, it appears that these bats depend upon sound to find food. Their large ears are apparently used to listen for the low-frequency sounds of prey-generated movements, such as the sound of an insect scuffling along the ground or calls the insects may make. Slit-faced bats sometimes catch their prey in the air, but primarily snatch their prey from a surface, such as a leaf or branch.

The broad wings of slit-faced bats enable them to fly slowly and hover, then pluck insects off ground or vegetation surfaces. When bats, such as the large slit-faced bat, catch and kill larger prey such as small vertebrates, they carry them off to their feeding perch. These bats can hunt either lying in wait on their perches or from slow, continuous flight low to the ground. When they eat insects, they typically drop their wings and legs.

Like all bats, slit-faced bats are active in the night hours and they roost (settle or rest) during the day hours. Most species shelter alone, in pairs, or in small family groups or colonies (group of animals of the same type living together). Roosting sites for slit-faced bats are diverse, and may include hollow trees, dense foliage, rocky outcrops, caves, buildings, ruins, abandoned wells, and porcupine and aardvark burrows.

Slit-faced bats have one offspring per year, typically at the beginning of the rainy season. Female large slit-faced bats leave their young behind in the roost when they set out at night to hunt. They return several times throughout the night to feed their young.

SLIT-FACED BATS AND PEOPLE

There is no known special relationship between slit-faced bats and people.

From the Greeks

The name *Nycteris* comes from the Greek word *nykteros,* meaning nocturnal.

CONSERVATION STATUS

The IUCN lists the Javan slit-faced bat and the Ja slit-faced bat as Vulnerable, facing a high risk of extinction in the wild. Three other species are listed as Near Threatened, not currently threatened, but may become so.

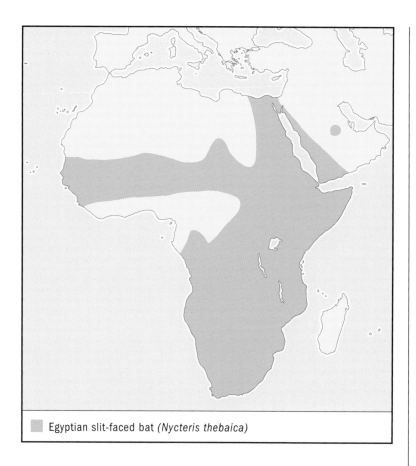

Egyptian slit-faced bat *(Nycteris thebaica)*

EGYPTIAN SLIT-FACED BAT
Nycteris thebaica

Physical characteristics: A distinctive feature of the Egyptian slit-faced bat is its long ears. The bat has long, fine fur that is gray to red. Its underparts are lighter in color. These bats are also called common slit-faced bats. They are medium-size bats, with an adult weighing about 0.2 to 0.4 ounces (7 to 12 grams)—about the weight of five pennies.

Geographic range: Egyptian slit-faced bats are found in Africa.

Habitat: These bats live in the open savanna woodlands of sub-Saharan Africa, in the dry or arid (extremely dry) areas of Africa. These bats can live in a wide range of habitats, with roosts including caves, under mines, buildings, and tree hollows.

When the female Egyptian slit-faced bat leaves the roost at night to hunt, she takes her young with her and then sets them in another area while she hunts. (Brock Fenton. Reproduced by permission.)

Diet: Egyptian slit-faced bats typically diet on arthropods, such as spiders, crickets, and scorpions, as well as insects, such as moths and beetles.

Behavior and reproduction: When foraging for food, Egyptian slit-faced bats pick their prey off the ground and vegetation surfaces, such as leaves or branches, as well as while flying. They can fly slowly and maneuver well, which allows them to hunt close to the ground and in dense vegetation.

These bats use echolocation and simply listening to detect their prey. Their large ears enable the bats to pick up sounds like the scuffling of some insects or the beating of wings. The purpose of the bird-like chirps they make while searching for their prey at night is unknown.

The roosts of Egyptian-slit faced bats include caves, areas under roads, mines, hollow trees, and roofs. They can be seen hanging from veranda (a structure like a porch) rooftops in temporary night roosts as they rest from their foraging. Observations have spotted colonies ranging in size from several and several hundred individuals.

Females produce a single offspring each year after gestating (being pregnant) for about 150 days. When the female leaves the roost at night to hunt, she takes her young with her and then sets them in another area while she hunts. Both sexes reach reproductive maturity at about their second year of life.

Egyptian-slit faced bats and people: There is no known significant relationship with people.

Conservation status: The IUCN does not consider Egyptian slit-faced bats to be threatened. ∎

FOR MORE INFORMATION

Books:

Fenton, M. Brock. *Bats.* New York: Checkmark Press, 2001.

Fenton, M. Brock. *The Bat: Wings in the Night Sky.* Buffalo, NY: Firefly Books, 1998.

Nowak, Ronald M. "Slit-faced Bats, or Hollow-faced Bats." *Walker's Mammals of the World 5.1 Online.* Baltimore: Johns Hopkins University Press, 1997. http://www.press.jhu.edu/books/walkers_mammals_of_the_world/chiroptera/chiroptera.nycteridae.nycteris.html (accessed on July 4, 2004).

Richardson, Phil. *Bats.* London: Whittet Books, 1985.

Ruff, Sue, and Don E. Wilson. *Bats.* New York: Benchmark Books, 2001.

Schober, Wilfried, and Eckard Grimmberger. *The Bats of Europe and North America.* Neptune City, NJ: T.F.H. Publications, Inc., 1997.

Periodicals:

Schnitzler, Hans-Ulrich, and Elisabeth K. V. Kalko. "Echolocation by Insect-Eating Bats." *Bioscience* (July 2001): 557.

Kerner, Sarah. "In the Bat Cave." *Boys' Life* (June 2003): 18.

Web sites:

Jacob, Davids. "Bats of the Western Cape." Cape Bat Action Team (Cape Bat). http://www.museums.org.za/sam/resources/mammal/bats.htm (accessed on July 4, 2004).

French, Barbara. "Where the Bats Are Part II: Other Animals' Shelters." Bat Conservation International, Inc. http://www.batcon.org/batsmag/v17n3-5.html (accessed on July 4, 2004).

Myers, Phil, and Bret Weinstein. "Family Nycteridae (slit-faced bats)." *Animal Diversity Web.* http://animaldiversity.ummz.umich.edu/site/accounts/information/Nycteridae.html (accessed on July 4, 2004).

Taylor, Peter. "Bats: Nature's Agricultural Allies" *Science in Africa.* http://www.scienceinafrica.co.za/2003/may/bats.htm (accessed on July 4, 2004).

Class: Mammalia
Order: Chiroptera
Family: Megadermatidae
Number of species: 5 species

family
CHAPTER

PHYSICAL CHARACTERISTICS

False vampire bats are medium-sized to large bats with a head and body length of 2.6 to 5.5 inches (6.5 to 14.0 centimeters). Their wingspans can reach 3 feet (1 meter). The Australian false vampire bat, also called the Australian ghost bat, is among the largest of the microchiropteran (my-kro-keer-OP-ter-an) bats. Microchiroptera is one of the two suborders of bats and includes most of the bats in the world.

False vampire bats have large ears joined by a band of skin across the forehead and noseleafs, which are fleshy protrusions from the nose. The heart-nosed bats have a leaf-like nose that is heart-shaped.

Megadermatids (meg-ah-der-MAT-ids; bats in the family Megadermatide) have a tail that is either short or absent. These bats typically have relatively short and broad wings.

Their fur tends to be long and gray in color, although the yellow-winged bats have bright yellow or orange wings and ears, with bluish fur. False vampire bats have twenty-six or twenty-eight teeth. The flesh-eating, or carnivorous, mega-dermatids, such as the Australian false vampire bats, have sharp and strong canine teeth for tearing flesh and crushing bones.

GEOGRAPHIC RANGE

Megadermatids are found in Africa, Asia, east India, Philippines, and Australia.

HABITAT

Megadermatids live in open, dry habitats in Australia, and in open woodlands. They also live in the very dry or arid areas of Africa and India. Typical habitats for heart-nosed bats include dry lowlands, coastal strip habitats, and sometimes river valleys.

DIET

Many of the megadermatid species are also known as false vampire bats because people mistakenly believed that they eat blood. Megadermatids eat insects or small vertebrates (animals with backbones), and none of them feed only on blood. The carnivorous species, such as the Australian false vampire bats, eat small vertebrates that include fish, frogs, lizards, birds, mice, or other bats. The Asian false vampire bats have a diverse diet, feeding on everything from insects, spiders, fish, birds, and frogs, to rodents and even occasionally smaller bats. False vampire bats are among the top predators (hunters) of the forest, hunting mainly birds, other bats, and rodents.

Yellow-winged bats eat insects on the ground or while flying. They feed on large and small insects, including moths and butterflies, grasshoppers, beetles, flies, and mosquitoes.

BEHAVIOR AND REPRODUCTION

Megadermatids make echolocation (eck-oh-loh-KAY-shun) calls through the nose. Echolocation is a technique of sending out sounds and then using the reflection or echoes of the sound to detect objects. In bats these sounds are too high-pitched for humans to hear. Megadermatids use their large noseleaf to focus the sound outwards.

Megadermatids roost (settle or rest) in caves, rock crevices, buildings, and trees. Roosting habits vary from solitary to colonial. The Asian false vampire bats roost in caves, buildings, and hollow trees in small groups, although one particularly large colony of nearly 2,000 was reported in India. Eating a wide range of foods from insects to birds, these bats maneuver (mah-NOO-ver) well as they snatch their food.

False vampire bats commonly kill the prey (animals hunted for food) by biting the head and crushing the skull. False vampires share their prey with other members of the family group, consisting of a pair of adults and their non-breeding young. The Australian false vampire bat drops on small mammals from above, and envelops them with its wings before biting the head and neck. They carry their prey to a high point or back to the roost.

Heart-nosed bats hang upside down on a low perch while they scan the area for their meals. This bat eats beetles, centipedes, scorpions, and small bats. From its perch, typically 10 to 16 feet (3 to 5 meters) above ground, this bat twists its body 180°, using its eyes and ears to search for prey. When it spots a meal, the bat swoops down and snatches the prey, carrying it back to its perch. There, the bat removes the legs and wings before eating the body.

Some megadermatids, such as the yellow-winged bats, appear to be monogamous (muh-NAH-guh-mus), meaning that the male and female pair up, which is unusual in bats and mammals. Heart-nosed bats mate in monogamous pairs for the breeding season. They make an effort to keep the same mate during the following breeding seasons. Mated pairs have a breeding site that the male defends. Prior to foraging for their food in the evening, the male of the heart-nosed and false vampire bats sing from perches.

Megadermatids give birth to a single offspring during each breeding period. In yellow-winged bats, following a gestation (pregnancy) of about three months, most births of the single offspring occur in April. False vampire bats also have a gestation period of about three months, and give birth at the beginning of the rainy season. Sometimes, an older member of the family may remain to sit with the young while the adults hunt.

MEGADERMATIDS AND PEOPLE

People are destroying the natural habitat of megadermatids, causing many of these species' populations to decrease.

CONSERVATION STATUS

The IUCN lists the heart-nosed bat as being Near Threatened, not currently threatened, but may become so; and the Australian false vampire bat as Vulnerable, facing a high risk of extinction in the wild.

KEEPING WARM

Ghost bats cannot stand getting cold. Studies suggest that these bats need to keep their body temperatures between 95 and 102.2°F (35 to 39°C). When surrounding temperatures are higher or lower, these bats need to need to increase or decrease their metabolic rate to keep warm or stay cool. They move between a number of caves, depending upon the weather, which means they need multiple cave sites where they can roost. Females especially need to keep warm while they are pregnant.

Australian false vampire bat *(Macroderma gigas)*

AUSTRALIAN FALSE VAMPIRE BAT
Macroderma gigas

Physical characteristics: Australian false vampire bats are among the largest of the bats. They have forearms that range from 3.7 to 4.6 inches (9.6 to 11.8 centimeters) long, and weigh 2.6 to 5 ounces (74 to 144 grams). Their head and body length is 3.9 to 5.1 inches (10 to 13 centimeters). Females are smaller than males.

These bats are also called ghost bats, because their fur is light brown to gray to almost white. In some areas, ghost bats have an ashy gray back and white underparts. These bats have wide ears that meet above the head and are fused. They have large eyes relative to their heads, along with prominent noseleafs.

Australian false vampire bats typically roost in caves and abandoned mines. (© B. G. Thomson/Photo Researchers, Inc. Reproduced by permission.)

Geographic range: Australian false vampire bats are found in northern Australia, mainly north Queensland, along the north central coast, and in the northwest.

Habitat: Australian false vampire bats live in both arid regions and rainforest areas, such as north Queensland. They typically roost in caves and abandoned mines.

Diet: The Australian false vampire bat is Australia's only carnivorous bat. These bats eat large insects, such as cockroaches, and vertebrates, such as reptiles, frogs, birds, small mammals, and other bat species.

Behavior and reproduction: Australian false vampire bats commonly hang from a branch and wait for their prey to pass on the ground below. The bats then drop down, envelop the prey with their wings and kill it by biting its head and neck. They also catch prey while in flight. Australian false vampire bats eat large amounts of food and consume much of their prey, including its flesh, bones, teeth, fur, small feathers, and the exoskeletons of insects.

Australian false vampire bats move to the warmer northern Australia area when the weather becomes cooler, and then back to the cooler southern areas when the weather becomes warm. These bats do use echolocation, yet they appear to capture their prey with their extremely sensitive hearing and vision. Their echolocation calls are less than one millisecond long. Australian false vampire bats roost alone or in small groups. During the breeding season, for the most part, females gather in colonies, while males gather into their own colonies. Yet some studies have found that some males are always present with the females. There are typically fewer than 100 bats in a group.

Australian false vampire bats generally mate in April or May and gestate for about three months. The females bear a single offspring. Mothers stay with their young and also fly with them to forage (search) for food during the first several weeks of life. Both sexes reach reproductive maturity at about their second year of life.

Austalian false vampire bats and people: Australian Aborigines, the early inhabitants of Australia, have a spiritual connection to the Austalian false vampire bats. Mining operations are destroying their roosting sites, causing a decline in their population. These bats are also extremely sensitive to any disturbance. People that enter a ghost-bat cave colony may cause the group to become nervous and leave.

Conservation status: Australian false vampire bats have declined in population because people have destroyed their habitats. They are categorized as Vulnerable by the IUCN. ■

FOR MORE INFORMATION

Books:

Fenton, M. Brock. *Bats.* New York: Checkmark Press, 2001.

Fenton, M. Brock. *The Bat: Wings in the Night Sky.* Buffalo, NY: Firefly Books, 1998.

Nowak, Ronald M. "Australian Giant False Vampire Bat, or Ghost Bat." *Walker's Mammals of the World 5.1 Online.* Baltimore: Johns Hopkins University Press, 1997. http://www.press.jhu.edu/books/walker/ chiroptera/chiroptera.megadermatidae.macroderma.html (accessed on July 4, 2004).

Richardson, Phil. *Bats.* London: Whittet Books, 1985.

Ruff, Sue, and Don E. Wilson. *Bats.* New York: Benchmark Books, 2001.

Schober, Wilfried, and Eckard Grimmberger. *The Bats of Europe and North America.* Neptune City, NJ: T.F.H. Publications, Inc., 1997.

Web sites:

"Bat." *MSN Encarta Online Encyclopedia 2004.* http://encarta.msn. com/encyclopedia_761557637/Bat.html (accessed on July 4, 2004).

French, Barbara. "False Vampires and Other Carnivores." Bat Conservation International, Inc. http://www.batcon.org/batsmag/v15n2-5.html (accessed on July 4, 2004).

Hester, L., and P. Myers. "Family Megadermatidae (False Vampire Bats)." Animal Diversity Web. http://animaldiversity.ummz.umich.edu/site/ accounts/information/Megadermatidae.html (accessed on July 4, 2004).

"Yellow-winged bat—*Lavia frans.*" American Zoo. http://www.americazoo .com/goto/index/mammals/63.htm (accessed on July 4, 2004).

HORSESHOE BATS
Rhinolophidae

Class: Mammalia
Order: Chiroptera
Family: Rhinolophidae
Number of species: 69 species

family

CHAPTER

phylum

class

subclass

order

monotypic order

suborder

▲ **family**

PHYSICAL CHARACTERISTICS

The name "horseshoe" bats comes from the distinctive shape of their nose. Many species of bats have fleshy folds of skin around their nostrils called a noseleaf. In the horseshoe bats, the lower part of its noseleaf is shaped like a horseshoe or a U-shape. This lower section covers the bat's upper lip. The upper part of the noseleaf, above the nostril, is pointed. In some species, such as Hildebrandt's horseshoe bat, the noseleaf is hairy.

Horseshoe bat species range widely in size, from small to moderate. The smaller species of these bats can have a head and body length of 1.4 inches (3.5 centimeters) and the larger species can measure 4.3 inches (11 centimeters). They weigh from 0.15 ounces (4.3 grams; less than the weight of two pennies) to 13.8 ounces (35 grams).

The fur on horseshoe bats can be a variety of colors, including gray-brown and reddish brown fur. Other bats can have gray, black, dark brown, yellow, or bright orange-red fur. Their fur is long and soft. These bats have large ears that are typically pointy and can move independently of one another. Their eyes are relatively small. The wings are broad with rounded ends.

GEOGRAPHIC RANGE

Horseshoe bats are found in temperate (areas with moderate temperatures) and tropical regions of the Old World, meaning the part of the world made up of Australia, Africa, Asia, and Europe. These bats are found in southern Europe, Africa, and southern Asia to northern and eastern Australia, including many

Pacific islands. They do not live in the arid (extremely dry) ranges of Africa. In many areas, these bats have extremely small ranges.

HABITAT

Horseshoe bats live in a wide variety of areas, such as forests, savannas, open areas, and occasionally in deserts. Horseshoe bats can live in areas that are cooler than many other bats can survive. They also have a wide variety of places in which they roost, meaning rest or settle. Primary roosting sites include caves and hollow trees. Other roosting sites include buildings, houses, mines, holes, and tunnels. Some of these bats roost in open areas. Research indicates that the roosting sites for these bats may be important factors in determining where they decide to live.

DIET

Horseshoe bats eat insects and spiders.

BEHAVIOR AND REPRODUCTION

Like all bats, horseshoe bats are nocturnal, meaning they are active at night. They begin foraging for their food later in the evening than most other bats, typically hunting about 20 feet (6 meters) above the ground. Horseshoe bats have a fluttering or hovering flight. These bats will catch prey (animals hunted for food) both in flight and on surfaces, such as leaves or branches. Some species also sit on some type of perch, such as a branch, and snatch insects as they fly past. When foraging, or searching, for food on surfaces, called gleaning, these bats find prey on branches, leaves, rocks, and the ground. The bats will eat the insect in flight if they are small enough. If the prey is a large insect, they may take their prey back to a roost or a feeding perch. They can catch the insect in their wings and store it in their cheek.

To locate their prey, horseshoe bats use echolocation (eck-oh-loh-KAY-shun), a technique in which they send out sounds and listen to the sounds that bounce back to locate objects. Horseshoe bats echolocate through their noses, as opposed to most bats, which send out echolocation calls through their mouths. Using echolocation, horseshoe bats can detect the flutter of insects' wings.

Most species gather together to roost, from small colonies of about twenty individuals, to large colonies of up to 2,000 individuals. One species in particular, the woolly horseshoe bat, roosts in pairs. These bats hang freely when they roost, not huddling next to one another to keep warm as do many other bats. When roosting, these bats wrap their wings around themselves, enclosing their entire body.

SPECIES RECOVERY

With a population that has dwindled down to an estimated 5,000 individuals, the greater horseshoes are one of England's most rare bats. Concerned about extinction, the country has taken steps to help this species once again flourish. In 1998 the English Nature Greater Horseshoe Bat Project was launched with the prime goal to increase the species population by 25 percent by the year 2010. With awareness, education, and specially designated roosting sites, the number of recorded births in 2003 had reached record levels (228). Warmer winters and a reduction in the use of chemicals and pesticides in farming also contributed to population growth.

Species that live in northern areas may hibernate (deep sleep in which an animal conserves energy) during the winter. Other species go into torpor every day. Torpor is a period of inactivity in which an animal's heart rate slows down to conserve energy. At least one species is migratory, meaning they travel to warmer areas when the weather becomes cool. Many species that hibernate can awaken easily and change their hibernating sites occasionally, sometimes flying almost a mile (1,500 meters) or more to a new place.

In some species, including ones that hibernate, females mate during the fall, but fertilization does not occur until the spring. In other species, mating and fertilization occur in the spring. For bats that live in tropical areas, females give birth during the warm summer months. In some species, males and females live together all year, while females form separate colonies in other species. Gestation (pregnancy) ranges from seven weeks to slightly over five months. Bats typically have one offspring per season, and the babies are independent at six to eight weeks of age.

HORSESHOE BATS AND PEOPLE

People have caused the decline in many species of horseshoe bats by destroying their habitat. Altering or disturbing these bats' habitat can indirectly reduce their prey. The use of insecticides, a chemical used to kill or control insects, has also reduced the population of the bats' prey.

CONSERVATION STATUS

Most species of horseshoe bats are in danger of a decline in population or have already experienced population loss. Researchers know little about some species of these bats and so their conservation status is not known. Out of the species listed in the IUCN Red List, thiry-eight species, there is one species listed as Critically Endangered, facing an extremely high risk of extinction, dying out, in the wild; and two as Endangered, facing a very high risk of extinction in the wild. There are also species that are not considered endangered globally but are in danger of extinction in specific areas, such as the greater horseshoe bat, which is regarded as endangered in Europe.

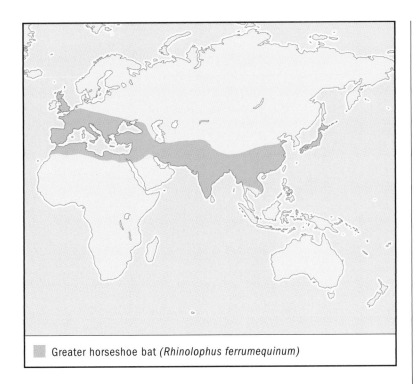

Greater horseshoe bat (*Rhinolophus ferrumequinum*)

GREATER HORSESHOE BAT
Rhinolophus ferrumequinum

Physical characteristics: The greater horseshoe bats are among the largest species of its family. The length of their head and body combined ranges from 2.2 to 3.1 inches (5.6 to 7.9 centimeters), and its wingspan is from 13.8 to 15.6 inches (35 to 40 centimeters). These bats have large, pointed ears, small eyes, and a flattened face, with a distinct horseshoe-shaped fleshy disc nose. Fur is fine and silky, typically light brown to grayish, with a reddish color. The wings and ears are light gray. Offspring are born gray and turn reddish brown as they grow.

Geographic range: Greater horseshoe bats are found in southern Europe, Great Britain, India, and southern Asia to southern China and Japan. In the United Kingdom they are primarily found only in southwest England and south Wales.

Habitat: These bats live in forest, as well as open land, such as pastures. They roost in caves, mine tunnels, and large buildings.

Greater horseshoe bats can catch their prey, such as this moth, while they are flying. (© Stephen Dalton/Photo Researchers, Inc. Reproduced by permission.)

Diet: Greater horseshoe bats eat small- to medium-sized insects, including beetles, moths, and flies.

Behavior and reproduction: With their broad wings, greater horseshoe bats fly slowly. These bats can feed by flying low to the ground and catching prey in flight. They also can wait for their prey on a perch, snatching the insect as it passes. They take large prey to a regular feeding perch.

Greater horseshoe bats emerge from their roosts about half an hour before sunset. Between warmer months, May to August, they typically return to their roost after about an hour and remain there until they emerge for a second round of foraging at about dawn. From late August until May they may remain at their roost all night.

Greater horseshoe bats hibernate. They may start hibernating near the entrance of caves, then move to sites deeper within the cave as the weather becomes cooler. The moistness of the caves prevents the bats from losing too much water from their bodies.

Greater horseshoe bats breed in autumn, from September to October, and give birth from June to July (where they've been studied in Europe). Females give birth to one young, after a gestation period of about seventy-five days. The mother hangs upside down while giving birth and the infant is born into her overlapped wings. They can live for up to thirty years.

Greater horseshoe bats and people: People have caused the decline of the greater horseshoe bats by disturbing or destroying their roosts and prey (with pesticide use). In Great Britain, it is estimated that the greater horseshoe bat population has decreased by 90 percent since 1900.

Conservation status: The IUCN Red List classifies the greater horseshoe bat as Near Threatened, meaning it is not yet threatened, but could become so, around the world. But in some areas, such as Europe, this species is considered endangered by national or regional conservation groups. ■

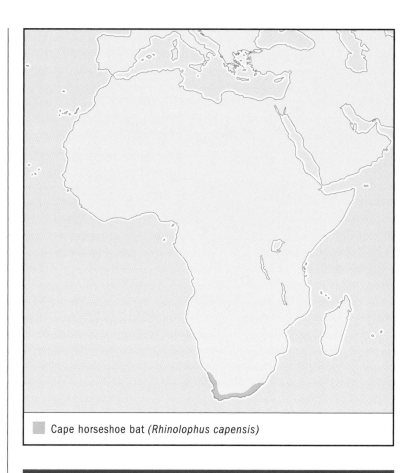

Cape horseshoe bat *(Rhinolophus capensis)*

CAPE HORSESHOE BAT
Rhinolophus capensis

Physical characteristics: The cape horseshoe bat is small to medium in size, with a head and body length of about 2.4 inches (6.2 centimeters). Its fur on the upper side and wings are dark brown, the back is lighter brown and the underside is brown to cream in color. It has the distinctive horseshoe ring around the nose, with a large, wavy triangular leaf extending from the horseshoe up between the eyes.

Geographic range: Cape horseshoe bats are found along the coastline of southern Africa.

Habitat: Cape horseshoe bats live along the coast. They are found in coastal and sea caves.

Diet: Cape horseshoe bats eat mainly beetles.

Behavior and reproduction: These bats catch their prey while flying slowly and low to the ground. They also can hunt from perches, waiting for prey to pass. When roosting, they usually hang individually, rather than in dense clusters.

They mate in spring, August through September, and young are born from November to December.

Cape horseshoe bats and people: There is no known, significant relationship between these bats and people.

Conservation status: The IUCN lists the cape horseshoe bat as Vulnerable. ■

FOR MORE INFORMATION

Books:

Fenton, M. Brock. *Bats.* New York: Checkmark Press, 2001.

Fenton, M. Brock. *The Bat: Wings in the Night Sky.* Buffalo, NY: Firefly Books, 1998.

Nowak, Ronald M. "Horseshoe Bats." *Walker's Mammals of the World 5.1 Online.* Baltimore: Johns Hopkins University Press, 1997. http://www.press.jhu.edu/books/walkers_mammals_of_the_world/chiroptera/chiroptera.rhinolophidae.rhinolophus.html (accessed on July 5, 2004).

Raabe, Emily. *Horseshoe Bats.* New York, NY: Powerkids Press, 2003.

Richardson, Phil. *Bats.* London: Whittet Books, 1985.

Ruff, Sue, and Don E. Wilson. *Bats.* New York: Benchmark Books, 2001.

Periodicals:

Griffin, Donald R. "Return to the Magic Well: Echolocation Behavior of Bats and Responses of Insect Prey." *BioScience* (July, 2001): 555.

"Horseshoe Bats Sound Out the Choicest Prey." *New Scientist* (March, 2003): 36.

Thi Dao, Nguyen. "My Life as a Forest Creature: Growing Up with the Cuc Phuong National Park. (This Land)." *Natural History* (March, 2003): 70.

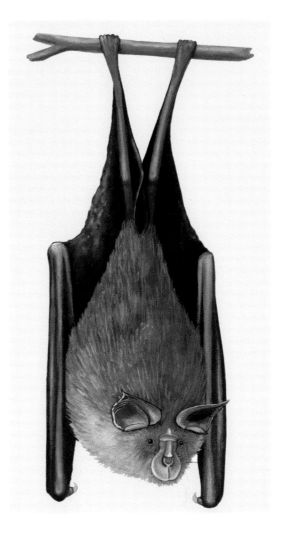

Cape horseshoe bats live along the coast of southern Africa, in coastal and sea caves. (Illustration by Emily Damstra. Reproduced by permission.)

Web sites:

"Bats in Australia." Australian Museum. http://www.amonline.net.au/bats/records/bat15.htm (accessed on July 5, 2004).

Myers, Phil. "Family Rhinolophidae (Horseshoe Bats and Old World Leaf-Nosed Bats)." Animal Diversity Web. http://animaldiversity.ummz.umich.edu/site/accounts/information/Rhinolophidae.html (accessed on July 5, 2004).

Roberts, G. M., and A. M. Hutson. "Greater Horseshoe Bat: *Rhinolophus ferrumequinum* The Bat Conservation Trust. http://www.bats.org.uk/batinfo/gr_horse.htm (accessed on July 5, 2004).

"Greater Horseshoe Bat." BBC Science and Nature: Animals. http://www.bbc.co.uk/nature/wildfacts/factfiles/284.shtml (accessed on July 5, 2004).

"Greater Horseshoe Bat: *Rhinolophus ferrumequinum*." UK Biodiversity Action Plan. http://www.ukbap.org.uk/ukplans.aspx?ID=550 (accessed on July 5, 2004).

OLD WORLD LEAF-NOSED BATS

Hipposideridae

Class: Mammalia

Order: Chiroptera

Family: Hipposideridae

Number of species: 66 species

family

CHAPTER

PHYSICAL CHARACTERISTICS

Also called roundleaf bats, Old World leaf-nosed bats vary greatly in size. They have a combined head and body length that ranges from 1.1 to 4.3 inches (2.8 to 11 centimeters). One species, Commerson's leaf-nosed bat, is one of the largest insect-eating bats of all the microchiroptera (my-kro-keer-OP-ter-ah; one of two bat categories that includes most of the bats in the world), with a wingspan of about 2 feet (0.6 meters). These bats are closely related to and share many of the features of horseshoe bats. They have a fleshy fold of skin around their nostrils called a noseleaf, which is leaf-like in appearance. The lower part of the noseleaf is shaped like a horseshoe or U-shape, with leaf-like flaps of skin above that protrude outwards.

The ears of these bats vary in size. They do not have a tragus (TRAY-gus), a flap of skin in front of the ear opening, which is common in many bats. These bats have only two bones in each toe. Their tail length ranges from nothing to approximately 2.4 inches (6 centimeters). Fur color ranges widely among the species, from reddish and yellowish to brown and cream. In several species, males and females have different fur colors, as well as different body and noseleaf sizes.

GEOGRAPHIC RANGE

Old World leaf-nosed bats are found in tropical (hot and humid weather) and subtropical areas of the Old World, meaning the part of the world made up of Australia, Africa, Asia, and Europe. They are found in Africa and southern Asia, east to the Philippine Islands, the Solomon Islands, and Australia.

phylum

class

subclass

order

monotypic order

suborder

▲ **family**

TO GROUP OR NOT TO GROUP

The first accounts of Old World leaf-nosed bats came in 1831, and the family's classification still remains uncertain. Some scientists consider Old World leaf-nosed bats a subfamily of horseshoe bats. Other researchers maintain that both groups are distinct families, as they are in this reference.

HABITAT

These bats live in a range of habitats that include deserts and rainforests. They roost (settle or rest) in caves, underground openings, buildings, and hollow trees. One species, the fulvous (FUL-vus) leaf-nosed bat, has been found in burrows of a large porcupine in Africa.

DIET

Old World leaf-nosed bats eat insects, although little is known about the specific insects that make up their diet.

BEHAVIOR AND REPRODUCTION

There is little information on the behavior and reproduction habits of many Old World leaf-nosed bat species. Most roost in groups that range widely in size: from about twelve to groups of hundreds, to approximately 5,000. Some species appear to roost singly. The primary roosting sites of these bats are caves and tunnels, yet many roost in tree hollows and buildings.

Old World leaf-nosed bats are nocturnal, or active at night, as are all bats. When they emerge from their roosts at night, they use echolocation (eck-oh-loh-KAY-shun) to forage, search, for food. Echolocation is the process of detecting objects by sending out sounds and listening to the sounds that bounce back from the objects. Old World leaf-nosed bats fly with their mouth closed and send out sounds through their nose, as opposed to most bats that use their mouths. These bats can send out sound in one frequency and listen to the sounds bounced back on another frequency.

Observations show they catch their prey in flight. Many hunt close to the ground, such as the Old World leaf-nosed bat of the Congo.

These bats mate during the fall and females do not become fertilized until the following year. Females generally give birth to a single offspring each year. When the offspring become independent and sexually mature depends upon the species and where they live.

OLD WORLD LEAF-NOSED BATS AND PEOPLE

These bats eat many insects that are considered pests to people. Some species have been harmed by humans destroying their habitat.

CONSERVATION STATUS

Some of the species in this family are common and others are rare and vulnerable to threats. Since little is known about many species in this family, the vulnerability of these bats is not fully understood. Out of the species that the IUCN lists, two are classified as Critically Endangered, facing an extremely high risk of extinction, dying out, in the wild; fifteen as Vulnerable facing a high risk of extinction, and twenty-three as Near Threatened, not currently threatened, but could become so.

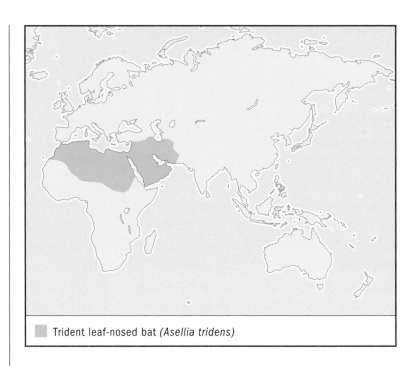

Trident leaf-nosed bat (Asellia tridens)

TRIDENT LEAF-NOSED BAT
Asellia tridens

Physical characteristics: These bats have a feature on their nose that resembles a trident, which is a spear with three prongs. The nose-leaf is made up of the horseshoe-shaped lower part, the triangle-shaped central part, and three spear-like projections. The nostrils are located in the front, and there is a frontal sac behind the noseleaf. The ears are large and nearly hairless. Fur color ranges and includes grayish, pale yellow, and orange-brown. Some trident leaf-nosed bats in Egypt have medium- to dark tan-colored fur. These bats have large ears and pale faces.

Geographic range: These bats are found in Morocco, Algeria, Egypt, Libya, Sudan, the Arabian Peninsula, and Pakistan.

Habitat: These bats live in arid (extremely dry) environments. They have often been observed roosting in caves and artificial structures, such as tunnels and old temples. Species have also been spotted roosting in underground tunnels and under the iron roof of a shed in Iraq in June, when the temperature inside the shed was an estimated 100.4°F (38°C).

Diet: Trident leaf-nosed bats eat beetles, bees, ants, and wasps.

Behavior and reproduction: Trident leaf nosed bats catch their prey (animals hunted for food) primarily while they are flying. They also may snatch up prey from the ground and other surfaces. These bats forage in vegetated areas and can travel far across desert areas for food.

Roosts of several hundred individuals have been observed. One researcher in 1980 discovered a roost of about 5,000 individuals. When exiting and entering roosts, these bats have been observed flying in small groups and low to the ground. In Iraq, these bats travel to cellars and tombs when they hibernate, from mid-September to mid-November. They then return to their summer roosts in April.

Trident leaf-nosed bats and people: By destroying their local habitats, there is some evidence that humans have caused a decrease in the bats' population.

Conservation status: The trident leaf-nosed bat is not considered to be threatened.

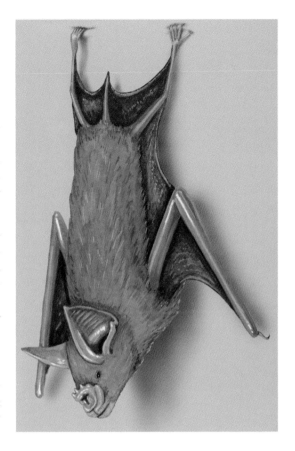

Trident leaf-nosed bats live in very dry areas, and may travel far across the desert in search of food. (Illustration by Joseph E. Trumpey. Reproduced by permission.)

FOR MORE INFORMATION

Books:

Fenton, M. Brock. *Bats.* New York: Checkmark Press, 2001.

Fenton, M. Brock. *The Bat: Wings in the Night Sky.* Buffalo, NY: Firefly Books, 1998.

Nowak, Ronald M. "Old World Leaf-nosed Bats." *Walker's Mammals of the World 5.1 Online.* Baltimore: Johns Hopkins University Press, 1997. http://www.press.jhu.edu/books/walkers_mammals_of_the_world/chiroptera/chiroptera.hipposideridae.html (accessed on July 5, 2004).

Ruff, Sue, and Don E. Wilson. *Bats.* New York: Benchmark Books, 2001.

Schober, Wilfried, and Eckard Grimmberger. *The Bats of Europe and North America.* Neptune City, NJ: T.F.H. Publications, Inc., 1997.

Periodicals:

Barr, Brady, and Margaret Zackowitz. "Going Batty." *National Geographic World* (October 2001): 12.

Schnitzler, Hans-Ulrich, and Elisabeth K. V. Kalko. "Echolocation by Insect-Eating Bats." *Bioscience* (July 2001): 557.

Web sites:

"Bat." World Almanac for Kids. http://www.worldalmanacforkids.com/explore/animals/bat.html (accessed on July 5, 2004).

Van Ryckegham, Alain. "How Do Bats Echolocate and How Are They Adapted to This Activity?" ScientificAmerican.com. http://www.sciam.com/askexpert_question.cfm?articleID=000D349B-6752-1C72-9EB7809EC588F2D7 (accessed on July 5, 2004).

"Jungle: Virtual Jungle Survival." BBC Science and Nature. http://www.bbc.co.uk/nature/programmes/tv/jungle/vjsurvival.shtml (accessed on July 5, 2004).

Class: Mammalia

Order: Chiroptera

Family: Phyllostomidae

Number of species: 151 species

family
CHAPTER

PHYSICAL CHARACTERISTICS

American leaf-nosed bats, also called New World leaf-nosed bats, are made up of diverse species. They range from small to large, with a combined head and body length of 1.6 to 5.3 inches (4 to 13.5 centimeters). This family includes the largest species of bat in the Western Hemisphere, the spectral vampire bat. These bats have a wingspan of about 3 feet (1 meter).

Some species have visible tails that are as long as 2.2 inches (5.5 centimeters), and others have no tail. These bats have noseleafs, meaning fleshy protrusions on the nose. Some of these species have noseleafs that are almost as long as the head, such as the sword-nosed bat. In most species, the noseleaf is a relatively simple structure shaped like a spear. Many species have bumps, warts, and other protrusions on the head near the nose-leaf or on the chin.

The size and shape of these bats' heads vary widely and reflect their diverse feeding habits. Fruit-eating bats, for example, may have a medium-sized noseleaf, flat faces, and wide teeth to crush fruit. Bats in this family that lap up nectar (sweet liquid produced by plants) have a small noseleaf, long tongue, and small teeth. Species in this family that eat meat are generally large and have sharp teeth.

Fur color of American leaf-nosed bats is generally brown or gray, with the exception of one species, the white bat. Some species have color patterns that include stripes on the head or back, or white tufts of fur on the shoulders.

phylum

class

subclass

order

monotypic order

suborder

▲ **family**

GEOGRAPHIC RANGE

These bats are also called New World leaf-nosed bats because of where they are found. The New World is made up of North America, Central America, and South America. American leaf-nosed bats are found in the southwestern United States south to northern Argentina, the West Indies, and central Chile.

HABITAT

Most American leaf-nosed bats live in the forest. They can live in forests that range from the dry to the tropical (hot and humid). Some species live in deserts. Many species roost (settle or rest) in caves or the hollows of trees. Other roosts include hollow logs, under tree roots, mines, tree foliage, and houses. Some species form tents out of leaves, settling under the tent for protection and rest.

DIET

American leaf-nosed bats eat a broad range of foods and groups in the family are generally categorized by diet. Most species eat animals, with the smaller species eating insects and other arthropods (a group of invertebrates that have a segmented body and jointed limbs) and the larger species feeding on frogs, lizards, birds, and other bats. Other species eat nectar and fruit. Some bats frequently eat insects and fruit. Just three species feed on blood.

BEHAVIOR AND REPRODUCTION

American leaf-nosed bats typically form colonies (groups), yet the numbers in the groups vary widely both within and among species. Sizes of groups range from pairs to colonies made up of several hundred thousand individuals.

All species of American leaf-nosed bats use echolocation (eck-oh-loh-KAY-shun) to detect objects and catch their prey (animals hunted for food). Echolocation is when an animal emits (sends out) high-pitched sounds that bounce off an object and return to the animal, which can then tell where the object is. These bats emit echolocation calls through their nose rather than their mouth.

Mating and reproduction vary widely among the species. Spectral vampire bats mate monogamously (muh-NAH-guh-mus-lee), meaning a male and female mate only with one another. The most common mating system is harem polygynous (HARE-um puh-LIJ-uh-nus), meaning one male mates with multiple females. Females in this family have one offspring either once or twice a year.

AMERICAN LEAF-NOSED BATS AND PEOPLE

Many of these bats are important pollinators for plants, meaning they disperse pollen, the fine grains that contain the male reproductive cells of seed plants. These bats help forests' and plants' continued survival. Through deforestation and destroying these bats' natural habitat, people have caused the decline in many of these bats' populations. Much of the negative myths and superstitions about bats come from the three species in this family that feed on blood. These vampire bats are considered pests to many farmers and feared for the spread of rabies.

CONSERVATION STATUS

Out of the seventy-one listed species, the 2003 IUCN Red List categorizes four species as Endangered (facing a very high risk of extinction, or dying out, in the wild) and twenty-five species as Vulnerable (facing a high risk of extinction in the wild).

BATTY FOLKLORE

Ancient artwork and hieroglyphics (high-ruh-GLI-fix; a writing system that uses pictures instead of letters) have shown that many cultures in the New World had stories about bats in this family. Representations of bats show these bats have a characteristic noseleaf. Many show bat traits added to a human figure. In New World myth and art, the underworld, the world of the dead, was one of the most important themes. Bat imagery was common because bats share several themes in the underworld, such as they are active in the dark, and they roost in caves, which were considered openings to the underworld. Vampire bats specifically were also part of folklore for the Mayans, who revered a vampire bat god. "Camazotz," the death bat, killed dying men on their way to the center of the Earth. Hieroglyphics and graphic drawings of the vampire bat are found throughout the Maya ruins in southern Mexico, Guatemala, and Honduras.

California leaf-nosed bat *(Macrotus californicus)*

CALIFORNIA LEAF-NOSED BAT
Macrotus californicus

Physical characteristics: California leaf-nosed bats are small to medium sized, with a head and body length combined of 2.1 to 2.5 inches (5.3 to 6.4 centimeters). They have a visible tail that ranges from 1.4 to 1.6 inches (3.5 to 4.1 centimeters). These bats have a large noseleaf, large ears, and broad wings. Their fur is brown or gray. The underside is lighter, typically a brown or tan color.

Geographic range: California leaf-nosed bats are one of only a few species of this family found in the United States. These bats are found in southern California and Arizona, as well as northwestern Mexico. There is also a record of the bat being found in Texas.

Habitat: California leaf-nosed bats live in arid (extremely dry) habitats. They roost in caves, mines, and abandoned buildings. They often roost in well-lit areas. They select mines and caves that stay warm in the winter months due to the heat from the Earth.

Diet: These bats eat insects, such as crickets, moths, beetles, and a variety of other arthropods.

Behavior and reproduction: California leaf-nosed bats gather in colonies of hundreds to thousands. Smaller groups have also been found.

To locate prey, California leaf-nosed bats use both echolocation and the sounds made by the prey. They also can use vision to find prey, and when they do, they stop producing echolocation calls. They capture their prey both while flying and from gleaning, picking the prey off surfaces such as vegetation and the ground. After they catch it, they take the prey to a roost to eat. They only eat certain parts of the prey, dropping legs, wings, and other parts of the insect on the ground.

These bats mate in August, September, and October. Males attract females by flapping their wings and vocal sounds. Females form maternity colonies, and the female has one offspring the following spring.

California leaf-nosed bats and people: The disturbance of these bats' natural habitats through mining has caused a decrease in these bats' population.

Conservation status: The California leaf-nosed bat is listed as Vulnerable. ■

California leaf-nosed bats live in extremely dry places, and feed on insects and other arthropods. (© Merlin D. Tuttle/ Bat Conservation International/ Photo Researchers, Inc. Reproduced by permission.)

Vampire bat *(Desmodus rotundus)*

VAMPIRE BAT
Desmodus rotundus

Physical characteristics: Vampire bats have a combined head and body length of about 2.7 to 3.7 inches (6.8 to 9.3 centimeters). One of these bats' striking features is their pointed front teeth. These bats have dark grayish brown fur, which is lighter on the underside. Ears are pointy and there is no visible tail. The thumb is clawed. Females are generally larger than males.

Geographic range: Vampire bats are found in northern Mexico to central Chile, Argentina, Uruguay, and Trinidad.

Habitat: Vampire bats live in warm climates, in both tropical and subtropical (nearly tropical, with warm temperatures and little rainfall) areas. They are commonly found where there is plenty of livestock. These bats are found roosting in caves, mines, tree hollows, and occasionally abandoned buildings.

Diet: Vampire bats feed on blood. These bats need about 2 tablespoons (29.6 milliliters) of blood each day; this is about 60 percent of the bat's body weight. Bats need to feed nightly.

Behavior and reproduction: Vampire bats are social animals; they roost in colonies that can range from twenty to 100 individuals. Much larger colonies of thousands have also been found.

Vampire bats approach their intended food source stealthily. They can walk, run, and hop along the ground, using their strong hind limbs and thumbs. At night, when vampire bats emerge to hunt for food, their victims are often sleeping. The bat will land beside the sleeping animal and then climb up until it finds a feeding spot. With its sharp front incisor teeth, the bat pierces the animal's skin and laps up blood from the wound. Vampire bats have chemicals in their saliva that stops blood from clotting. The bite rarely wakes a sleeping victim.

These bats occasionally will share the blood with other bats from its colony. After one female grooms another, the female being groomed may regurgitate (re-GER-jih-tate; throw up) part of her blood meal for the grooming female. It is also common to see females regurgitate food for their offspring.

Vampire bats mate year round. Females typically give birth to one offspring in April to May, or October to November. The offspring remain with their mothers for several months after they are weaned. They often share blood from the same wounds with their mothers.

Vampire bats and people: The fact that these bats feed on blood, combined with mythological stories about vampires, has caused many people to fear all bats. While the fears are largely myths, vampire bats can transmit rabies to humans and animals. These bats have caused tens of millions of dollars of damage to livestock farmers by transmitting rabies. They are considered pests in many livestock areas where they live. Also, researchers are investigating the anti-clotting properties of these bats' saliva to help with people who have strokes, in which a blood clot in the bloodstream cuts off blood supply to a part of the brain.

Conservation status: In areas with lots of livestock, vampire bats flourish. These are not considered threatened animals. ∎

Pallas's long-tongued bat (*Glossophaga soricina*)

PALLAS'S LONG-TONGUED BAT
Glossophaga soricina

Physical characteristics: Pallas's long-tongued bat is named for its most distinctive feature: its long tongue. It is a relatively small bat, with a head and body length combined of 1.8 to 2.3 inches (4.5 to 5.9 centimeters). Its visible tail is short, only about a quarter of an inch (0.6 centimeters). Fur color is dark brown to reddish brown, and the underside is paler. These bats have a long, narrow snout, small eyes, and short, rounded ears.

Geographic range: Pallas's long-tongued bats are found in northern Mexico, Paraguay, northern Argentina, Trinidad, Grenada, and Jamaica.

Pallas's long-tongued bats are important to their ecosystems because they disperse seeds and pollinate flowers, such as this banana flower. (© Merlin D. Tuttle/Bat Conservation International/Photo Researchers, Inc. Reproduced by permission.)

Habitat: These bats live in lowland habitats. They are more commonly found in dry forests than in wet forests. Bats roost in a variety of sites, including caves, hollows in trees, mines, and abandoned houses.

Diet: Pallas's long-tongued bats feed on nectar, pollen, and insects. When those foods are scarce, they will eat fruit as well.

Behavior and reproduction: Pallas's long-tongued bats often share their roosting sites with other species. They are social animals, forming colonies of several hundred individuals to a few thousand. Smaller colonies have also been found. The bats use their long, narrow tongues to lap nectar from plants. Individuals forage for food independently.

Females give birth to a single offspring twice each year. Females form maternity colonies. The seasons of birth vary depending upon where the bats live. In Costa Rica, births occur in December to February, then in April to June.

Pallas's long-tongued bat and people: Pallas's long-tongued bats are important to the ecosystem because of their role in dispersing seeds as well as pollinating night-blooming cacti (KACK-tie or KACK-tee; plural of cactus) and many other species of plants.

Conservation status: These bats are not threatened. ■

White bat (*Ectophylla alba*)

WHITE BAT
Ectophylla alba

Physical characteristics: These bats are relatively small, with a combined head and body length of 1.6 to 1.9 inches (4 to 4.7 centimeters). They are named for the color of their fur. The hair over their entire body is white to a light gray tinge. A ring of dark gray hair surrounds the eyes. Ears and noseleaf are yellow.

Geographic range: White bats are found from eastern Honduras to western Panama.

Habitat: White bats live in moist or wet tropical forests. They roost in makeshift tents about 6.5 feet (2 meters) above the ground.

Diet: White bats eat figs and other fruits.

White bats roost in a "tent" they made from a heliconia leaf in the rainforest of Costa Rica. (© Michael & Patricia Fogden/Corbis. Reproduced by permission.)

Behavior and reproduction: White bats modify leaves of plants in the relatively low-growing plants of forests to make roosts. These bats chew the large leaves, nipping the center so that the two sides of the leaf fold downward to form a "tent," under which the bats gather. The bats have been found roosting singly and in groups of two, four, and six.

White bat females apparently bear only a single young. In Costa Rica, females give birth in April. The males were observed sharing a tent with females until the young were born.

White bats and people: There is no known connection between white bats and people.

Conservation status: The IUCN Red List categorizes the white bat as Near Threatened, or close to becoming threatened. ∎

FOR MORE INFORMATION

Books:

Fenton, M. Brock. *Bats.* New York: Checkmark Press, 2001.

Fenton, M. Brock. *The Bat: Wings in the Night Sky.* Buffalo, NY: Firefly Books, 1998.

Raabe, Emily. *Vampire Bats.* New York: Powerkids Press, 2003.

Ruff, Sue, and Don E. Wilson. *Bats.* New York: Benchmark Books, 2001.

Schober, Wilfried, and Eckard Grimmberger. *The Bats of Europe and North America.* Neptune City, NJ: T.F.H. Publications, Inc., 1997.

Periodicals:

Clayton, Julie. "Wanted: Bloodsuckers; After Millions of Years of Bloody Enmity, Humans are Turning to Leeches, Ticks and Vampire Bats for Help. Julie Clayton Meets Our New Medical Allies." *New Scientist* (July 13, 2001): 42.

"Discovering Bats Beyond the Belfry." *Business Times* (November 9, 2001).

Seppa, N. "Compound in Bat Saliva May Aid Stroke Patients." *Science News* (January 18, 2003): 37.

"Stroke Patients get Vampire's Kiss." *Current Science* (April 11, 2003): 13.

"Vampire Bats Don't Learn From Bad Lunch." *Science News* (March 15, 2003): 173.

Web sites:

"The Secret Life of Bats." Fathom. http://www.fathom.com/course/21701775/session5.html (accessed on June 21, 2004).

Tomlinson, Denise. "Natural History of the Vampire Bat." The Organization for Bat Conservation at Cranbrook Institute of Science. http://www.batconservation.org/content/meetourbats/vampire.htm (accessed on June 21, 2004).

"Phyllostomidae." Animal Diversity Web. http://animaldiversity.ummz.umich.edu/site/accounts/information/Phyllostomidae.html (accessed on June 21, 2004).

"Vampire Bats." NationalGeographic.com. http://www.nationalgeographic.com/kids/creature_feature/0110/vampirebats.html (accessed on June 21, 2004).

phylum

class

subclass

order

monotypic order

suborder

▲ **family**

PHYSICAL CHARACTERISTICS

Moustached bats are named for their moustache-like distinctive feature. Above their upper lip, they have tufts of stiff hair. Their lips are large, with flaps and folds of skin on the bottom. When their mouth is open it appears to form a funnel. There are three common names for species in this family: moustached bats, ghost-faced bats, and naked-backed bats.

These bats are relatively small to medium size. The size of these bats' forearms range in length from approximately 1.4 inches (3.6 centimeters) to 2.6 inches (6.6 centimeters).

Moustached bats have a small bump on their nose and their eyes are relatively small. All bats in this family have a tail. Ears vary in size and shape but always have a tragus (TRAY-gus), meaning a flap of skin at the bottom of the external ear. In some species, the wings connect to the body at a point high along the middle of the back, making the surface of the back appear naked. These bats are commonly referred to as naked-backed bats. Ghost-faced bats can be easily identified by the folds of skin that reach from ear to ear, across the chin.

The fur of moustached bats can be gray, bright orange, brown, or reddish brown. Within species, individuals can vary widely in color. The fur color of some species in this family may change in different seasons. Fur in this family is short, fine, and thick.

GEOGRAPHIC RANGE

Moustached bats are found from the southern United States, including Arizona and southern Texas, through to Mexico,

Central America, and South America to Brazil, and much of the West Indies.

HABITAT

These bats generally live in tropical (hot and humid) habitats below 10,000 feet (3,000 meters). They live in the rainforest, forest, and in open areas. They generally roost in caves, mines, tunnels, and the hollows of trees. Some of these bats have been found in houses.

DIET

Moustached bats feed on a wide range of insects, including flies, beetles, moths, and mosquitoes.

BEHAVIOR AND REPRODUCTION

Moustached bats generally roost together in large colonies. Observations of the Parnell's moustached bats have found approximately 5,000 individuals roosting together.

NEW FAMILY: NEW NAME

Mormoopidae have a complex history of how they became their own family. These bats were first described in the early 1800s. For most of the twentieth century, this group was usually considered a subfamily of the Phyllostomidae, and given the name Chilonycterinae. (Some authorities continue to classify the mormoopids as only a subfamily of Phyllostomidae.) Mormoopidae became accepted as a distinct family and in 1972 was given its own name and family.

Moustached bats, like all bats, are nocturnal, meaning they are active at night. At night they emerge to forage for food by using echolocation, the detection of an object by listening to reflected sounds that are called out. They catch their prey (animals hunted for food) while flying. In forested habitats, these bats often search for prey, animals they hunt for food, along trails and roads and fly low, within 3.3 feet (1 meter) of the ground. The wings of these bats are associated with the ability to maneuver, fly rapidly, and remain in the air for long periods of time.

At the beginning of the rainy season, females give birth to a single young each year. Gestation (pregnancy) lasts approximately sixty days.

MOUSTACHED BATS AND PEOPLE

These bats can eat large numbers of nocturnal insects, including many that are harmful to crops and ones that are considered pests, such as mosquitoes. Humans are causing the loss of population among some species of these bats by destroying their habitat.

CONSERVATION STATUS

The IUCN lists two species as Near Threatened, meaning they are not currently threatened, but could become so. MacLeay's moustached bat is listed as Vulnerable, meaning it faces a high risk of extinction.

Parnell's moustached bat *(Pteronotus parnellii)*

PARNELL'S MOUSTACHED BAT
Pteronotus parnellii

SPECIES ACCOUNT

Physical characteristics: Like other bats in this family, Parnell's moustached bat has distinctive stiff hairs around its mouth. The fur color is medium to dark brown. These bats are relatively small with forearms ranging from 2.2 to 2.5 inches (5.5 to 6.3 centimeters). They have wingspan of about 13.4 to 13.8 inches (34 to 35 centimeters).

Geographic range: These bats are found throughout the Greater Antilles, Central America, southern Mexico, northern South America

Parnell's moustached bats roost in mines and caves, generally in large chambers and passageways far from the cave entrance. (Illustration by Barbara Duperron. Reproduced by permission.)

east of the Andes, northern Colombia, Venezuela, Brazil, Peru, and the Guianas.

Habitat: Parnell's moustached bats roost in mines and caves, generally in large chambers and passageways far from the cave entrance. These bats live in habitats ranging from arid to humid, tropical forests.

Diet: Parnell's moustached bats eat insects, primarily beetles and moths.

Behavior and reproduction: Parnell's moustached bats are extremely active. They are most active in the early evening. Observations of these bats in Mexico saw them emerging from their roost shortly after sunset. Some of the bats returned within one and a half hours, but most appeared to remain away from the roost for five to seven hours. The total number of bats in the cavern system was estimated at 400,000 to 800,000 individuals. It was estimated that these bats consumed between 4,190 and 8,380 pounds (1,900 to 3,805 kilograms) of insects each night.

These bats have a body temperature that varies with the environment, called heterothermic (het-ur-oh-THER-mic). When they are feeding, their body temperature remains high. When at rest, their body temperature and heart rate lower, thus conserving energy. When their heart rate slows down to conserve energy, the bats are going into torpor. Protected in their roost, Parnell's moustached bats can go into torpor from several hours to several months. If they go into a long-term torpor during the winter months it is considered hibernation.

These bats catch their prey while flying and can detect insects through dense vegetation. They are the only species of New World (North America, Central America, and South America) bat to have developed specialized echolocation calls. Structures within the ears of these bats work with the nerve cells to allow the bat to hear narrow and specific frequencies. This distinctive call enables the bat to sense the speed things move at, and thus relate its hearing to moving objects.

The only time males and females roost together during the year is when they are mating. Females have one offspring a year after a gestation period of approximately fifty days. Babies have no fur. Most of these bats usually give birth at the start of the rainy season, even though some may mate several months earlier.

Parnell's moustached bats and people: The relatively large bats of this species consume large numbers of insects, many of which are considered pests to humans, such as mosquitoes. One bat is capable of consuming over 1,000 insects per night. Occasional reports have connected these bats with rabies, a viral disease that affects the nervous system and can be deadly. Rabies is usually transmitted by the bite of an infected animal.

Conservation status: The IUCN does not list these bats as threatened. ■

FOR MORE INFORMATION

Books:

Fenton, M. Brock. *Bats.* New York: Checkmark Press, 2001.

Fenton, M. Brock. *The Bat: Wings in the Night Sky.* Buffalo, NY: Firefly Books, 1998.

Ruff, Sue, and Don E. Wilson. *Bats.* New York: Benchmark Books, 2001.

Schober, Wilfried, and Eckard Grimmberger. *The Bats of Europe and North America.* Neptune City, NJ: T.F.H. Publications, Inc., 1997.

Periodicals:

Schnitzler, Hans-Ulrich, and Elisabeth K. V. Kalko. "Echolocation by Insect-Eating Bats." *Bioscience* (July, 2001): 557.

DeBaca, Robert S., and Clyde Jones. "The Ghost-faced Bat, *Mormoops megalophylla,* (Chiroptera: Mormoopidae) from the Davis Mountains, Texas." *The Texas Journal of Science* (February, 2002): 89.

Web sites:

Bat Conservation International, Inc. Discover the Secret World of Bats. http://www.batcon.org (accessed on July 5, 2004).

Weinstein, Bret, and Phil Myers. "Family Mormoopidae (Ghost-faced Bats, Moustached Bats, and Naked-backed Bats)." Animal Diversity Web. http://animaldiversity.ummz.umich.edu/site/accounts/information/ Mormoopidae.html (accessed on July 5, 2004).

Class: Mammalia

Order: Chiroptera

Family: Noctilionidae

Number of species: 2 species

family

CHAPTER

PHYSICAL CHARACTERISTICS

Bulldog bats' lips are similar in appearance to a bulldog's. The lips are thick and the upper one hangs over the bottom lip, forming pouches. Their upper lip is split in the middle. The nose, which sticks out slightly over the lip, is long and thick. The ears are pointed and relatively large. Both species have long legs, and large feet with well-developed claws. The bats have long, narrow wings. They also have a visible tail. Bulldog bats have a strong odor, often described as fishy.

Bulldog bats are relatively large bats, having a combined head and body length that ranges from approximately 2.2 to 5.2 inches (5.7 to 13.2 centimeters). Males are larger than females.

Bulldog bat fur is typically short and slightly curly. Fur colors range from bright orange to orange-brown and gray-brown. There can be a pale stripe running down their backs. The undersides of these bats are lighter in color. At one point researchers thought that male bulldog bats were different in color than females. Males were said to be bright yellow, brown, and orange, and females a brown or gray color. Research has shown that fur color may vary among the species as a whole, and is not necessarily distinct between the sexes.

GEOGRAPHIC RANGE

Bulldog bats are found in Mexico, Central America, and South America as far south as Argentina. The greater bulldog bat also lives on islands in the West Indies.

HABITAT

Bulldog bats are found living near water and in other moist habitats. Greater bulldog bats generally roost, settle or rest, in dark caves, often located on the seashore, and the hollows of trees. Lesser bulldog bats roost in hollow trees, and in buildings.

DIET

Both species of bulldog bats eat insects, but greater bulldog bats feed primarily on fish, along with frogs and crustaceans, fresh-water and saltwater animals with no back-bone, such as shrimp. The greater bulldog bat is one of only a handful of bats known to eat fish. Lesser bulldog bats feed primarily on insects.

BEHAVIOR AND REPRODUCTION

Like all bats, bulldog bats rest during the day. While bulldog bats may sometimes leave their roost in the late afternoon, they are most likely to begin foraging for food at dusk, sunset. Both species catch their prey, animals hunted for food, using echolocation (eck-oh-loh-KAY-shun), the technique of detecting objects from calling out sounds and listening to the echo reflected from the object. These bats use echolocation to detect prey in flight, on the surface of the water, or directly below the water's surface.

After bulldog bats catch their prey they either eat the insect in flight or tuck away the partially-chewed food in their cheeks. These bats have pouches in their cheeks that can stretch to hold extra food. By storing the food, bulldog bats do not have to return to their roost after each catch. Mother and father bulldog bats can store food in their cheeks to bring to their young.

Bulldog bats are found living in colonies or groups of about thirty individuals up to several hundred. One kind of colony has young male bats. Another type of colony is made up of males, females, and their young. When they begin foraging for food, groups of up to fifteen leave their colony at the same time.

Female bulldog bats generally give birth to one offspring once a year. In general, bulldog bats mate in November and

FLYING WITH BIRDS

Look closely at a group of pelicans during the day and you might spot a few greater bulldog bats, or fisherman bats, in their midst. While these bats generally feed at dusk and during the night, observers have also seen them in the late afternoon flying alongside pelicans over water. Pelicans are large aquatic birds that eat fish. The bats probably catch small fish disturbed by the pelicans.

December, and then give birth in April through June. Births have also been recorded in the fall. The newborns can fly and become independent after one month. Both the male and female look after the baby, an unusual behavior for bats.

BULLDOG BATS AND PEOPLE

Bulldog bats eat insects that many people may consider pests. Water pollutants and habitat destruction are likely to harm the population of bulldog bats.

CONSERVATION STATUS

Bulldog bat species are not listed as threatened.

Greater bulldog bat (*Noctilio leporinus*)

GREATER BULLDOG BAT
Noctilio leporinus

Physical characteristics: The greater bulldog bat, also called the fishing bat, is a relatively large bat. These bats have a wingspan of almost three feet (1 meter), and a combined head and body length ranging from 4.6 to 5 inches (11.9 to 12.7 centimeters) Males are larger than females. Their feet and claws are much larger than the lesser bulldog bats, and their claws are very sharp. The fur is short and repels water.

Geographic range: Greater bulldog bats are found in parts of Central and South America, and throughout many islands on the Caribbean.

Habitat: Greater bulldog bats live in lowland and moist habitats that are near a water source, including the seashore, lakes, river basins, and ponds.

Diet: Greater bulldog bats eat primarily fish. They also eat crab and insects, including winged ants, crickets, and scarab beetles.

Behavior and reproduction: Greater bulldog bats typically roost in caves near a water source and in tree hollows. They roost in colonies of up to several hundred individuals bats. Each colony may have a distinctive odor. They emerge at dusk to forage for food in groups of five to fifteen.

Greater bulldog bats use echolocation to detect the ripples along the water's surface, which indicates a fish swimming. Groups of these bats zigzag low over the water and send out chirpy echolocation calls. The bats can track fish movement by predicting their speed and direction. Then they drag their sharp claws through the ripples and snatch the fish with their large, sharp claws. Once out of the water, the fish is carried to a perch, where the bat eats it. Greater bulldog bats may also capture insects and crustaceans on the surface of the water. Prey is either eaten in flight, stored in its cheeks, or carried to a roost to be eaten.

These bats have powerful wings. If they drop into the water while they are foraging they can use their wings like paddles. Once they have gained enough speed in the water the bat lifts itself up into flight.

Female greater bulldog bats generally have a single offspring each year. The breeding season may vary regionally. In the Northern Hemisphere, mating typically begin in November and the young are born in May and June.

Greater bulldog bats and people: The health of a population of greater bulldog bats may act as an indication of water pollution.

Conservation status: Greater bulldog bats are not listed as threatened. ∎

FOR MORE INFORMATION

Books:

Fenton, M. Brock. *Bats.* New York: Checkmark Press, 2001.

Fenton, M. Brock. *The Bat: Wings in the Night Sky.* Buffalo, NY: Firefly Books, 1998.

Nowak, Ronald M. "Bulldog Bats, or Fisherman Bats." *Walker's Mammals of the World 5.1 Online.* Baltimore: Johns Hopkins University Press, 1997. http://www.press.jhu.edu/books/walkers_mammals_of_the_world/chiroptera/chiroptera.noctilionidae.noctilio.html (accessed on June 22, 2004).

Raabe, Emily. *Bulldog Bats.* New York: Powerkids Press, 2003.

Richardson, Phil. *Bats.* London: Whittet Books, 1985.

Ruff, Sue, and Don E. Wilson. *Bats.* New York: Benchmark Books, 2001.

Schober, Wilfried, and Eckard Grimmberger. *The Bats of Europe and North America.* Neptune City, NJ: T.F.H. Publications, Inc., 1997.

Periodicals:

Pennisi, Elizabeth. "Gone Batty: Illuminating the Murky World of Tropical Bats." *Science News* (April 30, 1994): 284.

Schnitzler, Hans-Ulrich, and Elisabeth K. V. Kalko. "Echolocation by Insect-Eating Bats." *BioScience* (July 2001): 557.

Web sites:

Myers, P. "Noctilionidae." Animal Diversity Web. http://animaldiversity.ummz.umich.edu/site/accounts/information/Noctilionidae.html (accessed on June 22, 2004).

Pederson, Scott. "Bulldog or Fisherman Bat: *Noctilio leporinus.*" Bathead. http://biomicro.sdstate.edu/pederses/guidenlep.html (accessed on June 22, 2004).

Simmons, Nancy. "*Noctilio albiventris minor,* Lesser Bulldog Bat." DigiMorph. http://digimorph.org/specimens/Noctilio_albiventris/whole (accessed on June 22, 2004).

Class: Mammalia

Order: Chiroptera

Family: Mystacinidae

Number of species: 2 species

family

CHAPTER

PHYSICAL CHARACTERISTICS

New Zealand short-tailed bats are small to medium-sized bats. Their head and body length ranges from 2.3 to 3.5 inches (5.8 to 8.9 centimeters). They can weigh from 0.4 to 1.2 ounces (11 to 35 grams). As their name suggests, these bats have a short tail. The nose or snout of New Zealand short-tailed bats is relatively long and it sticks out over the lips.

These bats have unique wing membranes, the thin pieces of skin that form their wings. The parts of the wing membranes that run along the body are thick and leathery. When not flying, these bats can fold their wings beneath this thick membrane part.

Fur color on these bats is typically brown-gray or brown-black, with the tips of the hairs being white to grayish. This gives the bat a frosted look. The fur is velvety, short, and thick. New Zealand short-tail bats have relatively large ears. These bats have thick bodies with short, strong legs. The claws on their feet are pointy and sharp. The thumbs have a large claw with a talon, a sharp hooked claw, at the end and each of the toe claws also has a talon.

GEOGRAPHIC RANGE

New Zealand short-tailed bats are found on New Zealand and some of its offshore islands. New Zealand is made up of two large and many smaller islands in the southwest Pacific Ocean, east of Australia.

phylum

class

subclass

order

monotypic order

suborder

▲ **family**

HABITAT

New Zealand short-tailed bats are found in moist forests, where they roost, settle or rest. These bats also forage, search, for food along low-growing shrubbery and the coastline. The greater short-tailed bat was once found on two islands but it was last sighted in 1967 and is considered extinct.

DIET

New Zealand short-tailed bats eat a broad range of foods. They are omnivores, meaning they eat both plants and animals, which is unusual in bats. Their diet includes flying and resting arthropods, animals without a backbone with jointed legs and segmented bodies, fruit, nectar, and pollen. The bat has a relationship with a rare and parasitic plant, called woodrose, or pua reinga. The flower produces nectar on the forest floor. As the bats move around eating the nectar they pollinate the plants. New Zealand short-tailed bats are the woodrose's only pollinator. Researchers have also observed New Zealand short-tailed bats sometimes feeding on birds and carrion, animals that have already been killed.

BEHAVIOR AND REPRODUCTION

New Zealand short-tailed bats are active on the ground more than any other species of bat. Like all other bats, they are nocturnal, meaning they are active at night. Several hours after dusk, they begin foraging for food by running along the ground, up trees, and along tree branches.

These bats typically roost in the hollow trees of forests. They have also been found roosting in caves, houses, and in burrows, holes that they dig in the ground. Observations have shown that these bats roost in large groups of 100 to 500 individuals during the day. They also may roost in far smaller groups, and sometimes singly. When the weather becomes cooler, the bats go into a state of inactivity called torpor, but they will come out of their roosts on warmer winter nights to forage, or search, for food.

To find food, New Zealand short-tailed bats use echolocation (eck-oh-loh-KAY-shun), a technique in which the bats detect objects by sending out high-pitched calls and then listening to the reflected sound. They also find prey, animals hunted for food, by listening for movements and using their sense of smell. They commonly hunt prey on the forest floor, often forming burrows or holes under leaf litter in the ground to forage for food. When they tuck their wings away, these bats use the front arms like front legs, which helps them move along the ground.

Female New Zealand short-tailed bats give birth to one offspring once a year. The timing of mating and births appears to vary according to their location. Limited observations of the greater New Zealand short-tailed bat suggest that a single young may be born from spring to autumn.

NEW ZEALAND SHORT-TAILED BATS AND PEOPLE

People have caused a population decline in the New Zealand short-tailed bats, primarily through introducing predators, animals that hunt the bats for food, and destroying the bats' natural habitat. In stories the Maori (MAH-oo-ree), the original settlers of New Zealand, associate bats with a mythical, night-flying bird that foreshadows death or disaster.

RAT TROUBLE

Before humans arrived on New Zealand there were no predators of bats and they were free to roam on the ground. When the Maori, the first settlers of New Zealand, arrived they brought Polynesian rats with them. Polynesian rats were predators of New Zealand bats and they quickly spread. By the early 1800s, when European settlers arrived in New Zealand, the greater short-tailed bat had been devastated. It was extinct over 98 percent of its habitat and only survived on two small rat-free islands. The lesser short-tailed bat was not affected as badly.

The lesser short-tailed bats play an important role in the continued life of plants in New Zealand. As they feed on nectar and other plant material, they move from plant to plant and spread pollen, the fine grains that contain the male reproductive cells of seed plants. They are the only pollinators of the woodrose, an endangered and unique flower. These bats also are predators on insects that people may consider pests.

CONSERVATION STATUS

The World Conservation Union (IUCN) lists the lesser New Zealand short-tailed bat as Vulnerable, facing a high risk of extinction, and greater New Zealand short-tailed bat as Extinct, no longer existing. The lesser New Zealand short-tailed bat is known to be present on several islands. Populations have declined to about ten populations that may contain only a few thousand individuals.

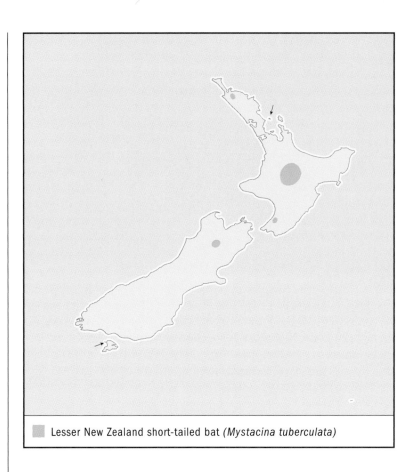

Lesser New Zealand short-tailed bat (*Mystacina tuberculata*)

LESSER NEW ZEALAND SHORT-TAILED BAT
Mystacina tuberculata

Physical characteristics: Lesser New Zealand short-tailed bats are a relatively small species of bat. The length of their body and head together ranges from 2.3 to 2.6 inches (5.8 to 6.6 centimeters). The wingspan of these bats is 11 to 11.4 inches (28 to 29 centimeters). There are three subspecies of the lesser New Zealand short-tailed bat, and all vary in size. The bats that live in the south are larger than those that live in the north.

Also called a northern short-tailed bat and the New Zealand long-eared bat, these bats have fur that is short, thick, and velvet-like. Their fur is typically brown-gray or dark brown in color. The hairs have white on the tips, which gives these bats a frosted appearance. These

bats have large, simple ears. The thumbs and each of the toe claws have a talon at the end.

The lesser New Zealand short-tailed bat is the only pollinator of the woodrose, an endangered and unique flower in New Zealand. (Illustration by Barbara Duperron. Reproduced by permission.)

Geographic range: Lesser New Zealand short-tailed bats live on New Zealand and some of its offshore islands. Fossil evidence suggests that these bats once lived on all the islands of New Zealand. In recent years, populations of these bats decreased to only an estimated ten locations on several islands.

Habitat: Lesser New Zealand short-tailed bats are found primarily in the moist, native forests of New Zealand. They often roost in the hollows of trees but have also been found roosting in houses, caves, and burrows. They have been observed foraging for food and flying along coastlines and in grassy areas with low shrubbery.

Diet: Lesser New Zealand short-tailed bats have a wide range of food options. They eat both flying and non-flying arthropods, nectar, pollen, fruit, and other plant materials. Observations have also spotted these bats eating both young and adult birds, along with the meat of animals that are already dead.

Behavior and reproduction: Unlike most bats, the lesser New Zealand short-tailed bat spends much of its time scurrying about on the ground, up trees, and along branches. Their ability to fold their wings up prevents them from injury as they move about. When they fold up their wings the bats can walk on their hind legs and use their front arms. These bats still fly but it is not known how much they use flight.

These bats roost in large groups of 100 to 150 individuals or more, and also to roost in small groups. They emerge several hours after dark to search for food. These bats chew out cavities, holes, and tunnels to use as roosts.

Researchers are still working to understand these bats' mating and reproduction. The bats have a breeding season in which males and females separate. At dark, males travel to the hollows in trees where they call out a high-pitched call or song. Females visit and mate with the males each evening, before they begin foraging for food. Females give birth to one offspring each year. In the northern populations the young are born in the summer, January and December; in the southern populations they are born later, April to May. Newborn bats are furless and born with their eyes open. They are able to fly in four to six weeks, and reach adult size at eight to twelve weeks.

Lesser New Zealand short-tailed bats and people: Because Lesser New Zealand short-tailed bats eat pollen, nectar, and other plant materials, they play a significant role in the continued survival of many plant species. People have had a significant impact in the decline of the population by introducing bat predators, such as Polynesian rats. The introduction of other species has also indirectly harmed the bat population. The Australian brush-tailed possum was introduced to start a fur industry, and one method of killing the possum is with cyanide poison that often contains added fruit smells to lure the animal. Since the lesser short-tailed bat spends a great deal of time on the forest floor, this poison can attract the bats. It is unknown how many bats have been killed by this method. People have also caused the decline of these bats by clearing the forests where these bats live.

Conservation status: Lesser New Zealand short-tailed bats are protected by law and listed by the Department of Conservation of New Zealand as a species of highest conservation priority. The New Zealand Red Data Books lists this species as Vulnerable to Endangered, facing a very high risk of extinction in the wild in the near future. The IUCN lists the lesser short-tailed bat as Vulnerable. ■

FOR MORE INFORMATION

Books:

Fenton, M. Brock. *Bats.* New York: Checkmark Press, 2001.

Fenton, M. Brock. *The Bat: Wings in the Night Sky.* Buffalo, NY: Firefly Books, 1998.

Nowak, Ronald M. "New Zealand Short-tailed bats." *Walker's Mammals of the World 5.1 Online.* Baltimore: Johns Hopkins University Press, 1997. http://www.press.jhu.edu/books/walkers_mammals_of_the_world/chiroptera/chiroptera.mystacinidae.mystacina.html (accessed on July 5, 2004).

Richardson, Phil. *Bats.* London: Whittet Books, 1985.

Ruff, Sue, and Don E. Wilson. *Bats.* New York: Benchmark Books, 2001.

Schober, Wilfried, and Eckard Grimmberger. *The Bats of Europe and North America.* Neptune City, NJ: T.F.H. Publications, Inc., 1997.

Periodicals:

Flannery, Tim. "A Lost Menagerie." *Natural History* (November 2001): 66.

"Hunt for the Short Tailed Bat." *Wairarapa Times* (February 26, 2000).

Jones, G., P. I. Webb, J. A. Sedgeley, and C. F. O'Donnell. "Mysterious *Mystacina:* How the New Zealand Short-Tailed Bat (*Mystacina tuberculata*) Locates Insect Prey." *Journal of Experimental Biology* (December 2003): 4209–4216.

Web sites:

Daniel, Mike. "New Zealand's Unique Burrowing Bats Are Endangered." Bat Conservation International, Inc. http://www.batcon.org/batsmag/v2n3-1.html (accessed on July 5, 2004).

"New Zealand Short-tailed bats." BBC Science and Nature. http://www.bbc.co.uk/nature/wildfacts/factfiles/668.shtml (accessed on July 5, 2004).

Weinstein, B., and P. Myers. "Family Mystacinidae (New Zealand Short-tailed Bats)." Animal Diversity Web. http://animaldiversity.ummz.umich.edu/site/accounts/information/Mystacinidae.html (accessed on July 5, 2004).

family

CHAPTER

PHYSICAL CHARACTERISTICS

Funnel-eared bats get their name from the shape of their ears, which are large and formed like a funnel. They are small and slim with relatively long legs that can be longer than the head and body combined. Combined the head and body is approximately 2 inches (5 centimeters) long. Their wings are long and slender with a slender tail that is completely enclosed in a tail membrane. They also have small eyes.

Adult males have a large structure typically in the center of the forehead called the natalid (NAT-ah-lid) organ. The function of this is uncertain.

The fur of these bats is soft and long with color ranging from gray, yellowish, reddish, to deep chestnut. One species, the Mexican funnel-eared bat, has two color phases, or types: one in which fur is light, tan to pinkish light brown, and the other in which fur is darker, a yellowish or reddish brown. The belly is paler in both phases.

GEOGRAPHIC RANGE

The five species of funnel-eared bats are found in several areas. One species is found in northern Mexico, eastern Brazil, and specific Caribbean islands. Another species occurs in northern South America and nearby islands. The other three species are found on islands in the Caribbean.

HABITAT

These bats live in lowland forests that are dry and deciduous, forests where the trees lose their leaves at the end of the growing season. In general, they are found below 984 feet (300 meters). In Venezuela, these bats were found in habitats from sea level to about 8,200 feet (2,500 meters). Typically, these bats roost, rest or settle, in the darkest areas of caves and mine tunnels. They also have been found roosting in tree hollows.

DIET

These bats feed on small insects.

BEHAVIOR AND REPRODUCTION

Funnel-eared bats form colonies, groups, of up to 300 individuals. Some observations have also found fewer than a dozen individuals. These bats often roost with other families of bats. Northern populations may travel to warmer areas in the winter. Some species of bats have been observed hanging singly, alone.

Since they are nocturnal, active at night, funnel-eared bats leave their roost about half an hour after sunset to forage, search, for food. They use echolocation (eck-oh-loh-KAY-shun) to locate their prey, animals hunted for food. Echolocation is the detection of objects by emitting, sending out, sounds and listening to the returning sounds that bounce off objects. These bats flutter their wings rapidly while flying, like a moth, and can maneuver (mah-NOO-ver) easily. This allows them to enter and exit dense plant growth.

Females bear a single offspring late in the dry season, when they establish separate maternity colonies. Little is known about the mating behavior of these bats, but findings show that males mate with more than one female during the season.

FUNNEL-EARED BATS AND PEOPLE

Bacteria that cause fevers in humans have been isolated in one species of funnel-eared bat, the Trinidadian funnel-eared bat. Many bats, such as this one, have bacteria or other organisms associated with their droppings, waste, that can lead to diseases in people.

CONSERVATION STATUS

The World Conservation Union (IUCN) lists Gervais's funnel-eared bat as Near Threatened (not currently threatened, but could become so in the future), and the Bahaman funnel-eared bat as Vulnerable, facing a high risk of extinction in the wild.

WHAT A BABYFACE

The genus (JEE-nus) name *Natalus* comes from the Latin word *natus* meaning to be born. (*Natus* is also the root word for nature.) These bats were given this name because they are small and look like newborns even as adults.

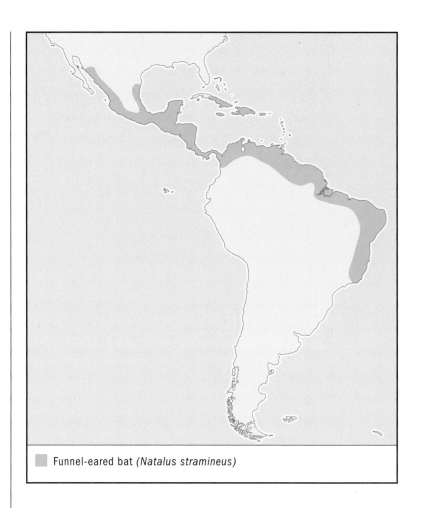

Funnel-eared bat *(Natalus stramineus)*

FUNNEL-EARED BAT
Natalus stramineus

Physical characteristics: Funnel-eared bats, also called Mexican funnel-eared bats, have the funnel-shaped ears that are characteristic of the family. They have long, slender hind legs. They have black, stiff hairs above the upper lip, appearing like a moustache, and white hairs below the lower lip. The natalid organ is shaped like a bell and covers the muzzle, the snout.

Fur color occurs in both a light and a dark phase. The light phase is generally a light to medium tan and the dark phase is a reddish brown. The belly is paler in both phases, and of a similar color.

Geographic range: Funnel-eared bats are found in northern Mexico to eastern Brazil, Cuba, Jamaica, Lesser Antilles, and Tres Marias islands off western Mexico.

Habitat: Funnel-eared bats generally live in deciduous forests. They may also live in moister forest areas.

Diet: Funnel-eared bats feed on insects.

Behavior and reproduction: These bats were found roosting in large colonies with thousands of individuals in Venezuela. At high altitudes, some colonies may go into torpor, a dormant state, during the cooler months.

In general, bats of this species roost in the darkest areas of caves and mines. Females form maternity roosts during the breeding season. Gestation, pregnancy, lasts approximately ten months. Offspring are born weighing more than 50 percent of the mother's weight.

Funnel-eared bats roost in the darkest areas of caves and mines. (© Merlin D. Tuttle, Bat Conservation International. Reproduced by permission.)

Funnel-eared bats and people: There is no known special significance between funnel-eared bats and people.

Conservation status: Funnel-eared bats are not considered threatened by the IUCN. ∎

FOR MORE INFORMATION

Books:

Fenton, M. Brock. *Bats.* New York: Checkmark Press, 2001.

Fenton, M. Brock. *The Bat: Wings in the Night Sky.* Buffalo, NY: Firefly Books, 1998.

Nowak, Ronald M. "Funnel-eared Bats." *Walker's Mammals of the World 5.1 Online.* Baltimore: Johns Hopkins University Press, 1997. http://www.press.jhu.edu/books/walkers_mammals_of_the_world/chiroptera/chiroptera.natalidae.natalus.html (accessed on July 5, 2004).

Richardson, Phil. *Bats.* London: Whittet Books, 1985.

Ruff, Sue, and Don E. Wilson. *Bats.* New York: Benchmark Books, 2001.

Schober, Wilfried, and Eckard Grimmberger. *The Bats of Europe and North America.* Neptune City, NJ: T.F.H. Publications, Inc., 1997.

Web sites:

"Discover the Secret World of Bats." Bat Conservation International, Inc. http://www.batcon.org (accessed on July 5, 2004).

Simmons, Nancy. "*Natalus stramineus,* Mexican Funnel-eared Bat." Digi-Morph. http://www.digimorph.org/specimens/Natalus_stramineus/head/ (accessed on July 5, 2004).

Weinstein, B. and P. Myers. "Family Natalidae: Funnel eared bats." Animal Diversity Web. http://animaldiversity.ummz.umich.edu/site/accounts/information/Natalidae.html (accessed on July 5, 2004).

CHAPTER

PHYSICAL CHARACTERISTICS

Smoky bats are also commonly called thumbless bats. While they do have a thumb, it is small, enclosed in the edge of the wing, and can appear invisible. Other bats, on the other hand, use their thumbs to grip surfaces while crawling, and to hang right side up while giving birth. Smoky bats are among the smallest of bats, having a head and body length combined of 1.4 to 2.6 inches (3.5 to 5.8 centimeters). Their forearms are about 1.2 to 1.6 inches (3 to 4 centimeters) long. Females are slightly larger than males.

These bats appear delicate, with broad wings that are relatively long. The snout is pig-like in appearance, being short and turned up at the tip. Set close together, the nostrils are oval or triangular. Ears resemble funnel-eared bats. They are separate, large, and funnel-shaped, reaching almost to the jaw line. These bats have tiny eyes that are hidden by fur and their large ears. They also have long legs and short feet, with claws on the end of their feet. The tail is relatively long, but it does not reach past the edge of the tail membrane (layer of thin skin).

The fur is generally coarse. The smoky bat has triangular, wart-like fleshy projections around its mouth and lips.

GEOGRAPHIC RANGE

The two species of the family are found in different areas. The thumbless bat is found west of the Andes, from central coastal Ecuador south to northern Chile. The smoky bat is found in Costa Rica, lowland Brazil, Peru and Trinidad.

BAT RELATIVES

There are no known fossils in this family. In general, bats do not fossilize well because of their small, delicate skeletons. Scientists consider the smoky bats to be most closely related to Central and South American disk-winged bats and funnel-eared bats.

HABITAT

Furipterids (members of the family Furipteridae) live in diverse habitats. The thumbless bat has been found living in lowland rainforests to the arid (extremely dry) deserts of South America to cultivated land. The smoky bat appears to have a narrower range of habitats, found primarily in lowland, moist forests. Many of these bats live in isolated populations. They are found primarily in caves, tree hollows, and human-made structures.

DIET

Bats in this family feed on insects, primarily moths and butterflies.

BEHAVIOR AND REPRODUCTION

Little is known about the species of bats in this family. Because they are small, agile flyers in isolated populations, smoky bats are difficult to catch and study. It is known that these bats roost in colonies (groups) between 100 and 300 individuals.

Like all bats, the smoky bats become active at night (nocturnal). The long and broad shape of their wings allows them to fly slowly and with great agility to forage, search, for moths and butterflies. This also gives them the ability to forage for prey (animals eaten for food) in dense forest undergrowth.

SMOKY BATS AND PEOPLE

People have caused the decline of the species in this family due to harming their natural habitats.

CONSERVATION STATUS

The World Conservation Union (IUCN) Red List categorizes the thumbless bat species as Vulnerable, meaning it is facing a high risk of extinction in the wild. The smoky bat is not considered threatened.

Smoky bat *(Furipterus horrens)*

SMOKY BAT
Furipterus horrens

Physical characteristics: The smoky bat is the smaller of the two species in this family. Head and body length is approximately 1.3 to 1.6 inches (3.3 to 4 centimeters), and their forearms can range from 1.2 to 1.6 inches (3 to 4 centimeters). These bats weigh about 0.1 ounces (3 grams)—only slightly more than the weight of a penny. Females are larger than males by about 10 to 15 percent.

These bats have dense fur. Fur on the head is long and thick. Fur color ranges from brownish gray, dark gray, to a slate blue. Color on the belly is paler. The fur on these bats' head is long and thick. It covers the head and reaches to the snout, almost concealing the

mouth. Ears are dark and stiff, and the snout is black.

Geographic range: These bats are found from Costa Rica to southern Brazil, including Venezuela and Colombia. They are also found on Trinidad but they have not been found on any other Caribbean island.

Habitat: These bats live primarily in humid rainforests of Costa Rica south to Brazil. They often live near streams. They have also been found in evergreen forests and clear areas. They have been found in caves, hollows in trees, and beneath rotting logs.

Diet: Smoky bats eat small moths.

Behavior and reproduction: These bats fly slowly and flutter similar to the way moths fly. These bats wait for complete darkness before they leave their roost to begin foraging. They search for prey beneath the forest canopy, at heights ranging from 3.2 to 16.4 feet (1 to 5 meters).

Colony size varies but it appears these bats do group together in relatively large numbers. One colony observed contained fifty-nine individuals. Another found colony contained approximately 250 individuals divided into groups of four to thirty roosting in holes in the walls. In another cave there were 150 bats roosting separately from one other.

Discovered colonies primarily include males, females, and young. Observations have also found there are all-male colonies, suggesting that females may have separate sites to raise their young.

Smoky bats and people: There is no known connection between smoky bats and people.

Conservation status: These bats are not considered threatened. ■

FOR MORE INFORMATION

Books:

Fenton, M. Brock. *Bats.* New York: Checkmark Press, 2001.

Fenton, M. Brock. *The Bat: Wings in the Night Sky.* Buffalo, NY: Firefly Books, 1998.

The smoky bat has a reduced thumb that is enclosed in the wing membrane. (Photograph by Maarten Vonhof. Reproduced by permission.)

Nowak, Ronald M. "Smoky Bats, or Thumbless Bats." *Walker's Mammals of the World 5.1 Online.* Baltimore: Johns Hopkins University Press, 1997. http://www.press.jhu.edu/books/walkers_mammals_of_the_world/chiroptera/chiroptera.furipteridae.html (accessed on July 5, 2004).

Richardson, Phil. *Bats.* London: Whittet Books, 1985.

Ruff, Sue, and Don E. Wilson. *Bats.* New York: Benchmark Books, 2001.

Web sites:

"Discover the Secret World of Bats." Bat Conservation International, Inc. http://www.batcon.org (accessed on July 5, 2004).

Simmons, Nancy. "*Furipterus horrens* Thumbless Bat." DigiMorph. http://www.digimorph.org/specimens/Furipterus_horrens/whole (accessed on July 5, 2004).

Weinstein, B., and P. Myers. "Family Furipteridae (Smoky Bats and Thumbless Bats." Animal Diversity Web. http://animaldiversity.ummz.umich.edu/site/accounts/information/Furipteridae.html (accessed on July 5, 2004).

DISK-WINGED BATS

Thyropteridae

Class: Mammalia

Order: Chiroptera

Family: Thyropteridae

Number of species: 2 species

family

C H A P T E R

phylum

class

subclass

order

monotypic order

suborder

▲ family

PHYSICAL CHARACTERISTICS

These bats are about the size of a person's thumb, having a head and body length that ranges from 1.2 to 2.3 inches (3 to 5.7 centimeters). They weigh from 0.10 to 0.17 ounces (3 to 5 grams), about the same weight as one to two pennies.

These bats are also called New World sucker-footed bats, named after the suction cup-like feature found on their feet. These bats have circular suction cup disks with short stalks on the soles of the feet and the bottom of their thumbs. The disks on the thumb are larger than those on the feet. They also have a well-developed claw on their thumb.

Bats in this family have small eyes. There is a small wart-like projection above the nostrils, and there is no noseleaf (leaf-shaped fleshy protrusion). The tail juts out freely past the membrane (thin layer of skin), so it is visible. The ears are large and shaped like a funnel. The muzzle is long and slender. Nostrils are circular and set relatively far apart.

Species in this family have long, fluffy hair. Fur color ranges from a medium reddish brown to slightly darker. The undersides of these bats are white or brown. The ears can be either black or yellow.

GEOGRAPHIC RANGE

These bats are found in Central and South America, east of the Andes, including southern Nicaragua to the Guianas and Peru, and southern Mexico to Bolivia and southern Brazil, and Trinidad.

HABITAT

Disk-winged bats live in the moist parts of forests. They are common in many areas, and in Costa Rica there are up to four colonies (groups) for every 2.5 acres (1 hectare). They generally roost (rest or settle) in a curled leaf of some plant, such as the heliconia plant or the banana tree, before the leaf opens.

DIET

Disk-winged bats eat insects.

BEHAVIOR AND REPRODUCTION

Disk-winged bats use only their suction-like disks to grip and stick to the smooth surfaces of the curled-up leaves in which they roost. They do not use their feet or claws to touch the surface of the leaves.

These bats can support their entire weight with the suction of a single disk. Sweat glands keep the disks' undersurfaces moist, which helps provide the vacuum seal for sticking to the surface. Beneath each disk is a muscle that controls the vacuum. This muscle can create the seal and, when the bat wants to come unstuck, the muscle also undoes the seal. These bats will also lick their disks to help with the suction. Studies have found that these bats have lost the ability to roost on rough surfaces, such as trees and rocks.

SUCKER COUSINS?

One of the puzzling features of the disk-winged bats is their relationship to the Old World sucker-footed bat. Both families of bats feature suction-like disks that allow them to grip onto vertical, smooth surfaces. Yet the Old World sucker-footed bat is found primarily in the rainforests of Madagascar, far away from where New World disk-winged bats are found. The Old World bat also has suction cups on its thumbs and roosts in young, rolled leaves, but their suction cups are thought to be the result of an evolutionary convergence with the suction cups of the New World bats. This means that both groups of bats evolved the suction cups separately, not as a result of their relationship to one another. Unfortunately, there is no fossil record for the New World disk-winged bats.

Generally only one or two disk-winged bats roost in the same leaf, yet observers have found as many as eight individuals in one leaf. Roosting inside curled leaves protects them from the weather and predators. Leaves open within days, and groups must change roosts often.

Like all bats, these bats are nocturnal, meaning that they are active at night. When more than one bat roosts in a leaf, these bats spread out evenly, one above the other. In Costa Rica, a study reported that group sizes ranged from one to nine, and averaged six bats. Generally, the same group moves together from one old leaf to a new roosting site. Bats in this family have been found roosting with bats in another family, the proboscis bat.

Unlike most other bats, individuals in this family typically hang with their head upward. Disk-winged bats use echolocation (eck-oh-loh-KAY-shun) to find prey (animals hunted for food) and detect objects. Echolocation is a process for locating objects by emitting, sending out, sounds, which are reflected back to the bat by objects in the sound's path.

Females roost together in hollow logs to give birth. Males in this family are thought to be polygynous (puh-LIJ-uh-nus), meaning they mate with more than one female during the mating season.

DISK-WINGED BATS AND PEOPLE

People have caused the decline in this family's population due to disturbing and destroying their natural habitat. Because they feed on insects, these bats eat many insects that people may consider pests.

CONSERVATION STATUS

Although these bats are common in some areas, the IUCN lists *Thyroptera lavali* as Vulnerable. In 1999, findings observed that *Thyroptera lavali* was restricted to a small area in extreme northeastern Peru.

Spix's disk-winged bat *(Thyroptera tricolor)*

SPIX'S DISK-WINGED BAT
Thyroptera tricolor

Physical characteristics: Fur color of Spix's disk-winged bats ranges from dark brown to reddish brown. Their undersides are a cream or yellow, and their ears are blackish. The sides of their bodies are an intermediate color, which is why they were given the name tricolor, which means to have three colors. These bats weight about 0.14 ounces (4 grams). They have a head and body length combined of 1 to 1.5 inches (2.7 to 3.8 centimeters). Females are slightly larger than males.

Geographic range: Spix's disk-winged bats are found in tropical forests from Veracruz, Mexico to southeast Brazil.

Spix's disk-winged bat roosts with its head upright. Most other bats, besides disk-winged bats, hang upside down. (Brock Fenton. Reproduced by permission.)

Habitat: Spix's disk-winged bats have been found in rainforests, swamps, and clearings. They have generally been found living below 2,625 feet (800 meters) and have not been recorded living above 4,265 feet (1,300 meters).

Diet: Spix's disk-winged bats feed on insects, such as small beetles and flies. Spix's bats eat about 20 percent of its weight each night.

Behavior and reproduction: This species roosts in young, partly uncurled leaves. They are found roosting in leaves of heliconia plants, recognizable by their large leaves. Roosts contain about six individual bats, composed of one or more adult males, several females and several juveniles of both sexes. Female Spix's bats have been observed taking their offspring for the evening flight in search of food.

These bats are polygynous, meaning that the bats mate with more than one female at a time. These bats breed twice annually. Gestation (pregnancy) lasts about two months. For the first month of life offspring either remain in the roosts or cling to their mothers when they go out to feed, even though young can weigh up to 46 percent of the mother's weight. Offspring can generally fly after one month.

Spix's disk-winged bats and people: Aside from eating insects some people consider pests, these bats have no known significant relationship with people.

Conservation status: These bats are not considered threatened. ■

FOR MORE INFORMATION

Books:

Fenton, M. Brock. *Bats.* New York: Checkmark Press, 2001.

Fenton, M. Brock. *The Bat: Wings in the Night Sky.* Buffalo, NY: Firefly Books, 1998.

Nowak, Ronald M. "Disk-winged Bats, or New World Sucker-footed Bats." *Walker's Mammals of the World 5.1 Online.* Baltimore: Johns Hopkins University Press, 1997. http://www.press.jhu.edu/books/walkers_mammals_of_the_world/chiroptera/chiroptera.thyropteridae.thyroptera.html (accessed on July 5, 2004).

Richardson, Phil. *Bats.* London: Whittet Books, 1985.

Ruff, Sue and Don E. Wilson. *Bats.* New York: Benchmark Books, 2001.

Schober, Wilfried and Eckard Grimmberger. *The Bats of Europe and North America.* Neptune City, NJ: T.F.H. Publications, Inc., 1997.

Periodicals:

Reebs, Stephen. "Sticky Situation." *Natural History* (June 2002): 16.

Milius, Susan. "Save Our Sounds: In Some Libraries, Noise is Good." *Science News* (September 14, 2002): 16.

Web sites:

Clarke, Diana. "Nomads of the New World Tropics." The Sun and Your Skin. http://yourskinandsun.com/article1091.html (accessed on July 5, 2004).

"Discover the Secret World of Bats." Bat Conservation International, Inc. http://www.batcon.org (accessed on July 5, 2004).

Weinstein, B., and P. Myers. "Family Thyropteridae (Disc-Winged Bats)." *Animal Diversity Web.* http://animaldiversity.ummz.umich.edu/site/accounts/information/Thyropteridae.html (accessed on July 5, 2004).

**OLD WORLD
SUCKER-FOOTED BAT**

Myzopodidae

Class: Mammalia

Order: Chiroptera

Family: Myzopodidae

One species: Old World
sucker-footed bat
(*Myzopoda aurita*)

PHYSICAL CHARACTERISTICS

Also known as the Madagascar sucker-footed bat, the sucker-footed bat family has only one known species. Bats in this family are small to medium in size, having a head and body length combined of 2.3 inches (5.7 centimeters), and a tail length of approximately 1.9 inches (4.8 centimeters). The tail extends beyond the tail membrane (layer of thin skin). The bat weighs about 0.3 ounces (8 grams).

Old World sucker-footed bat is named after the suction-like pads or disks on their wrists and ankles. These pads are horseshoe shaped. They are attached directly to the feet and ankles, without a stalk as in the disk-winged bats.

Old World sucker-footed bats have large ears, which are about 1.2 to 1.4 inches (3 to 3.5 centimeters) long. The ears do not have a tragus (TRAY-gus), which is a small flap of flesh in front of the opening of the ear. The upper lip extends beyond the lower lip. Their thumbs are small and have a vestigial (ves-TIJ-ee-al; not fully developed) claw.

These bats are occasionally called golden bats because of their fur color. Their moderately thick fur is brown to golden brown in color with some reddish shades.

GEOGRAPHIC RANGE

This species has been found only in Madagascar. It has been observed primarily from areas that stretch the full length of the east coast, and one area on the west coast. There are fewer than twenty localities where this bat has been recorded.

phylum

class

subclass

order

monotypic order

suborder

▲ **family**

HABITAT

Old World sucker-footed bats are found primarily in the rainforests along eastern Madagascar.

DIET

An examination of one bat's droppings found that moths were its main food source. It is not known what other prey (animals eaten for food) or other foods the bats may eat.

BEHAVIOR AND REPRODUCTION

Little is known about the behavior and mating habits of these bats. Their suction disks allow them to cling onto smooth surfaces, yet they do not appear to hold the bat's body as tightly to a vertical surface as those of the disk-winged bats. The bats probably use the pads to hold on to the smooth, hard stems and leaves of palms and other smooth surfaces.

They have been found roosting (resting or settling) in the unrolled leaf of a traveler's palm. One bat was discovered over a small stream, another in a vanilla plantation, and one in a sparsely forested area over a path close to a stream. These bats have also been recorded flying over urban areas. They probably roost in a variety of palm species and other similar types of plants.

Like all bats, Old World sucker-footed bats are nocturnal, meaning that they are active at night. One bat was caught in a net about one hour after sunset.

Old World sucker-footed bats can maneuver (mah-NOO-ver) well in flight. They have been observed spending long periods of time hovering over freshly dug and planted paddy fields, as well as within forest clearings. It is assumed they were feeding in these areas.

These bats use echolocation (eck-oh-loh-KAY-shun) to capture their prey. Echolocation is the process for locating objects by emitting, or sending out, sounds, which are reflected back to the bat by objects in the sound's path. Old World sucker-footed bats emit relatively long echolocation calls with complex frequency modulated (FM) calls.

No information is available about this species' mating and breeding habits.

OLD WORLD SUCKER-FOOTED BATS AND PEOPLE

These bats are considered extremely rare and the IUCN defines the loss of forest due to human interference as the most likely threat to this species.

CONSERVATION STATUS

Old-World sucker footed bats are considered one of the world's rarest species. The IUCN Red List categorizes these bats

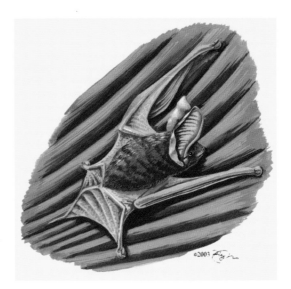

Old World sucker-footed bat (Myzopoda aurita). (Illustration by Jonathan Higgins. Reproduced by permission.)

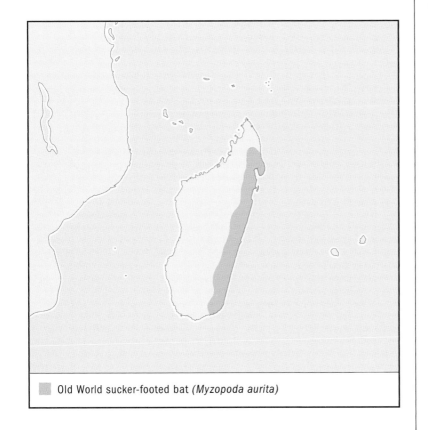

Old World sucker-footed bat (*Myzopoda aurita*)

as Vulnerable, meaning they are facing a high risk of extinction in the wild.

FOR MORE INFORMATION

Books:

Fenton, M. Brock. *Bats.* New York: Checkmark Press, 2001.

Fenton, M. Brock. *The Bat: Wings in the Night Sky.* Buffalo, NY: Firefly Books, 1998.

Nowak, Ronald M. "Old World Sucker-footed Bat." *Walker's Mammals of the World 5.1 Online.* Baltimore: Johns Hopkins University Press, 1997. http://www.press.jhu.edu/books/walkers_mammals_of_the_world/ chiroptera/chiroptera.myzopodidae.myzopoda.html (accessed on July 5, 2004).

Richardson, Phil. *Bats.* London: Whittet Books, 1985.

Ruff, Sue, and Don E. Wilson. *Bats.* New York: Benchmark Books, 2001.

Russ, Jon, and Daniel Bennett, eds. *The Bats of Madagascar: A Field Guide with Descriptions of Echolocation Calls.* Glossop, U.K.: Viper Press, 2001. http://mampam.50megs.com/bats/madagascar/2000/ mad2000. pdf (accessed on July 5, 2004).

Schober, Wilfried, and Eckard Grimmberger. *The Bats of Europe and North America.* Neptune City, NJ: T.F.H. Publications, Inc., 1997.

Web sites:

Myers, P. "Family Myzopodidae (Old World Sucker-Footed Bat)." Animal Diversity Web. http://animaldiversity.ummz.umich.edu/site/accounts/ information/Myzopodidae.html (accessed on July 5, 2004).

Simmons, Nancy. "*Myzopoda aurita,* Old World Sucker-Footed Bat." DigiMorph. http://www.digimorph.org/specimens/Myzopoda_aurita/head/ (accessed on July 5, 2004).

**FREE-TAILED BATS AND
MASTIFF BATS**

Molossidae

Class: Mammalia

Order: Chiroptera

Family: Molossidae

Number of species: 90 species

PHYSICAL CHARACTERISTICS

Molossids (mol-LOSS-ids; members of the family Molossidae) range widely in size from small to moderately large bats. They have a forearm length of approximately 1.1 to 3.4 inches (2.7 to 8.5 centimeters), and weigh from 0.2 to 3.8 ounces (5 to 167 grams). Free-tailed bats are named for their thick tail that extends far beyond the tail membrane (thin layer of skin). The mastiff bats are named after their facial resemblance to the mastiff dog.

Some species of molossids have a distinctive wrinkled upper lip, while others have a smooth upper lip. Muzzles of all these bats are generally short and wide and often have wide, fleshy lips that may have folds or creases. Many have a distinctive pad over their noses. The upper surface of this pad often has small horn-like projections. Ears of free-tailed bats are relatively short and thick, often joined across the forehead and point directly forward. The eyes of these bats are relatively small, while the lips are large. All species have long and narrow wings that are thick and, along with the tail, are covered in a leathery membrane. Molossids also have short, strong legs and broad feet. On the outer toes of each foot are curved bristles that the bat uses for grooming its fur.

Molossids generally have short, velvety fur. One group of bats in this family is called the hairless bats because their hair is so short that the animal appears to be naked. Some species have a crest of hairs on the top of the head that stands upright. Fur color may be gray, tan, black, or brown. Many species have

phylum

class

subclass

order

monotypic order

suborder

▲ **family**

two color phases, or types, a reddish one and brownish or black-ish color phase.

GEOGRAPHIC RANGE

Molossids are found throughout the world's warmer areas. They are primarily found in South America and Africa, as well as from southern Europe and southern Asia through Malaysia, and east to the Fiji Islands. They are also found in the central and southern part of the United States, south through the West Indies, Mexico, and Central America to the southern half of South America. Except for one other family of bats, the Vespertilionidae, molossids are found in the widest geographic area.

HABITAT

With molossids spread out all over the world, they are found living in a wide range of habitats. They are commonly found in both natural and urban areas. These bats are most plentiful in arid (extremely dry) and semi-arid conditions. They prefer to live in temperatures that are at least 110°F (43°C). These bats roost (rest or settle) in sites such as caves, tunnels, build-ings, hollow trees, foliage, decayed logs, and holes in the ground. They also shelter under bark, rocks, and iron rooftops.

DIET

Molissids eat a variety of insects, such as moths and ones with hard shells, such as beetles and stinkbugs.

BEHAVIOR AND REPRODUCTION

Molossids are generally strong flyers that can fly quickly for long periods of time. Like all bats, these bats are nocturnal, meaning they are active at night. These bats fly all night, whereas other bats typically fly a short time during the night. They can fly six or seven hours without stopping.

Molossids catch their prey using echolocation (eck-oh-loh-KAY-shun), a technique where the bat detects objects by re-ceiving the reflection of sounds it produces. They fly with their mouths open and send out echolocation calls. They forage, search for food, in groups and head towards large swarms of insects. They also look for food around streetlights, which at-tract insects, such as moths. They generally catch their prey while they are flying.

THAT'S A LOT OF GUANO

A colony with thousands or millions of bats will produce a lot of guano, and people have been putting these droppings to use for a long time. Before people began to sell guano as fertilizer, the Confederate Army was using guano during the Civil War (1861–1865), as a source of gunpowder. It is thought that this guano was collected from the Brazilian free-tailed bat. In the late 1800s came the discovery of the millions of bats in Carlsbad Caverns, New Mexico, and their associated guano, which was valuable. In the early 1900s mining operations started in the caves, using mining cars to transport guano to the cave entrance. Most of the guano was shipped to southern California to help the developing citrus industry. In about twenty years of operation, over 100,000 tons of guano was taken from Carlsbad Cavern. Six companies attempted to make a profit in this venture, but all failed due largely to high transportation costs. Bat droppings in Carlsbad Caverns over the past 17,000 years have formed guano deposits covering several thousand square feet to a depth of almost 50 feet (15 meters)!

Because they live in warm areas, molossids do not need to hibernate (become inactive in the cooler months to conserve energy). Some of these bats travel to even warmer areas in the winter.

Molossids have a range of roosting habits, from solitary to social, living in large colonies (groups) of millions of individuals. Between those two extremes, sizes of colonies range from hundreds to thousands of individuals. Most of these bats do form colonies in the size of a few tens to several hundred individuals. Molossids generally return to their roosting sites every year. Their colonies generally give off a strong, musky odor.

Little is known about the mating habits of most molossids. Most species are considered polygynous (puh-LIJ-uh-nus), meaning the male mates with more than one female during the mating season. Females of most species appear to produce one offspring per year. Two young are born on rare occasions, and the black mastiff bat in Trinidad possibly has two litters per year. During pregnancy, females generally form maternity colonies that are separate from the males. In these colonies, females relocate and nurse their young independently.

MOLOSSIDS AND PEOPLE

Like many insect-eating bats, molossids eat many insects that humans consider to be pests. The one hundred million Mexican free-tailed bats that live in Texas in the summer eat an estimated 1,000 tons (907 metric tons) of insects each night, many of which destroy crops. In California and other areas, farmers build bats houses to attract these bats so they will eat the pests. People also collect the bat droppings (guano; GWAH-no) of molossid bats that live in large colonies, using the guano as a fertilizer as it is rich in nitrogen. Some species of these bats have also been associated with spreading disease, such as rabies. Rabies is a viral infection that attacks the nervous system and can be deadly.

People have caused the decrease in population of molossids by destroying and disturbing their natural habitat. These bats have also been harmed through eating insects that have come into contact with pesticides, chemicals designed to control pests.

CONSERVATION STATUS

The survival of many of these species is under threat. The IUCN lists Gallagher's free-tailed bat, Niangara free-tailed bat, and Wroughton free-tailed bat, as Critically Endangered, meaning they face an extremely high risk of extinction in the wild. The Incan little mastiff bat is listed as Endangered, meaning it faces a very high risk of extinction in the wild. Fifteen other species are listed as Vulnerable, meaning they face a high risk of extinction in the wild.

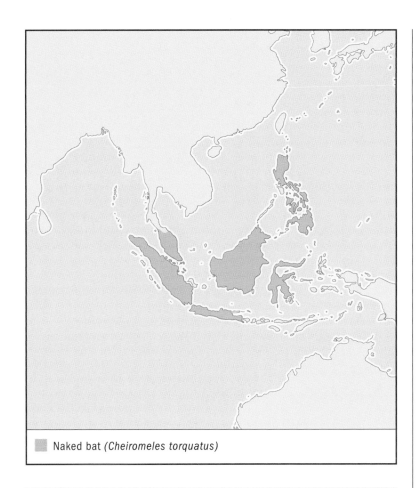

Naked bat (*Cheiromeles torquatus*)

NAKED BAT
Cheiromeles torquatus

Physical characteristics: Naked bats are the largest molossids, with a head and body length ranging from 4.5 to 5.8 inches (11.5 to 14.5 centimeters). They weigh from 3.2 to 5.7 ounces (96 to 170 grams). Also called naked bulldog bats, these bats are almost completely hairless. They have scattered short hairs and bits of longer hair around a scent gland on their neck. This haired gland produces a strong, foul odor.

These bats have loose, dark gray, brown, or black skin. A naked bat has bristles on its toes, which it uses for cleaning and grooming. Another distinguishing characteristic of the bat is the pocket of skin along its sides. These flaps of skin form a wing pouch that the bat

folds its wings into when it rests. Ears are separate and their lips are smooth. Big toes have a flat nail instead of the typical claw.

Geographic range: Naked bats are found in Southeast Asia, including Malaysia, Borneo, Java, Sumatra, the Philippines, and surrounding islands.

Habitat: These bats live in tropical forests and several live on islands. They roost in caves, rock crevices, tree hollows, and holes in the ground.

Diet: Naked bats feed on insects, primarily termites and winged ants.

Behavior and reproduction: Naked bats are strong, fast fliers. They fly high above the forest canopy (the tops of trees) or above clearings to forage, or search, for food. When they fold their wings into their pouch, these bats can move about relatively easily on all four limbs.

This species of bat roosts in large colonies. Nearly a thousand individuals were observed in a hollow tree, and a colony of about 20,000 was observed in a cave in Borneo.

There are usually two offspring. The young are most likely left in the roost when the parents leave to forage for food in the evening.

Naked bats and people: In certain areas, most of the forest habitat of the naked bat has been destroyed by development, logging, and cultivation. People have hunted these bats for food and killed them because they mistakenly believed these bats were harming their crops.

Conservation status: The IUCN Red List categorizes these bats as Near Threatened, not currently threatened, but could become so. In specific areas, this species has significantly declined, and is protected by law. ■

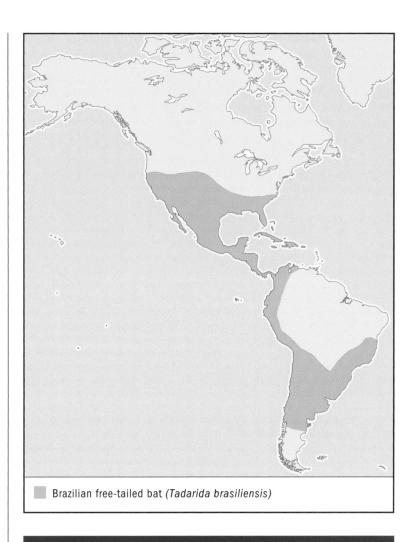

Brazilian free-tailed bat *(Tadarida brasiliensis)*

BRAZILIAN FREE-TAILED BAT
Tadarida brasiliensis

Physical characteristics: Also called the Mexican free-tailed bat, Brazilian free-tailed bats are small to medium in size, with a total head and body length of approximately 3.8 inches (9.5 centimeters).

Geographic range: Brazilian free-tailed bats are found in the southern half of the United States, as well as Mexico, Central America, South America to southern Chile and Argentina, and much of the Lesser and Greater Antilles.

Habitat: Brazilian free-tailed bats are primarily found in arid and semi-arid habitats. They are also found in urban areas, moist forests, and grassland areas. These bats roost in caves, mine tunnels, tree hollows, and under bridges. They also are frequently found in and around buildings.

Diet: These bats feed on a range of insects, including moths, beetles, weevils, mosquitoes, flying ants, and leafhoppers.

Behavior and reproduction: Brazilian free-tailed bats are best known for their immense roosting colonies. While roosts of several dozen have been found, these bats also roost in colonies that reach the millions. A colony that lives in Bracken Cave, Texas, makes up the largest colony of mammals in the world, with an estimated twenty million individuals in this summertime maternity colony. They fly high above the ground when foraging for prey, except when sweeping over a body of water to drink.

Brazilian free-tailed bats may roost in colonies of millions of bats. These are some of the largest colonies of mammals in the world. (John Hoffman/Bruce Coleman Inc. Reproduced by permission.)

Mating among these bats is considered promiscuous (prah-MISS-kyoo-us), meaning males and females mate with more than one other bat. Females bear a single offspring once a year in May to July. In maternity roosts where millions of bats are packed tightly together, mothers are able to identify and nurse their own young.

Brazilian free-tailed bats and people: Many of the insects these bats eat are considered pests by humans. These bats are also known carriers of rabies.

Conservation status: Many of the large colonies have declined dramatically in numbers. The IUCN lists Brazilian free-tailed bats as Near Threatened. ■

FOR MORE INFORMATION

Books:

Fenton, M. Brock. *Bats.* New York: Checkmark Press, 2001.

Fenton, M. Brock. *The Bat: Wings in the Night Sky.* Buffalo, NY: Firefly Books, 1998.

Nowak, Ronald M. "Free-tailed Bats and Mastiff Bats." *Walker's Mammals of the World 5.1 Online.* Baltimore: Johns Hopkins University Press,

1997. http://www.press.jhu.edu/books/walkers_mammals_of_the_world/chiroptera/chiroptera.molossidae.html (accessed on July 5, 2004).

Raabe, Emily. *Free-Tailed Bats.* New York: Powerkids Press, 2003.

Richardson, Phil. *Bats.* London: Whittet Books, 1985.

Ruff, Sue, and Don E. Wilson. *Bats.* New York: Benchmark Books, 2001.

Schober, Wilfried, and Eckard Grimmberger. *The Bats of Europe and North America.* Neptune City, NJ: T.F.H. Publications, Inc., 1997.

Periodicals:

Bowers, Barbara. "Going to Bat for the Bats." *Audubon* (December 2003): 86

Finnegan, Lora J. "Bats about Bats." *Sunset* (July 1993): 38

Kerner, Sarah. "In the Bat Cave: These Guys Got an Up-close Look at One of the World's Most Misunderstood Creatures. Lesson Learned: Bats get a Bad Rap!" *Boys' Life* (June 2003): 18

McCracken, Gary F., and John K. Westbrook. "Bat Patrol: Scientists Discover That High-flying Mammals are Bad News for Bugs." *National Geographic* (April 2002): 114

Vine, Katy. "Pow (Going Batty)!" *Texas Monthly* (January 2004)

"Wings in the Dark." *Weekly Reader* (October 31, 2003): 4

Web sites:

"Natural Resources: The Bat Colony." Carlsbad Caverns National Park: National Park Service. http://www.nps.gov/cave/bats.htm (accessed on July 5, 2004).

"Discover the Secret World of Bats." Bat Conservational International, Inc. http://www.batcon.org (accessed on July 5, 2004).

Kee, Lim Gaik. "Bats are Pollinators not Pests." Nature Watch. http://habitatnews.nus.edu.sg/pub/naturewatch/text/a062b.htm (accessed on July 5, 2004).

"Malaysian Bat Conservation." EarthWatch Institute. http://www.earthwatch.org/expeditions/kingston/meetthescientists.html (accessed on July 5, 2004).

"Naked Bat *(Cheiromeles torquatus).*" The Forest Department: Sarawak, Malaysia. http://www.forestry.sarawak.gov.my/forweb/wildlife/mgmt/tpa/nbat.htm (accessed on July 5, 2004).

Myers, P. "Family Molossidae (Free-tailed Bats)." Animal Diversity Web. http://animaldiversity.ummz.umich.edu/site/accounts/information/Molossidae.html (accessed on July 5, 2004).

Class: Mammalia

Order: Chiroptera

Family: Vespertilionidae

Number of species: About 267 species

family

C H A P T E R

PHYSICAL CHARACTERISTICS

Although this group of bats is large and contains many different-looking species, they do share several characteristics. Compared to many other bats that have what might be described as bizarre noses with flaps and other fleshy decorations, the vespertilionid (ves-per-TILL-ee-on-id) bats have plain faces. They are even known as the "plain-faced bats." Some species have noses shaped like tubes, however, with nostrils at the end of the tube.

The "webbed tail," known as a patagium (pah-TAY-jee-um), is actually a membrane or a thin bit of skin that stretches between the hind legs and aids the bat in flight. In these bats, the patagium is hairless. Their ears are noticeable and sometimes quite large, and they also have tails at the middle of the patagium that can be as long as the body. All have an obvious outgrowth, called a tragus (TRAY-gus), arising from the bottom of the ear. Most of them have small eyes. Overall body length ranges from about 1.4 to 5.5 inches (3.5 to 14 centimeters) and weight from 0.01 to 1.6 ounces (2.5 to 45 grams).

GEOGRAPHIC RANGE

Vespertilionid bats live in temperate to tropical climates worldwide. They are absent from far northern North American and Eurasia, as well as Antarctica.

HABITAT

The habitat varies in this large group of animals. Many of them spend the day resting in caves, or in tight little places, like cracks in a house or a barn, underneath bark or in the hollow of a tree. Some even rest during the day, a behavior called roosting, inside curled leaves or in other sheltered spots within vegetation. At night, when they become active, the bats are often seen flying above open spaces, or over or near wetlands, rivers and streams, and lakes and ponds. During winter months, the bats typically hibernate. In colder climates, the bats overwinter in caves or other places with relatively stable temperatures. In warmer climates, they may simply choose a spot beneath a loose piece of bark or in the hollow of a tree.

DIET

The diet for most of the vespertilionid bats consists of insects, and many species eat their body weight in insects each night. A few species eat other things, including spiders, scorpions, fish, and lizards.

BEHAVIOR AND REPRODUCTION

Like other bats, the vespertilionid bats use sound waves to find their way through their habitat and to find food. They make high-pitched sounds, ones that we cannot hear, and then listen as the waves bounce off of objects and return to them as echoes. Using this method of "seeing" with sound, they can fly quickly between tree limbs and around objects, while also finding and identifying prey insects. It is common for a vespertilionid bat to notice a moth or other flying insect while both the bat and insect are in flight, then swoop in and capture the insect in midair. Using echolocation (eck-oh-loh-KAY-shun), they can also spot insects on plants and pick them off of leaves. Echolocation is particularly useful in these animals that rest during the day and look for food in the dark of night. A few species become active around sunset, sometimes even a little earlier, but most wait until the skies darken before they leave their roost and begin looking for food. Because they are such excellent and swift fliers, the vespertilionid bats avoid most predators. Occasionally an owl is able to catch one at night, but their biggest threat of predation (hunting by animals that eat them for food) comes from larger land animals that stumble upon a roost while the bats are resting.

Bats have a fairly set schedule with certain activities occurring during specific seasons. Mating occurs in the fall in most species. Some bats don't engage in any courtship rituals, but for the most part, scientists know little about these behaviors in most bats. In the fall, bats that live in cooler climates begin to disappear, probably to start migrating to warmer climates for the winter. Cool- and warm-climate bats typically participate in hibernation, although some warm-weather bats remain active all year. Some vespertilionid bats hibernate alone, and others hibernate together in large groups, often numbering a hundred or more. If the temperature rises sufficiently in the winter, the bats may awaken and fly about in search of food. When spring arrives, males typically strike out on their own, but females usually form colonies in roosts, which may be in caves or other hideaways, and share the duties associated with raising young, which are born in late spring to early summer. (A few warm-weather species may be able to have young at other times of the year.) Most mothers have one or two young, called pups, a year. A few species may have up to four pups at a time. The pups begin flying in about a month and then start hunting for insects on their own. Some remain with the colony for their first year, but others leave earlier.

BIRDS AREN'T THE ONLY ANIMALS TO MIGRATE

When people hear about a fall migration, they usually think of birds that fly south for the winter. Other animals, including bats, migrate, too. Some bats may fly several hundred miles (kilometers) to escape the winter cold. The noctule, a medium-sized bat from Europe and Asia, makes migrations of 400 miles (670 kilometers) or more each year—quite a feat for an animal that is only about 3 inches (7.6 centimeters) long in body length and weighs about an ounce (28 grams).

Bat behavior is a field with many unanswered questions. Although scientists know a good deal about the behavior of a few species, they know little about most of the vespertilionid bats.

VESPERTILIONID BATS AND PEOPLE

Humans frequently don't recognize the benefits of bats. Vespertilionid bats eat many insects, including mosquitoes, crop-damaging beetles, and other pest species. Just five bats can eat 15,000 or more insects in a single night. Besides their benefit in keeping insect populations in check, bats have become a part of the folklore of many cultures. Much of the folklore, including that portrayed in horror books and movies, describes bats as evil creatures bent on sucking blood. Vespertilionid bats engage in no such activity, and rarely even fly close to a human.

CONSERVATION STATUS

The Red List of the World Conservation Union (IUCN) contains two Extinct, died out, species; seven Critically Endangered, facing an extremely high risk of extinction in the wild; twenty Endangered, facing a very high risk of extinction in the wild; fifty-two Vulnerable, facing a high risk of extinction; and seventy-three Near Threatened, not currently threatened, but could become so. Those categories total 154 bats, more than half of all vespertilionid species. The U.S. Fish and Wildlife Service lists thirteen vespertilionid bats as endangered. For many of the species, habitat destruction and pesticide use are major reasons for their declines. Both organized and grassroots efforts are now under way to protect many bat populations. These include the preservation of roosting and hibernation sites.

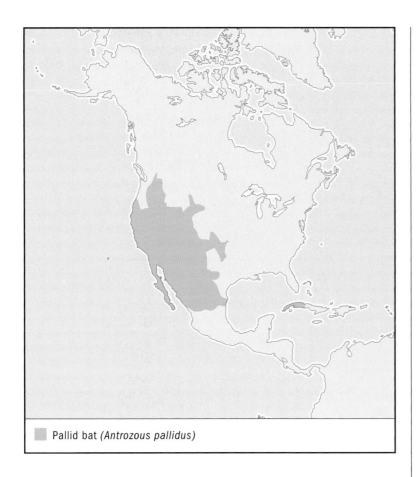

Pallid bat (*Antrozous pallidus*)

PALLID BAT
Antrozous pallidus

Physical characteristics: Unlike many of the dark-furred, small-eyed vespertilionid bats, the pallid bat is yellowish with larger eyes. It also has large ears. Adult size ranges from 3.6 to 5.5 inches (9.2 to 14 centimeters) in body length and 0.5 to 1 ounce (13 to 29 grams) in weight. Its tail is a little more than a third of its body length.

Geographic range: The pallid bat lives in western North America from southern Canada to northern Mexico, also western Cuba.

Habitat: Their daytime roosts are in cracks and crevices of rocky outcroppings and in caves, usually near a water source. At night, they

The pallid bat eats insects, scorpions, and other invertebrates, and possibly small lizards and mammals, such as mice. (© Merlin D. Tuttle/Bat Conservation International/Photo Researchers, Inc. Reproduced by permission.)

typically roost nearby in tree hollows, under bridges, or in some other hiding place.

Diet: These bats eat insects, scorpions, and other invertebrates (animals without backbones); possibly small lizards and mammals, such as mice.

Behavior and reproduction: They leave their daytime roosts after sunset, then begin looking for insects by flying between about 1 and 7 feet (30 centimeters to 2.1 meters) above the ground. They mate in fall to early winter, and females give birth to one or two pups in late spring to early summer. The young stay with their mothers in maternity roosts, and begin flying about a month and a half later.

Pallid bats and people: This species visits plants, probably in search of insects. In so doing, it picks up and delivers pollen, which helps fertilize plants.

Conservation status: The pallid bat is not threatened. ■

Western barbastelle (*Barbastella barbastellus*)

WESTERN BARBASTELLE
Barbastella barbastellus

Physical characteristics: This large-eared bat ranges from 1.8 to 2.4 inches (4.5 to 6.0 centimeters) in body length with a tail nearly as long, and 0.2 to 0.4 ounces (6 to 12 grams) in weight. Its back fur is black with white tips, and its belly fur is lighter.

Geographic range: The western barbastelle lives in central and northern Europe.

Habitat: These bats prefer upland forests, usually near water.

Diet: This species eats mainly flying insects, which they catch in midair. They will also swoop down to plants and pluck insects from their leaves.

Behavior and reproduction: This bat becomes active before sunset when it emerges from its daytime roosts in trees, caves, and other secluded spots. It is more solitary than many other vespertilionid bats,

with many individuals spending the summer alone. Females will sometimes form small maternity colonies. Hibernation begins in late fall. Many questions remain about this rather rare bat's behavior.

Western barbastelles and people: Like other insect-eating bats, the western barbastelle rids its habitat of many insects that humans might consider pests.

Conservation status: The IUCN Red List lists this bat as Vulnerable. ■

The western barbastelle lives in central and northern Europe, preferring upland forests, usually near water. (Illustration by Emily Damstra. Reproduced by permission.)

Little brown bat *(Myotis lucifugus)*

LITTLE BROWN BAT
Myotis lucifugus

Physical characteristics: Similar in appearance to the big brown bat, this species is a bit smaller. Its body length averages 3.1 to 3.7 inches (20 to 27 centimeters) with a tail a little less than half that size. It weighs 0.2 to 0.5 ounces (6 to 14 grams). The little brown bat is light to dark brown above with a lighter belly.

Geographic range: This bat lives in Canada, the United States, and Mexico.

Habitat: When they aren't flying in search of food, they do their summertime resting in tree hollows, underneath bark, or in barns, attics, and other such structures. During winter, they typically hibernate in caves.

Diet: Their diet consists mainly of flying insects.

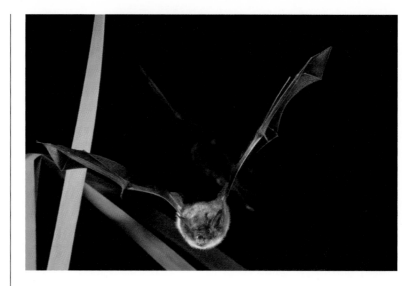

Behavior and reproduction: They mate in the late summer to early fall. The females typically have just one pup in late spring or during the first half of summer. The young grow quickly, but don't mate until at least the following year.

Little brown bats and people: Like many other insect-eating bats, the little brown bat helps to control pest insect populations.

Conservation status: This bat is not threatened.   ■

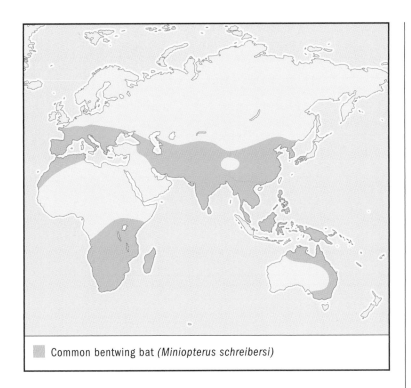

Common bentwing bat (*Miniopterus schreibersi*)

COMMON BENTWING BAT
Miniopterus schreibersi

Physical characteristics: Unlike other vespertilionid bats, bentwing bats have a long third finger that they can bend beneath their wing when they aren't flying. The common bentwing bat has a thick gray, yellow, or brown fur coat. It ranges from 2.0 to 3.1 inches (5.1 to 7.8 centimeters) in body length and weighs 0.3 to 0.6 ounces (8 to 16 grams). Its tail is about as long as its body.

Geographic range: This bat lives in Madagascar, southern and northwestern Africa, southern Europe, southern Asia, eastern and northern Australia, and New Guinea.

Habitat: They tend to prefer woodlands and fields that are near caves or other roosting sites.

Diet: Adult bats will eat up to a third of their body weight in flying insects every night.

Owls may sometimes catch common bentwing bats while they are flying for insects. (Brock Fenton. Reproduced by permission.)

Behavior and reproduction: They mate in the fall, and females typically give birth to one pup each summer. The females form large maternity roosts where they raise their young together. A roost can contain several thousand pups. The pups are old enough to mate and have their own families in about a year. Predators for common bentwing bats include owls that may occasionally catch the bats in the air, as well as snakes and cats that may find a roost.

Common bentwing bats and people: Like most other bats, the insect diet of this species helps to keep pests in check.

Conservation status: The IUCN Red List considers this species Near Threatened, likely due to predation and disturbance to maternal roosts. ■

FOR MORE INFORMATION

Books:

Altringham, J. *Bats: Biology and Behavior.* Oxford, U.K.: Oxford University Press, 1996.

Fenton, M. Brock. *Bats.* New York: Checkmark Books, 2001.

Kunz, T., and P. Racey eds. *Bat Biology and Conservation.* Washington, DC: Smithsonian Institution Press, 1998.

Kurta, A. *Mammals of the Great Lakes Region.* Ann Arbor: The University of Michigan Press, 1995.

Nowak, R. *Walker's Mammals of the World.* Baltimore: Johns Hopkins University Press, 1999.

Web sites:

IUCN 2003. 2003 IUCN Red List of Threatened Species. http://www.redlist.org (accessed July 5, 2004).

Endangered Species Program, U.S. Fish & Wildlife Service. http://endangered.fws.gov/ (accessed on July 5, 2004).

Species List by Biome

CONIFEROUS FOREST
American black bear
American pika
American water shrew
Asian elephant
Bobcat
Brown-throated three-toed
  sloth
Chimpanzee
Common bentwing bat
Coypu
Desert cottontail
Eastern mole
Edible dormouse
Ermine
Gambian rat
Geoffroy's spider monkey
Giant panda
Gray squirrel
Gray wolf
Greater sac-winged bat
Hairy-footed jerboa
Human
Indian crested porcupine
Kirk's dikdik
Lar gibbon
Little brown bat
Malayan moonrat
Mandrill
Moose

Mountain beaver
Mountain hare
Nine-banded armadillo
North American beaver
North American porcupine
Northern pika
Pacarana
Pallas's long-tongued bat
Pallid bat
Pileated gibbon
Puma
Red deer
Red panda
Red-shanked douc langur
Reindeer
Rhesus macaque
Serow
Siamang
Siberian musk deer
Snow leopard
Snowshoe hare
South African porcupine
Southern tree hyrax
Star-nosed mole
Striped skunk
Tasmanian devil
Three-striped night monkey
Tiger
Valley pocket gopher
Venezuelan red howler monkey

Virginia opossum
Weeper capuchin
Western barbastelle
White-tailed deer
White-throated capuchin

DECIDUOUS FOREST
Aardvark
African civet
American bison
American black bear
American least shrew
American pika
American water shrew
Ashy chinchilla rat
Asian elephant
Aye-aye
Bobcat
Bornean orangutan
Bridled nail-tailed wallaby
Brush-tailed phascogale
Brush-tailed rock wallaby
Capybara
Central American agouti
Chimpanzee
Collared peccary
Common bentwing bat
Common brush-tailed possum
Common genet

Common ringtail
Common tenrec
Common wombat
Cotton-top tamarin
Coypu
Crowned lemur
Degu
Desert cottontail
Eastern chipmunk
Eastern gray kangaroo
Eastern mole
Eastern pygmy possum
Edible dormouse
Ermine
Eurasian wild pig
European badger
Forest elephant
Forest hog
Funnel-eared bat
Gambian rat
Geoffroy's spider monkey
Giant panda
Goeldi's monkey
Gray squirrel
Gray wolf
Greater dog-faced bat
Greater glider
Greater horseshoe bat
Greater sac-winged bat
Ground pangolin
Human
Indian crested porcupine
Indian muntjac
Indian rhinoceros
Koala
Lar gibbon
Lesser Malay mouse deer
Lesser New Zealand short-
tailed bat
Lion
Little brown bat
Lord Derby's anomalure
Lowland tapir
Malayan moonrat
Mara
Mountain beaver
Mountain hare

North American beaver
North American porcupine
Northern raccoon
Numbat
Paca
Pacarana
Pallas's long-tongued bat
Parnell's moustached bat
Pileated gibbon
Puma
Pygmy glider
Red deer
Red fox
Red kangaroo
Red panda
Red-tailed sportive lemur
Rhesus macaque
Ringtailed lemur
Rock cavy
Senegal bushbaby
Serow
Siamang
Silky anteater
South African porcupine
Southern flying squirrel
Spotted hyena
Star-nosed mole
Striped skunk
Sugar glider
Three-striped night monkey
Tiger
Valley pocket gopher
Venezuelan red howler
monkey
Virginia opossum
Water buffalo
Weeper capuchin
Western barbastelle
Western European hedgehog
White rhinoceros
White-tailed deer
White-throated capuchin

DESERT

Australian jumping mouse
Bighorn sheep

Bobcat
Brazilian free-tailed bat
California leaf-nosed bat
Collared peccary
Damaraland mole-rat
Dassie rat
Desert cottontail
Dromedary camel
Egyptian slit-faced bat
Egyptian spiny mouse
Grant's desert golden mole
Gray wolf
Hairy-footed jerboa
Hardwicke's lesser mouse-
tailed bat
Human
Kirk's dikdik
Lion
Mzab gundi
Naked mole-rat
North American porcupine
Pallid bat
Parnell's moustached bat
Pink fairy armadillo
Pronghorn
Puma
Red fox
Rhesus macaque
San Joaquin pocket mouse
Savanna elephant
Short-beaked echidna
Southern marsupial mole
Spotted hyena
Striped skunk
Trident leaf-nosed bat
Valley pocket gopher
Virginia opossum
White-footed sportive lemur

GRASSLAND

Aardvark
Aardwolf
African civet
Alpaca
Alpine marmot
American bison

American black bear
American least shrew
American pika
Ashy chinchilla rat
Asian elephant
Australian false vampire bat
Australian jumping mouse
Black wildebeest
Black-bellied hamster
Black-tailed prairie dog
Brazilian free-tailed bat
Bridled nail-tailed wallaby
California leaf-nosed bat
Capybara
Central American agouti
Chimpanzee
Common bentwing bat
Common genet
Common tenrec
Coypu
Degu
Dwarf epauletted fruit bat
Eastern barred bandicoot
Eastern chipmunk
Eastern gray kangaroo
Eastern mole
Egyptian rousette
Egyptian slit-faced bat
Egyptian spiny mouse
Ermine
Eurasian wild pig
Forest elephant
Gambian rat
Giant anteater
Giant kangaroo rat
Giraffe
Grant's desert golden mole
Gray wolf
Greater bilby
Greater dog-faced bat
Greater horseshoe bat
Grevy's zebra
Ground pangolin
Hardwicke's lesser mouse-
   tailed bat
Hispaniolan solenodon
Hispid cotton rat

Human
Indian crested porcupine
Indian muntjac
Indian rhinoceros
Kiang
Lesser New Zealand short-
   tailed bat
Lion
Llama
Long-tailed chinchilla
Lowland tapir
Maned wolf
Mara
Naked bat
Nine-banded armadillo
Northern pika
Numbat
Paca
Pallas's long-tongued bat
Pallid bat
Parnell's moustached bat
Pearson's tuco-tuco
Pink fairy armadillo
Pronghorn
Przewalski's horse
Puma
Red deer
Red fox
Red kangaroo
Rock cavy
Rock hyrax
San Joaquin pocket mouse
Savanna elephant
Senegal bushbaby
Short-beaked echidna
Smoky bat
Snow leopard
South African porcupine
Spix's disk-winged bat
Spotted hyena
Springhare
Star-nosed mole
Striped skunk
Tasmanian wolf
Thomson's gazelle
Tiger
Valley pocket gopher

Vampire bat
Virginia opossum
Water buffalo
Western European hedgehog
Western red colobus
White rhinoceros
Yellow-streaked tenrec

LAKE AND POND
American water shrew
Babirusa
Capybara
Central American agouti
Common hippopotamus
Coypu
Duck-billed platypus
European otter
Greater bulldog bat
Malayan tapir
Muskrat
North American beaver
North American porcupine
Prehensile-tailed porcupine
Tiger

OCEAN
Antarctic fur seal
Beluga
Blue whale
Burmeister's porpoise
California sea lion
Common bottlenosed dolphin
Dugong
Franciscana dolphin
Galápagos sea lion
Gray whale
Harbor porpoise
Harp seal
Hawaiian monk seal
Humpback whale
Killer whale
Narwhal
North Atlantic right whale
Northern bottlenosed whale
Northern elephant seal
Northern minke whale

Pygmy right whale
Pygmy sperm whale
Shepherd's beaked whale
Sperm whale
Spinner dolphin
Steller's sea cow
Walrus
West Indian manatee

RAINFOREST
Australian false vampire bat
Aye-aye
Babirusa
Bald uakari
Bennett's tree kangaroo
Bornean orangutan
Brazilian free-tailed bat
Brown-throated three-toed
  sloth
Brush-tailed rock wallaby
Central American agouti
Checkered sengi
Chevrotains
Chimpanzee
Collared peccary
Colombian woolly monkey
Common brush-tailed possum
Common ringtail
Common squirrel monkey
Common tenrec
Common tree shrew
Cotton-top tamarin
Coypu
Crowned lemur
Cuban hutia
Eastern pygmy possum
Eurasian wild pig
Forest elephant
Fossa
Funnel-eared bat
Geoffroy's spider monkey
Giant anteater
Goeldi's monkey
Greater sac-winged bat
Ground cuscus
Hispaniolan solenodon

Hoffman's two-toed sloth
Human
Indian crested porcupine
Indian flying fox
Indian muntjac
Indri
Kitti's hog-nosed bat
Lar gibbon
Lesser New Zealand short-
  tailed bat
Lord Derby's anomalure
Lowland tapir
Malayan colugo
Malayan tapir
Mandrill
Masked titi
Milne-Edwards's sifaka
Monito del monte
Mountain beaver
Musky rat-kangaroo
Naked bat
North American beaver
Northern bettong
Northern greater bushbaby
Okapi
Old World sucker-footed bat
Paca
Pacarana
Philippine tarsier
Pileated gibbon
Potto
Prehensile-tailed porcupine
Proboscis monkey
Pygmy hippopotamus
Pygmy marmoset
Pygmy slow loris
Queensland tube-nosed bat
Red mouse lemur
Red-shanked douc langur
Rhesus macaque
Ring-tailed mongoose
Rock hyrax
Rufous spiny bandicoot
Short-beaked echidna
Siamang
Siberian musk deer
Silky anteater

Silky shrew opossum
Smoky bat
Southern pudu
Spiny rat
Spix's disk-winged bat
Sugar glider
Sumatran rhinoceros
Three-striped night monkey
Valley pocket gopher
Vampire bat
Venezuelan red howler
  monkey
Virginia opossum
Water opossum
Weeper capuchin
Western gorilla
Western red colobus
Western tarsier
White bat
White-faced saki
White-tailed deer
White-throated capuchin
Yellow-streaked tenrec

RIVER AND STREAM
American water shrew
Aye-aye
Babirusa
Baiji
Black-bellied hamster
Boto
Capybara
Central American agouti
Common hippopotamus
Common squirrel monkey
Coypu
Duck-billed platypus
European otter
Ganges and Indus dolphin
Greater bulldog bat
Greater cane rat
Lowland tapir
Malayan tapir
Mountain beaver
Muskrat
North American beaver

North American porcupine
Northern raccoon
Old World sucker-footed bat
Paca
Prehensile-tailed porcupine
Pygmy hippopotamus
Smoky bat
Tiger
Virginia opossum
Water opossum
West Indian manatee
White-footed sportive lemur

SEASHORE
Antarctic fur seal
California sea lion
Cape horseshoe bat
European otter
Galápagos sea lion
Grant's desert golden mole
Greater bulldog bat
Harp seal
Hawaiian monk seal
Honey possum
Lesser New Zealand short-
  tailed bat

Marianas fruit bat
Northern elephant seal
Pearson's tuco-tuco
Walrus

TUNDRA
American black bear
Ermine
Gray wolf
Hairy-footed jerboa
Human
Long-tailed chinchilla
Moose
Mountain hare
North American porcupine
Northern pika
Norway lemming
Polar bear
Red fox
Reindeer
Snowshoe hare
Striped skunk

WETLAND
American black bear

Bobcat
Bornean orangutan
Brazilian free-tailed bat
Capybara
Common squirrel monkey
Coypu
European otter
Giant anteater
Greater bulldog bat
Greater cane rat
Greater dog-faced bat
Indian flying fox
Malayan moonrat
Marianas fruit bat
North American beaver
Northern raccoon
Old World sucker-footed bat
Pacarana
Parnell's moustached bat
Proboscis monkey
Puma
Rhesus macaque
Spix's disk-winged bat
Star-nosed mole
Tiger
Valley pocket gopher

Species List by Geographic Range

AFGHANISTAN
Common bentwing bat
Dromedary camel
Eurasian wild pig
Gray wolf
Greater horseshoe bat
Hardwicke's lesser mouse-
  tailed bat
Red deer
Red fox
Rhesus macaque
Snow leopard
Trident leaf-nosed bat

ALBANIA
Blue whale
Common bentwing bat
Common bottlenosed dolphin
Edible dormouse
Eurasian wild pig
European badger
European otter
Gray wolf
Greater horseshoe bat
Humpback whale
Northern minke whale
Pygmy sperm whale
Red deer
Red fox
Sperm whale

ALGERIA
Blue whale
Common bentwing bat
Common bottlenosed dolphin
Common genet
Dromedary camel
Eurasian wild pig
European otter
Greater horseshoe bat
Humpback whale
Killer whale
Mzab gundi
Northern bottlenosed whale
Northern minke whale
Pygmy sperm whale
Red deer
Red fox
Sperm whale
Trident leaf-nosed bat

ANDORRA
European badger
Red fox

ANGOLA
Aardvark
African civet
Blue whale
Common bentwing bat

Common bottlenosed dolphin
Common genet
Dassie rat
Egyptian slit-faced bat
Gambian rat
Giraffe
Ground pangolin
Humpback whale
Kirk's dikdik
Lion
Northern minke whale
Pygmy sperm whale
South African porcupine
Sperm whale
Spinner dolphin
Spotted hyena
Springhare
Western gorilla
White rhinoceros

ANTARCTICA
Antarctic fur seal
Blue whale
Northern minke whale

ARGENTINA
Blue whale
Brazilian free-tailed bat
Brown-throated three-toed sloth

Burmeister's porpoise
Capybara
Central American agouti
Collared peccary
Common bottlenosed dolphin
Coypu
Franciscana dolphin
Giant anteater
Greater bulldog bat
Humpback whale
Killer whale
Llama
Lowland tapir
Maned wolf
Mara
Monito del monte
Northern minke whale
Pallas's long-tongued bat
Pearson's tuco-tuco
Pink fairy armadillo
Prehensile-tailed porcupine
Puma
Pygmy right whale
Red deer
Shepherd's beaked whale
Southern pudu
Sperm whale
Three-toed tree sloths
Vampire bat
Water opossum

ARMENIA
Common bentwing bat
Edible dormouse
Eurasian wild pig
European badger
Gray wolf
Red deer
Red fox

AUSTRALIA
Australian false vampire bat
Australian jumping mouse
Bennett's tree kangaroo
Blue whale
Bridled nail-tailed wallaby

Brush-tailed phascogale
Brush-tailed rock wallaby
Common bentwing bat
Common bottlenosed dolphin
Common brush-tailed possum
Common ringtail
Common wombat
Duck-billed platypus
Dugong
Eastern barred bandicoot
Eastern gray kangaroo
Eastern pygmy possum
Greater bilby
Greater glider
Honey possum
Humpback whale
Killer whale
Koala
Musky rat-kangaroo
Northern bettong
Northern minke whale
Numbat
Pygmy glider
Pygmy right whale
Pygmy sperm whale
Queensland tube-nosed bat
Red fox
Red kangaroo
Rufous spiny bandicoot
Short-beaked echidna
Southern marsupial mole
Sperm whale
Spinner dolphin
Sugar glider
Tasmanian devil
Tasmanian wolf

AUSTRIA
Alpine marmot
Common bentwing bat
Edible dormouse
Ermine
Eurasian wild pig
European badger
Greater horseshoe bat
Mountain hare

Red deer
Red fox
Western European hedgehog

AZERBAIJAN
Common bentwing bat
Edible dormouse
Eurasian wild pig
European badger
Gray wolf
Red deer
Red fox

BANGLADESH
Asian elephant
Blue whale
Common bentwing bat
Common bottlenosed dolphin
Eurasian wild pig
Ganges and Indus dolphin
Gray wolf
Greater horseshoe bat
Humpback whale
Indian crested porcupine
Indian flying fox
Indian muntjac
Indian rhinoceros
Northern minke whale
Pygmy sperm whale
Red fox
Rhesus macaque
Serow
Sperm whale
Spinner dolphin
Tiger

BELARUS
Black-bellied hamster
Edible dormouse
Ermine
Eurasian wild pig
European badger
Gray wolf
Moose
Mountain hare

Red deer
Red fox

BELGIUM
Black-bellied hamster
Blue whale
Common bottlenosed dolphin
Edible dormouse
Ermine
Eurasian wild pig
European badger
Greater horseshoe bat
Harbor porpoise
Humpback whale
Killer whale
North Atlantic right whale
Northern minke whale
Pygmy sperm whale
Sperm whale
Western European hedgehog

BELIZE
Blue whale
Brazilian free-tailed bat
Central American agouti
Collared peccary
Common bottlenosed dolphin
Funnel-eared bat
Geoffroy's spider monkey
Giant anteater
Greater bulldog bat
Greater dog-faced bat
Greater sac-winged bat
Hispid cotton rat
Humpback whale
Nine-banded armadillo
Northern minke whale
Paca
Pallas's long-tongued bat
Parnell's moustached bat
Pygmy sperm whale
Silky anteater
Sperm whale
Spinner dolphin
Spix's disk-winged bat
Vampire bat

Virginia opossum
Water opossum
White-tailed deer

BENIN
Aardvark
African civet
Blue whale
Common bottlenosed dolphin
Common genet
Gambian rat
Humpback whale
Lord Derby's anomalure
Northern minke whale
Pygmy sperm whale
Rock hyrax
Senegal bushbaby
South African porcupine
Sperm whale
Spinner dolphin

BHUTAN
Asian elephant
Common bentwing bat
Gray wolf
Greater horseshoe bat
Indian crested porcupine
Red fox
Red panda
Rhesus macaque
Serow
Snow leopard
Water buffalo

BOLIVIA
Alpaca
Ashy chinchilla rat
Boto
Brazilian free-tailed bat
Brown-throated three-toed
  sloth
Capybara
Central American agouti
Collared peccary
Coypu
Giant anteater
Goeldi's monkey

Greater bulldog bat
Greater dog-faced bat
Greater sac-winged bat
Hoffman's two-toed sloth
Llama
Lowland tapir
Maned wolf
Nine-banded armadillo
Pacarana
Pallas's long-tongued bat
Puma
Pygmy marmoset
Silky anteater
Spix's disk-winged bat
Three-toed tree sloths
Vampire bat
White-faced saki
White-tailed deer

BOSNIA AND HERZEGOVINA
Common bentwing bat
Edible dormouse
Eurasian wild pig
European badger
Greater horseshoe bat
Red deer
Red fox

BOTSWANA
Aardvark
Aardwolf
African civet
Common genet
Common hippopotamus
Damaraland mole-rat
Egyptian slit-faced bat
Giraffe
Ground pangolin
Lion
Savanna elephant
Springhare

BRAZIL
Bald uakari
Blue whale

Boto
Brazilian free-tailed bat
Brown-throated three-toed
  sloth
Burmeister's porpoise
Capybara
Central American agouti
Collared peccary
Common bottlenosed dolphin
Common squirrel monkey
Coypu
Franciscana dolphin
Funnel-eared bat
Giant anteater
Goeldi's monkey
Greater bulldog bat
Greater dog-faced bat
Greater sac-winged bat
Hoffman's two-toed sloth
Humpback whale
Killer whale
Lowland tapir
Maned wolf
Masked titi
Nine-banded armadillo
Northern minke whale
Paca
Pacarana
Pallas's long-tongued bat
Parnell's moustached bat
Prehensile-tailed porcupine
Pygmy marmoset
Pygmy right whale
Pygmy sperm whale
Red deer
Rock cavy
Silky anteater
Smoky bat
Sperm whale
Spinner dolphin
Spix's disk-winged bat
Three-striped night monkey
Three-toed tree sloths
Vampire bat
Venezuelan red howler
  monkey
Water opossum

Weeper capuchin
White-faced saki
White-tailed deer

BULGARIA
Common bentwing bat
Edible dormouse
Eurasian wild pig
European badger
Gray wolf
Greater horseshoe bat
Harbor porpoise
Red deer
Red fox

BURKINA FASO
Aardvark
African civet
Common genet
Egyptian slit-faced bat
Rock hyrax
Senegal bushbaby

BURUNDI
Aardvark
African civet
Common bentwing bat
Common genet
Egyptian slit-faced bat
Gambian rat
Lord Derby's anomalure
Senegal bushbaby
South African porcupine

CAMBODIA
Asian elephant
Blue whale
Common bentwing bat
Common bottlenosed dolphin
Dugong
Eurasian wild pig
Greater horseshoe bat
Humpback whale
Indian muntjac
Lesser Malay mouse deer

Malayan tapir
Northern minke whale
Pileated gibbon
Pygmy sperm whale
Serow
Sperm whale
Spinner dolphin

CAMEROON
Aardvark
African civet
Blue whale
Chimpanzee
Common bottlenosed dolphin
Common genet
Dwarf epauletted fruit bat
Egyptian rousette
Forest elephant
Forest hog
Gambian rat
Greater cane rat
Humpback whale
Lord Derby's anomalure
Mandrill
Northern minke whale
Potto
Pygmy sperm whale
Rock hyrax
Senegal bushbaby
South African porcupine
Sperm whale
Spinner dolphin
Western gorilla
Western red colobus

CANADA
American bison
American black bear
American least shrew
American pika
American water shrew
Beluga
Bighorn sheep
Black-tailed prairie dog
Bobcat
California sea lion

Eastern chipmunk
Eastern mole
Ermine
Gray squirrel
Gray wolf
Harbor porpoise
Harp seal
Killer whale
Little brown bat
Moose
Mountain beaver
Muskrat
Narwhal
North American beaver
North American porcupine
North Atlantic right whale
Northern bottlenosed whale
Northern raccoon
Pallid bat
Polar bear
Pronghorn
Puma
Red deer
Red fox
Reindeer
Snowshoe hare
Southern flying squirrel
Star-nosed mole
Striped skunk
Virginia opossum
Walrus
White-tailed deer

CENTRAL AFRICAN REPUBLIC
Aardvark
African civet
Chimpanzee
Common genet
Dwarf epauletted fruit bat
Egyptian rousette
Forest elephant
Gambian rat
Giraffe
Greater cane rat
Lord Derby's anomalure

Rock hyrax
Senegal bushbaby
South African porcupine
Western gorilla
White rhinoceros

CHAD
Aardvark
African civet
Common genet
Dromedary camel
Egyptian slit-faced bat
Gambian rat
Ground pangolin
Mzab gundi
Rock hyrax
Senegal bushbaby
Spotted hyena
Trident leaf-nosed bat
White rhinoceros

CHILE
Alpaca
Ashy chinchilla rat
Blue whale
Brazilian free-tailed bat
Burmeister's porpoise
Common bottlenosed dolphin
Coypu
Degu
Humpback whale
Killer whale
Llama
Long-tailed chinchilla
Monito del monte
Northern minke whale
Pallas's long-tongued bat
Pearson's tuco-tuco
Pygmy right whale
Pygmy sperm whale
Red deer
Shepherd's beaked whale
Southern pudu
Sperm whale
Vampire bat

CHINA
Asian elephant
Baiji
Blue whale
Common bentwing bat
Common bottlenosed dolphin
Dugong
Edible dormouse
Ermine
European badger
Giant panda
Gray wolf
Greater horseshoe bat
Hairy-footed jerboa
Humpback whale
Indian muntjac
Kiang
Killer whale
Lar gibbon
Lesser Malay mouse deer
Moose
Mountain hare
Northern minke whale
Northern pika
Pygmy slow loris
Pygmy sperm whale
Red deer
Red fox
Red panda
Reindeer
Rhesus macaque
Serow
Siberian musk deer
Snow leopard
Sperm whale
Spinner dolphin
Tiger

COLOMBIA
Bald uakari
Blue whale
Boto
Brazilian free-tailed bat
Brown-throated three-toed sloth
Capybara

Central American agouti
Collared peccary
Colombian woolly monkey
Common bottlenosed dolphin
Common squirrel monkey
Cotton-top tamarin
Funnel-eared bat
Giant anteater
Goeldi's monkey
Greater bulldog bat
Greater sac-winged bat
Hispid cotton rat
Hoffman's two-toed sloth
Humpback whale
Killer whale
Llama
Lowland tapir
Nine-banded armadillo
Northern minke whale
Paca
Pacarana
Pallas's long-tongued bat
Parnell's moustached bat
Prehensile-tailed porcupine
Pygmy marmoset
Pygmy sperm whale
Silky anteater
Silky shrew opossum
Smoky bat
Sperm whale
Spinner dolphin
Spiny rat
Spix's disk-winged bat
Three-striped night monkey
Three-toed tree sloths
Vampire bat
Water opossum
White-faced saki
White-tailed deer
White-throated capuchin

CONGO
African civet
Blue whale
Common bottlenosed dolphin
Common genet

Dwarf epauletted fruit bat
Egyptian rousette
Egyptian slit-faced bat
Forest elephant
Forest hog
Humpback whale
Lord Derby's anomalure
Northern minke whale
Potto
Pygmy sperm whale
South African porcupine
Sperm whale
Spinner dolphin
Springhare
Western gorilla

COSTA RICA
American least shrew
Blue whale
Brazilian free-tailed bat
Brown-throated three-toed
  sloth
Central American agouti
Collared peccary
Common bottlenosed dolphin
Funnel-eared bat
Geoffroy's spider monkey
Giant anteater
Greater bulldog bat
Greater dog-faced bat
Greater sac-winged bat
Hispid cotton rat
Hoffman's two-toed sloth
Humpback whale
Killer whale
Nine-banded armadillo
Northern minke whale
Paca
Pallas's long-tongued bat
Parnell's moustached bat
Puma
Pygmy sperm whale
Silky anteater
Smoky bat
Sperm whale
Spinner dolphin

Spiny rat
Spix's disk-winged bat
Three-toed tree sloths
Vampire bat
Virginia opossum
Water opossum
White bat
White-tailed deer
White-throated capuchin

CROATIA
Blue whale
Common bentwing bat
Common bottlenosed dolphin
Edible dormouse
Eurasian wild pig
European badger
Greater horseshoe bat
Humpback whale
Northern minke whale
Pygmy sperm whale
Red deer
Red fox
Sperm whale

CUBA
Blue whale
Brazilian free-tailed bat
Central American agouti
Collared peccary
Common bottlenosed dolphin
Cuban hutia
Funnel-eared bat
Greater bulldog bat
Humpback whale
Killer whale
Northern minke whale
Pallid bat
Parnell's moustached bat
Pygmy sperm whale
Sperm whale
Spinner dolphin

CYPRUS
Blue whale

Common bottlenosed dolphin
Humpback whale
Northern minke whale
Pygmy sperm whale
Sperm whale

CZECH REPUBLIC
Black-bellied hamster
Common bentwing bat
Edible dormouse
Ermine
European badger
Greater horseshoe bat
Red deer
Red fox

DEMOCRATIC REPUBLIC OF THE CONGO
Aardvark
African civet
Blue whale
Checkered sengi
Chimpanzee
Common bentwing bat
Common bottlenosed dolphin
Common genet
Common hippopotamus
Dwarf epauletted fruit bat
Egyptian rousette
Egyptian slit-faced bat
Forest elephant
Forest hog
Gambian rat
Giraffe
Humpback whale
Lord Derby's anomalure
Mandrill
Northern minke whale
Okapi
Potto
Pygmy sperm whale
Rock hyrax
South African porcupine
Sperm whale

Spinner dolphin
Western gorilla
Western red colobus
White rhinoceros

DENMARK
Blue whale
Common bottlenosed dolphin
Ermine
Eurasian wild pig
European badger
Harbor porpoise
Humpback whale
Killer whale
North Atlantic right whale
Northern minke whale
Norway lemming
Pygmy sperm whale
Red deer
Red fox
Sperm whale
Western European hedgehog

DJIBOUTI
Aardvark
Blue whale
Common bottlenosed dolphin
Common genet
Dromedary camel
Dugong
Humpback whale
Northern minke whale
Rock hyrax
Senegal bushbaby
Sperm whale
Spinner dolphin

DOMINICAN REPUBLIC
Blue whale
Brazilian free-tailed bat
Common bottlenosed dolphin
Funnel-eared bat
Greater bulldog bat
Hispaniolan solenodon

Humpback whale
Killer whale
Northern minke whale
Parnell's moustached bat
Pygmy sperm whale
Sperm whale
Spinner dolphin

ECUADOR
Blue whale
Boto
Brazilian free-tailed bat
Brown-throated three-toed
  sloth
Capybara
Central American agouti
Collared peccary
Common bottlenosed dolphin
Galápagos sea lion
Giant anteater
Goeldi's monkey
Greater bulldog bat
Greater dog-faced bat
Greater sac-winged bat
Hoffman's two-toed sloth
Humpback whale
Killer whale
Llama
Lowland tapir
Nine-banded armadillo
Northern minke whale
Pacarana
Pallas's long-tongued bat
Pygmy marmoset
Pygmy sperm whale
Silky anteater
Silky shrew opossum
Sperm whale
Spinner dolphin
Spiny rat
Spix's disk-winged bat
Three-toed tree sloths
Vampire bat
Water opossum
White-faced saki
White-tailed deer

EGYPT
Blue whale
Common bottlenosed dolphin
Common genet
Dromedary camel
Egyptian rousette
Egyptian slit-faced bat
Egyptian spiny mouse
Eurasian wild pig
Greater horseshoe bat
Hardwicke's lesser mouse-
  tailed bat
Humpback whale
Northern minke whale
Pygmy sperm whale
Red fox
Rock hyrax
Sperm whale
Trident leaf-nosed bat

EL SALVADOR
Blue whale
Brazilian free-tailed bat
Brown-throated three-toed
  sloth
Collared peccary
Common bottlenosed dolphin
Funnel-eared bat
Geoffroy's spider monkey
Giant anteater
Greater bulldog bat
Greater sac-winged bat
Hispid cotton rat
Humpback whale
Killer whale
Nine-banded armadillo
Northern minke whale
Paca
Pallas's long-tongued bat
Parnell's moustached bat
Pygmy sperm whale
Silky anteater
Sperm whale
Spinner dolphin
Spix's disk-winged bat
Three-toed tree sloths

Vampire bat
Virginia opossum
Water opossum
White-tailed deer

EQUATORIAL GUINEA
African civet
Blue whale
Common bottlenosed dolphin
Common genet
Forest elephant
Humpback whale
Lord Derby's anomalure
Mandrill
Northern minke whale
Potto
Pygmy sperm whale
South African porcupine
Sperm whale
Spinner dolphin
Western gorilla

ERITREA
Aardvark
Blue whale
Common bottlenosed dolphin
Common genet
Dromedary camel
Dugong
Egyptian slit-faced bat
Humpback whale
Northern minke whale
Rock hyrax
Sperm whale
Spinner dolphin

ESTONIA
Blue whale
Common bottlenosed dolphin
Ermine
Eurasian wild pig
European badger
Gray wolf
Harbor porpoise
Humpback whale

Moose
Mountain hare
Northern minke whale
Red deer
Red fox
Sperm whale

ETHIOPIA
Aardvark
Common genet
Dromedary camel
Egyptian slit-faced bat
Forest hog
Grevy's zebra
Lion
Naked mole-rat
Rock hyrax
Senegal bushbaby
Thomson's gazelle

FINLAND
Blue whale
Common bottlenosed dolphin
Ermine
Eurasian wild pig
European badger
European otter
Gray wolf
Humpback whale
Moose
Mountain hare
Northern minke whale
Norway lemming
Red fox
Reindeer
Sperm whale
Western European hedgehog

FRANCE
Alpine marmot
Blue whale
Common bentwing bat
Common bottlenosed dolphin
Common genet
Edible dormouse

Ermine
Eurasian wild pig
European badger
European otter
Greater horseshoe bat
Harbor porpoise
Humpback whale
Killer whale
North Atlantic right whale
Northern bottlenosed whale
Northern minke whale
Pygmy sperm whale
Red deer
Red fox
Sperm whale
Western European hedgehog

FRENCH GUIANA
Blue whale
Capybara
Collared peccary
Common bottlenosed dolphin
Common squirrel monkey
Funnel-eared bat
Giant anteater
Greater bulldog bat
Greater dog-faced bat
Greater sac-winged bat
Humpback whale
Lowland tapir
Nine-banded armadillo
Northern minke whale
Paca
Pallas's long-tongued bat
Parnell's moustached bat
Prehensile-tailed porcupine
Pygmy sperm whale
Silky anteater
Smoky bat
Sperm whale
Spinner dolphin
Spix's disk-winged bat
Three-toed tree sloths
Vampire bat
Water opossum
Weeper capuchin

White-faced saki
White-tailed deer

GABON
African civet
Blue whale
Common bottlenosed dolphin
Common genet
Common hippopotamus
Dwarf epauletted fruit bat
Egyptian rousette
Forest elephant
Forest hog
Humpback whale
Lord Derby's anomalure
Mandrill
Northern minke whale
Potto
Pygmy sperm whale
South African porcupine
Sperm whale
Spinner dolphin
Western gorilla

GAMBIA
Aardvark
African civet
Blue whale
Common bottlenosed dolphin
Common genet
Gambian rat
Greater cane rat
Humpback whale
Killer whale
Northern minke whale
Pygmy sperm whale
Senegal bushbaby
South African porcupine
Sperm whale
Spinner dolphin
Western red colobus

GEORGIA
Common bentwing bat
Edible dormouse

Eurasian wild pig
European badger
Gray wolf
Harbor porpoise
Red deer
Red fox

GERMANY
Alpine marmot
Black-bellied hamster
Blue whale
Common bentwing bat
Common bottlenosed dolphin
Edible dormouse
Ermine
Eurasian wild pig
European badger
Greater horseshoe bat
Harbor porpoise
Humpback whale
Killer whale
North Atlantic right whale
Northern minke whale
Northern raccoon
Pygmy sperm whale
Red deer
Red fox
Sperm whale
Western European hedgehog

GHANA
Aardvark
African civet
Blue whale
Chimpanzee
Common bottlenosed dolphin
Common genet
Dwarf epauletted fruit bat
Egyptian rousette
Forest elephant
Forest hog
Gambian rat
Humpback whale
Lord Derby's anomalure
Northern minke whale
Potto

Pygmy sperm whale
Rock hyrax
Senegal bushbaby
South African porcupine
Sperm whale
Spinner dolphin
Western red colobus

GREECE
Blue whale
Common bentwing bat
Common bottlenosed dolphin
Edible dormouse
European badger
European otter
Gray wolf
Greater horseshoe bat
Harbor porpoise
Humpback whale
Northern minke whale
Pygmy sperm whale
Red deer
Red fox
Sperm whale

GREENLAND
Blue whale
Ermine
Harbor porpoise
Harp seal
Humpback whale
Killer whale
North Atlantic right whale
Northern bottlenosed whale
Northern minke whale
Polar bear
Reindeer
Walrus

GRENADA
Nine-banded armadillo
Pallas's long-tongued bat

GUAM
Marianas fruit bat

GUATEMALA
American least shrew
Blue whale
Brazilian free-tailed bat
Central American agouti
Collared peccary
Common bottlenosed dolphin
Funnel-eared bat
Geoffroy's spider monkey
Giant anteater
Greater bulldog bat
Greater dog-faced bat
Greater sac-winged bat
Hispid cotton rat
Humpback whale
Killer whale
Nine-banded armadillo
Northern minke whale
Paca
Pallas's long-tongued bat
Parnell's moustached bat
Puma
Pygmy sperm whale
Silky anteater
Sperm whale
Spinner dolphin
Spix's disk-winged bat
Vampire bat
Virginia opossum
Water opossum
White-tailed deer

GUINEA
Aardvark
African civet
Blue whale
Chimpanzee
Common bottlenosed dolphin
Common genet
Egyptian slit-faced bat
Forest hog
Gambian rat
Humpback whale
Killer whale
Northern minke whale
Pygmy hippopotamus

Pygmy sperm whale
Rock hyrax
Senegal bushbaby
South African porcupine
Sperm whale
Spinner dolphin

GUINEA-BISSAU
Aardvark
African civet
Blue whale
Common bottlenosed dolphin
Common genet
Forest hog
Gambian rat
Humpback whale
Killer whale
Northern minke whale
Pygmy sperm whale
Rock hyrax
Senegal bushbaby
South African porcupine
Sperm whale
Spinner dolphin
Western red colobus

GUYANA
Blue whale
Boto
Capybara
Collared peccary
Common bottlenosed dolphin
Common squirrel monkey
Funnel-eared bat
Giant anteater
Greater bulldog bat
Greater dog-faced bat
Greater sac-winged bat
Humpback whale
Lowland tapir
Nine-banded armadillo
Northern minke whale
Paca
Pallas's long-tongued bat
Parnell's moustached bat
Prehensile-tailed porcupine

Pygmy sperm whale
Silky anteater
Smoky bat
Sperm whale
Spinner dolphin
Spix's disk-winged bat
Three-toed tree sloths
Vampire bat
Water opossum
Weeper capuchin
White-faced saki
White-tailed deer

HAITI
Blue whale
Brazilian free-tailed bat
Common bottlenosed dolphin
Funnel-eared bat
Greater bulldog bat
Hispaniolan solenodon
Humpback whale
Killer whale
Northern minke whale
Parnell's moustached bat
Pygmy sperm whale
Sperm whale
Spinner dolphin

HONDURAS
American least shrew
Blue whale
Brazilian free-tailed bat
Brown-throated three-toed
  sloth
Central American agouti
Collared peccary
Common bottlenosed dolphin
Funnel-eared bat
Geoffroy's spider monkey
Giant anteater
Greater bulldog bat
Greater dog-faced bat
Greater sac-winged bat
Hispid cotton rat
Hoffman's two-toed sloth
Humpback whale

Killer whale
Nine-banded armadillo
Northern minke whale
Paca
Pallas's long-tongued bat
Parnell's moustached bat
Pygmy sperm whale
Silky anteater
Sperm whale
Spinner dolphin
Spiny rat
Spix's disk-winged bat
Three-toed tree sloths
Vampire bat
Virginia opossum
Water opossum
White bat
White-tailed deer
White-throated capuchin

HUNGARY
Black-bellied hamster
Common bentwing bat
Edible dormouse
Ermine
Eurasian wild pig
European badger
Greater horseshoe bat
Red deer
Red fox

ICELAND
Blue whale
Harbor porpoise
Humpback whale
Killer whale
North Atlantic right whale
Northern bottlenosed whale
Northern minke whale
Norway lemming

INDIA
Asian elephant
Blue whale
Common bentwing bat

Common bottlenosed dolphin
Dromedary camel
Dugong
Ermine
Eurasian wild pig
Ganges and Indus dolphin
Gray wolf
Greater horseshoe bat
Hardwicke's lesser mouse-
  tailed bat
Humpback whale
Indian crested porcupine
Indian flying fox
Indian muntjac
Indian rhinoceros
Kiang
Killer whale
Lion
Northern minke whale
Pygmy sperm whale
Red fox
Red panda
Rhesus macaque
Serow
Snow leopard
Sperm whale
Spinner dolphin
Tiger
Water buffalo

INDONESIA
Asian elephant
Babirusa
Blue whale
Bornean orangutan
Common bentwing bat
Common bottlenosed dolphin
Common tree shrew
Dugong
Eurasian wild pig
European otter
Humpback whale
Indian muntjac
Killer whale
Lar gibbon
Lesser Malay mouse deer

Malayan colugo
Malayan moonrat
Malayan tapir
Naked bat
Northern minke whale
Proboscis monkey
Pygmy sperm whale
Serow
Siamang
Sperm whale
Spinner dolphin
Sumatran rhinoceros
Tiger
Western tarsier

IRAN
Blue whale
Common bentwing bat
Common bottlenosed dolphin
Dromedary camel
Dugong
Edible dormouse
Egyptian rousette
Egyptian spiny mouse
Eurasian wild pig
European badger
Gray wolf
Greater horseshoe bat
Hairy-footed jerboa
Humpback whale
Indian crested porcupine
Killer whale
Northern minke whale
Pygmy sperm whale
Red deer
Red fox
Sperm whale
Spinner dolphin
Trident leaf-nosed bat

IRAQ
Dromedary camel
Egyptian spiny mouse
Eurasian wild pig
Gray wolf
Greater horseshoe bat

Red fox
Trident leaf-nosed bat

IRELAND
Blue whale
Common bottlenosed dolphin
Ermine
Eurasian wild pig
European badger
European otter
Harbor porpoise
Humpback whale
Killer whale
Mountain hare
North Atlantic right whale
Northern bottlenosed whale
Northern minke whale
Red deer
Red fox
Sperm whale
Western European hedgehog

ISRAEL
Blue whale
Common bottlenosed dolphin
Dromedary camel
Egyptian rousette
Egyptian slit-faced bat
Egyptian spiny mouse
Eurasian wild pig
Gray wolf
Hardwicke's lesser mouse-
  tailed bat
Humpback whale
Indian crested porcupine
Northern minke whale
Pygmy sperm whale
Red fox
Rock hyrax
Sperm whale
Trident leaf-nosed bat

ITALY
Alpine marmot
Blue whale

Common bentwing bat
Common bottlenosed dolphin
Edible dormouse
Ermine
Eurasian wild pig
European badger
Gray wolf
Greater horseshoe bat
Humpback whale
Killer whale
Mountain hare
Northern minke whale
Pygmy sperm whale
Red deer
Red fox
Sperm whale
Western European hedgehog

IVORY COAST
Aardvark
African civet
Blue whale
Chimpanzee
Common bottlenosed dolphin
Common genet
Dwarf epauletted fruit bat
Egyptian rousette
Forest elephant
Forest hog
Gambian rat
Humpback whale
Lord Derby's anomalure
Northern minke whale
Pygmy hippopotamus
Pygmy sperm whale
Rock hyrax
Senegal bushbaby
South African porcupine
Sperm whale
Spinner dolphin
Western red colobus

JAMAICA
Blue whale
Brazilian free-tailed bat
Common bottlenosed dolphin

Funnel-eared bat
Greater bulldog bat
Humpback whale
Killer whale
Northern minke whale
Pallas's long-tongued bat
Parnell's moustached bat
Pygmy sperm whale
Sperm whale
Spinner dolphin

JAPAN
Blue whale
Common bentwing bat
Common bottlenosed dolphin
Dugong
Ermine
Eurasian wild pig
European badger
European otter
Gray whale
Greater horseshoe bat
Harbor porpoise
Humpback whale
Killer whale
Marianas fruit bat
Mountain hare
Northern minke whale
Northern pika
Pygmy sperm whale
Reindeer
Siberian musk deer
Sperm whale
Spinner dolphin

JORDAN
Dromedary camel
Egyptian slit-faced bat
Egyptian spiny mouse
Eurasian wild pig
Gray wolf
Hardwicke's lesser mouse-
  tailed bat
Red fox
Rock hyrax
Trident leaf-nosed bat

KAZAKHSTAN
Black-bellied hamster
Common bentwing bat
Edible dormouse
Ermine
Eurasian wild pig
European badger
Gray wolf
Hairy-footed jerboa
Moose
Mountain hare
Red deer
Red fox
Snow leopard

KENYA
Aardvark
Aardwolf
African civet
Blue whale
Common bentwing bat
Common bottlenosed dolphin
Common genet
Dugong
Egyptian rousette
Egyptian slit-faced bat
Forest hog
Gambian rat
Giraffe
Greater cane rat
Grevy's zebra
Ground pangolin
Humpback whale
Kirk's dikdik
Lion
Lord Derby's anomalure
Naked mole-rat
Northern greater bushbaby
Northern minke whale
Potto
Pygmy sperm whale
Rock hyrax
Senegal bushbaby
South African porcupine
Sperm whale
Spinner dolphin

Springhare
Thomson's gazelle

KUWAIT
Egyptian spiny mouse
Gray wolf
Trident leaf-nosed bat

KYRGYZSTAN
Common bentwing bat
Edible dormouse
Ermine
Eurasian wild pig
European badger
Gray wolf
Red deer
Red fox
Snow leopard

LAOS
Asian elephant
Common bentwing bat
Eurasian wild pig
Greater horseshoe bat
Indian muntjac
Lesser Malay mouse deer
Malayan tapir
Pileated gibbon
Pygmy slow loris
Red fox
Red-shanked douc langur
Rhesus macaque
Serow

LATVIA
Blue whale
Common bottlenosed dolphin
Ermine
Eurasian wild pig
European badger
Gray wolf
Harbor porpoise
Humpback whale
Moose
Mountain hare

Northern minke whale
Red deer
Red fox
Sperm whale

LEBANON
Blue whale
Common bottlenosed dolphin
Dromedary camel
Egyptian spiny mouse
Hardwicke's lesser mouse-
  tailed bat
Humpback whale
Northern minke whale
Pygmy sperm whale
Sperm whale
Trident leaf-nosed bat

LESOTHO
Aardvark
African civet
Common bentwing bat
Common genet
Egyptian slit-faced bat
South African porcupine

LESSER ANTILLES
Blue whale
Brazilian free-tailed bat
Common bottlenosed dolphin
Funnel-eared bat
Greater bulldog bat
Humpback whale
Killer whale
Northern minke whale
Pygmy sperm whale
Sperm whale
Spinner dolphin

LIBERIA
Aardvark
African civet
Blue whale
Common bottlenosed dolphin

Common genet
Forest elephant
Forest hog
Humpback whale
Killer whale
Lord Derby's anomalure
Northern minke whale
Pygmy hippopotamus
Pygmy sperm whale
Rock hyrax
South African porcupine
Sperm whale
Spinner dolphin
Western red colobus

LIBYA
Blue whale
Common bottlenosed dolphin
Dromedary camel
Egyptian spiny mouse
Eurasian wild pig
Greater horseshoe bat
Humpback whale
Mzab gundi
Northern minke whale
Pygmy sperm whale
Red fox
Sperm whale
Trident leaf-nosed bat

LIECHTENSTEIN
Ermine
Eurasian wild pig
Greater horseshoe bat
Red deer
Red fox

LITHUANIA
Blue whale
Common bottlenosed dolphin
Edible dormouse
Ermine
Eurasian wild pig
European badger
Harbor porpoise

Humpback whale
Moose
Mountain hare
Northern minke whale
Red deer
Red fox
Sperm whale

LUXEMBOURG
Edible dormouse
Ermine
Eurasian wild pig
European badger
Greater horseshoe bat
Red deer
Red fox

MACEDONIA
Common bentwing bat
Edible dormouse
Eurasian wild pig
European badger
Gray wolf
Greater horseshoe bat
Red deer
Red fox

MADAGASCAR
Aye-aye
Blue whale
Common bentwing bat
Common bottlenosed dolphin
Common tenrec
Crowned lemur
Dugong
Fossa
Humpback whale
Indri
Killer whale
Milne-Edwards's sifaka
Northern minke whale
Old World sucker-footed bat
Pygmy sperm whale
Red mouse lemur

Red-tailed sportive lemur
Ringtailed lemur
Ring-tailed mongoose
Sperm whale
Spinner dolphin
White-footed sportive lemur
Yellow-streaked tenrec

MALAWI
Aardvark
African civet
Checkered sengi
Common bentwing bat
Common genet
Egyptian slit-faced bat
Gambian rat
Ground pangolin
South African porcupine

MALAYSIA
Asian elephant
Blue whale
Bornean orangutan
Common bentwing bat
Common bottlenosed dolphin
Common tree shrew
Dugong
Eurasian wild pig
Humpback whale
Indian muntjac
Killer whale
Lar gibbon
Lesser Malay mouse deer
Malayan colugo
Malayan moonrat
Malayan tapir
Naked bat
Northern minke whale
Proboscis monkey
Pygmy sperm whale
Serow
Siamang
Sperm whale
Spinner dolphin
Sumatran rhinoceros

MALI
Aardvark
African civet
Common genet
Dromedary camel
Egyptian rousette
Egyptian slit-faced bat
Gambian rat
Mzab gundi
Rock hyrax
Savanna elephant
Senegal bushbaby

MARIANA ISLANDS
Marianas fruit bat

MAURITANIA
Aardvark
Blue whale
Common bottlenosed dolphin
Dromedary camel
Humpback whale
Killer whale
Northern minke whale
Pygmy sperm whale
Sperm whale
Spinner dolphin

MEXICO
American black bear
American least shrew
Bighorn sheep
Black-tailed prairie dog
Blue whale
Bobcat
Brazilian free-tailed bat
Brown-throated three-toed
  sloth
California leaf-nosed bat
California sea lion
Central American agouti
Collared peccary
Common bottlenosed dolphin
Desert cottontail
Eastern mole

Funnel-eared bat
Geoffroy's spider monkey
Gray whale
Greater bulldog bat
Greater dog-faced bat
Greater sac-winged bat
Hispid cotton rat
Humpback whale
Killer whale
Little brown bat
Muskrat
Nine-banded armadillo
North American beaver
North American porcupine
Northern elephant seal
Northern minke whale
Northern raccoon
Paca
Pallas's long-tongued bat
Pallid bat
Parnell's moustached bat
Pronghorn
Puma
Pygmy sperm whale
Silky anteater
Sperm whale
Spinner dolphin
Spix's disk-winged bat
Striped skunk
Three-toed tree sloths
Valley pocket gopher
Vampire bat
Virginia opossum
Water opossum
White-tailed deer

MOLDOVA
Black-bellied hamster
Common bentwing bat
Edible dormouse
Eurasian wild pig
European badger
Gray wolf
Greater horseshoe bat
Red deer
Red fox

MONACO
European badger
Red fox

MONGOLIA
Ermine
Eurasian wild pig
Gray wolf
Hairy-footed jerboa
Moose
Mountain hare
Northern pika
Przewalski's horse
Red deer
Red fox
Reindeer
Siberian musk deer
Snow leopard

MOROCCO
Blue whale
Common bentwing bat
Common bottlenosed dolphin
Dromedary camel
Eurasian wild pig
European otter
Greater horseshoe bat
Harbor porpoise
Hardwicke's lesser mouse-
  tailed bat
Humpback whale
Killer whale
North Atlantic right whale
Northern bottlenosed whale
Northern minke whale
Pygmy sperm whale
Red deer
Red fox
Sperm whale
Spinner dolphin
Trident leaf-nosed bat

MOZAMBIQUE
Aardvark

African civet
Blue whale
Checkered sengi
Common bentwing bat
Common bottlenosed dolphin
Common genet
Common hippopotamus
Dugong
Egyptian rousette
Egyptian slit-faced bat
Gambian rat
Ground pangolin
Humpback whale
Killer whale
Lord Derby's anomalure
Northern minke whale
Pygmy sperm whale
Rock hyrax
South African porcupine
Sperm whale
Spinner dolphin
Springhare
White rhinoceros

MYANMAR
Asian elephant
Blue whale
Common bentwing bat
Common bottlenosed dolphin
Eurasian wild pig
Gray wolf
Greater horseshoe bat
Humpback whale
Indian flying fox
Indian muntjac
Kitti's hog-nosed bat
Lar gibbon
Lesser Malay mouse deer
Malayan moonrat
Malayan tapir
Northern minke whale
Pygmy sperm whale
Red fox
Red panda
Rhesus macaque
Serow

Sperm whale
Spinner dolphin
Tiger

NAMIBIA
Aardvark
African civet
Blue whale
Common bentwing bat
Common bottlenosed dolphin
Common genet
Common hippopotamus
Damaraland mole-rat
Dassie rat
Egyptian slit-faced bat
Giraffe
Grant's desert golden mole
Ground pangolin
Humpback whale
Killer whale
Kirk's dikdik
Northern minke whale
Pygmy sperm whale
Rock hyrax
Savanna elephant
Sperm whale
Springhare

NEPAL
Asian elephant
Common bentwing bat
Eurasian wild pig
Ganges and Indus dolphin
Gray wolf
Greater horseshoe bat
Indian crested porcupine
Indian muntjac
Indian rhinoceros
Kiang
Red fox
Red panda
Rhesus macaque
Serow
Snow leopard
Water buffalo

NETHERLANDS
Black-bellied hamster
Blue whale
Common bottlenosed dolphin
Ermine
Eurasian wild pig
European badger
Harbor porpoise
Humpback whale
Killer whale
Northern minke whale
Northern raccoon
Pygmy sperm whale
Red deer
Red fox
Sperm whale
Western European hedgehog

NEW ZEALAND
Blue whale
Brush-tailed rock wallaby
Common bottlenosed dolphin
Common brush-tailed possum
Dugong
Humpback whale
Killer whale
Lesser New Zealand short-
  tailed bat
Northern minke whale
Pygmy right whale
Pygmy sperm whale
Shepherd's beaked whale
Sperm whale

NICARAGUA
American least shrew
Blue whale
Brazilian free-tailed bat
Brown-throated three-toed
  sloth
Central American agouti
Collared peccary
Common bottlenosed dolphin
Funnel-eared bat
Geoffroy's spider monkey

Giant anteater
Greater bulldog bat
Greater dog-faced bat
Greater sac-winged bat
Hispid cotton rat
Hoffman's two-toed sloth
Humpback whale
Killer whale
Nine-banded armadillo
Northern minke whale
Paca
Pallas's long-tongued bat
Parnell's moustached bat
Pygmy sperm whale
Silky anteater
Sperm whale
Spinner dolphin
Spiny rat
Spix's disk-winged bat
Three-toed tree sloths
Vampire bat
Virginia opossum
Water opossum
White bat
White-tailed deer
White-throated capuchin

NIGER
Aardvark
Dromedary camel
Egyptian slit-faced bat
Gambian rat
Mzab gundi
Rock hyrax
Senegal bushbaby
Trident leaf-nosed bat

NIGERIA
Aardvark
African civet
Blue whale
Chimpanzee
Common bottlenosed dolphin
Common genet
Dwarf epauletted fruit bat

Egyptian rousette
Egyptian slit-faced bat
Gambian rat
Humpback whale
Lord Derby's anomalure
Northern minke whale
Potto
Pygmy sperm whale
Rock hyrax
Senegal bushbaby
South African porcupine
Sperm whale
Spinner dolphin
Western gorilla
Western red colobus

NORTH KOREA
Blue whale
Common bentwing bat
Common bottlenosed dolphin
Eurasian wild pig
Humpback whale
Killer whale
Northern minke whale
Northern pika
Pygmy sperm whale
Red deer
Siberian musk deer
Sperm whale
Spinner dolphin

NORWAY
Blue whale
Common bottlenosed dolphin
Ermine
Eurasian wild pig
European badger
European otter
Harbor porpoise
Humpback whale
Killer whale
Moose
Mountain hare
North Atlantic right whale
Northern bottlenosed whale

Northern minke whale
Norway lemming
Polar bear
Red deer
Red fox
Reindeer
Sperm whale
Western European hedgehog

OMAN
Blue whale
Common bottlenosed dolphin
Dromedary camel
Dugong
Egyptian rousette
Egyptian spiny mouse
Gray wolf
Humpback whale
Killer whale
Northern minke whale
Pygmy sperm whale
Rock hyrax
Sperm whale
Spinner dolphin
Trident leaf-nosed bat

PAKISTAN
Blue whale
Common bentwing bat
Common bottlenosed dolphin
Dromedary camel
Dugong
Eurasian wild pig
Ganges and Indus dolphin
Gray wolf
Greater horseshoe bat
Hardwicke's lesser mouse-
  tailed bat
Humpback whale
Indian flying fox
Indian muntjac
Indian rhinoceros
Kiang
Killer whale
Northern minke whale

Pygmy sperm whale
Red fox
Rhesus macaque
Snow leopard
Sperm whale
Spinner dolphin
Trident leaf-nosed bat

PANAMA
American least shrew
Blue whale
Brazilian free-tailed bat
Brown-throated three-toed
  sloth
Capybara
Central American agouti
Collared peccary
Common bottlenosed dolphin
Funnel-eared bat
Geoffroy's spider monkey
Giant anteater
Greater bulldog bat
Greater dog-faced bat
Greater sac-winged bat
Hispid cotton rat
Hoffman's two-toed sloth
Humpback whale
Killer whale
Nine-banded armadillo
Northern minke whale
Northern raccoon
Paca
Pallas's long-tongued bat
Parnell's moustached bat
Puma
Pygmy sperm whale
Silky anteater
Smoky bat
Sperm whale
Spinner dolphin
Spiny rat
Spix's disk-winged bat
Three-toed tree sloths
Vampire bat
Water opossum
White bat

White-tailed deer
White-throated capuchin

PAPUA NEW GUINEA
Blue whale
Common bentwing bat
Common bottlenosed dolphin
Dugong
Ground cuscus
Humpback whale
Killer whale
Northern minke whale
Pygmy sperm whale
Rufous spiny bandicoot
Short-beaked echidna
Sperm whale
Spinner dolphin
Sugar glider

PARAGUAY
Brazilian free-tailed bat
Brown-throated three-toed
  sloth
Capybara
Collared peccary
Coypu
Giant anteater
Greater bulldog bat
Maned wolf
Nine-banded armadillo
Paca
Pallas's long-tongued bat
Prehensile-tailed porcupine
Three-toed tree sloths
Vampire bat
Water opossum

PERU
Alpaca
Ashy chinchilla rat
Bald uakari
Blue whale
Boto
Brazilian free-tailed bat
Burmeister's porpoise

Capybara
Central American agouti
Collared peccary
Common bottlenosed
  dolphin
Giant anteater
Goeldi's monkey
Greater bulldog bat
Greater dog-faced bat
Greater sac-winged bat
Hoffman's two-toed sloth
Humpback whale
Killer whale
Llama
Lowland tapir
Maned wolf
Nine-banded armadillo
Northern minke whale
Pacarana
Pallas's long-tongued bat
Parnell's moustached bat
Pearson's tuco-tuco
Pygmy marmoset
Pygmy sperm whale
Silky anteater
Sperm whale
Spinner dolphin
Spix's disk-winged bat
Vampire bat
Water opossum
White-faced saki
White-tailed deer

PHILIPPINES
Blue whale
Common bentwing bat
Common bottlenosed
  dolphin
Dugong
Humpback whale
Naked bat
Northern minke whale
Philippine tarsier
Pygmy sperm whale
Sperm whale
Spinner dolphin

POLAND
Black-bellied hamster
Blue whale
Common bentwing bat
Common bottlenosed
  dolphin
Edible dormouse
Ermine
Eurasian wild pig
European badger
Greater horseshoe bat
Harbor porpoise
Humpback whale
Moose
Northern minke whale
Red deer
Red fox
Sperm whale

PORTUGAL
Blue whale
Common bentwing bat
Common bottlenosed
  dolphin
Common genet
Eurasian wild pig
European badger
European otter
Greater horseshoe bat
Harbor porpoise
Humpback whale
Killer whale
North Atlantic right whale
Northern bottlenosed whale
Northern minke whale
Pygmy sperm whale
Red deer
Red fox
Sperm whale
Western barbastelle
Western European hedgehog

PUERTO RICO
Blue whale
Brazilian free-tailed bat

Common bottlenosed
  dolphin
Funnel-eared bat
Greater bulldog bat
Humpback whale
Killer whale
Northern minke whale
Pygmy sperm whale
Sperm whale
Spinner dolphin

QATAR
Egyptian spiny mouse

ROMANIA
Black-bellied hamster
Common bentwing bat
Edible dormouse
Eurasian wild pig
European badger
Gray wolf
Greater horseshoe bat
Harbor porpoise
Red deer
Red fox

RUSSIA
Beluga
Black-bellied hamster
Blue whale
Common bentwing bat
Common bottlenosed
  dolphin
Edible dormouse
Ermine
Eurasian wild pig
European otter
Gray whale
Gray wolf
Harbor porpoise
Harp seal
Humpback whale
Killer whale
Moose
Mountain hare
Narwhal

Northern minke whale
Northern pika
Northern raccoon
Polar bear
Red deer
Red fox
Reindeer
Siberian musk deer
Snow leopard
Sperm whale
Tiger
Walrus
Western European hedgehog

RWANDA
Aardvark
African civet
Chimpanzee
Common bentwing bat
Common genet
Egyptian slit-faced bat
Gambian rat
Lord Derby's anomalure
Rock hyrax
Senegal bushbaby
South African porcupine

SAUDI ARABIA
Blue whale
Common bottlenosed dolphin
Dromedary camel
Dugong
Egyptian slit-faced bat
Egyptian spiny mouse
Gray wolf
Hardwicke's lesser mouse-
  tailed bat
Humpback whale
Indian crested porcupine
Northern minke whale
Pygmy sperm whale
Rock hyrax
Sperm whale
Spinner dolphin
Trident leaf-nosed bat

SENEGAL
Aardvark
African civet
Blue whale
Chimpanzee
Common bottlenosed dolphin
Common genet
Egyptian slit-faced bat
Gambian rat
Hardwicke's lesser mouse-
  tailed bat
Humpback whale
Killer whale
Northern minke whale
Pygmy sperm whale
Rock hyrax
Senegal bushbaby
South African porcupine
Sperm whale
Spinner dolphin
Western red colobus

SIERRA LEONE
Aardvark
African civet
Blue whale
Chimpanzee
Common bottlenosed dolphin
Common genet
Egyptian slit-faced bat
Forest hog
Gambian rat
Humpback whale
Killer whale
Lord Derby's anomalure
Northern minke whale
Potto
Pygmy hippopotamus
Pygmy sperm whale
Rock hyrax
Senegal bushbaby
South African porcupine
Sperm whale
Spinner dolphin
Western red colobus

SINGAPORE
Lesser Malay mouse deer

SLOVAKIA
Black-bellied hamster
Edible dormouse
Ermine
European badger
Greater horseshoe bat
Red deer
Red fox

SLOVENIA
Blue whale
Common bentwing bat
Common bottlenosed dolphin
Edible dormouse
Ermine
Eurasian wild pig
European badger
Greater horseshoe bat
Humpback whale
Northern minke whale
Pygmy sperm whale
Red deer
Red fox
Sperm whale

SOMALIA
Aardwolf
African civet
Blue whale
Common bentwing bat
Common bottlenosed dolphin
Common genet
Dromedary camel
Dugong
Egyptian slit-faced bat
Humpback whale
Kirk's dikdik
Naked mole-rat
Northern greater bushbaby
Northern minke whale
Pygmy sperm whale

Rock hyrax
Senegal bushbaby
South African porcupine
Sperm whale
Spinner dolphin

SOUTH AFRICA
Aardvark
Aardwolf
African civet
Black wildebeest
Blue whale
Cape horseshoe bat
Common bentwing bat
Common bottlenosed dolphin
Common genet
Damaraland mole-rat
Dassie rat
Egyptian rousette
Egyptian slit-faced bat
Gambian rat
Giraffe
Grant's desert golden mole
Ground pangolin
Humpback whale
Killer whale
Northern minke whale
Pygmy right whale
Pygmy sperm whale
Rock hyrax
Savanna elephant
Shepherd's beaked whale
South African porcupine
Southern tree hyrax
Sperm whale
Spinner dolphin
Springhare

SOUTH KOREA
Blue whale
Common bentwing bat
Common bottlenosed dolphin
Eurasian wild pig
Humpback whale
Killer whale

Northern minke whale
Pygmy sperm whale
Sperm whale
Spinner dolphin

SPAIN
Alpine marmot
Blue whale
Common bentwing bat
Common bottlenosed dolphin
Common genet
Edible dormouse
Eurasian wild pig
European badger
European otter
Gray wolf
Greater horseshoe bat
Harbor porpoise
Humpback whale
Killer whale
North Atlantic right whale
Northern bottlenosed whale
Northern minke whale
Pygmy sperm whale
Red deer
Red fox
Sperm whale
Western barbastelle
Western European hedgehog

SRI LANKA
Asian elephant
European otter
Indian crested porcupine
Indian flying fox
Indian muntjac

SUDAN
Aardvark
African civet
Blue whale
Chimpanzee
Common bottlenosed dolphin
Common genet

Common hippopotamus
Dromedary camel
Dugong
Dwarf epauletted fruit bat
Egyptian slit-faced bat
Gambian rat
Giraffe
Greater cane rat
Ground pangolin
Humpback whale
Northern minke whale
Pygmy sperm whale
Rock hyrax
Senegal bushbaby
South African porcupine
Sperm whale
Spinner dolphin
Spotted hyena
Thomson's gazelle
Trident leaf-nosed bat
White rhinoceros

SURINAME
Blue whale
Collared peccary
Common bottlenosed dolphin
Common squirrel monkey
Funnel-eared bat
Giant anteater
Greater bulldog bat
Greater dog-faced bat
Greater sac-winged bat
Humpback whale
Lowland tapir
Northern minke whale
Paca
Pallas's long-tongued bat
Parnell's moustached bat
Prehensile-tailed porcupine
Pygmy sperm whale
Silky anteater
Smoky bat
Sperm whale
Spinner dolphin
Spix's disk-winged bat
Three-toed tree sloths

Vampire bat
Water opossum
Weeper capuchin
White-faced saki
White-tailed deer

SWAZILAND
Aardvark
African civet
Common bentwing bat
Common genet
Egyptian slit-faced bat
Gambian rat
Giraffe
Ground pangolin
South African porcupine

SWEDEN
Blue whale
Common bottlenosed dolphin
Ermine
Eurasian wild pig
European badger
Gray wolf
Harbor porpoise
Humpback whale
Moose
Mountain hare
Northern minke whale
Norway lemming
Red deer
Red fox
Sperm whale
Western European hedgehog

SWITZERLAND
Alpine marmot
Common bentwing bat
Edible dormouse
Ermine
Eurasian wild pig
European badger
Greater horseshoe bat
Mountain hare
Red deer

Red fox
Western European hedgehog

SYRIA
Blue whale
Common bottlenosed dolphin
Dromedary camel
Egyptian spiny mouse
Eurasian wild pig
Gray wolf
Greater horseshoe bat
Hardwicke's lesser mouse-
tailed bat
Humpback whale
Northern minke whale
Pygmy sperm whale
Red deer
Red fox
Sperm whale
Trident leaf-nosed bat

TAJIKISTAN
Common bentwing bat
Edible dormouse
Ermine
Eurasian wild pig
European badger
Gray wolf
Greater horseshoe bat
Red deer
Red fox
Snow leopard

TANZANIA
Aardvark
African civet
Blue whale
Checkered sengi
Chimpanzee
Common bentwing bat
Common bottlenosed dolphin
Common genet
Common hippopotamus
Dugong
Egyptian rousette

Egyptian slit-faced bat
Gambian rat
Giraffe
Greater cane rat
Ground pangolin
Humpback whale
Killer whale
Kirk's dikdik
Lion
Lord Derby's anomalure
Northern greater bushbaby
Northern minke whale
Pygmy sperm whale
Rock hyrax
Senegal bushbaby
South African porcupine
Sperm whale
Spinner dolphin
Springhare
Thomson's gazelle

THAILAND
Asian elephant
Blue whale
Common bentwing bat
Common bottlenosed dolphin
Common tree shrew
Dugong
Eurasian wild pig
Greater horseshoe bat
Humpback whale
Indian muntjac
Kitti's hog-nosed bat
Lar gibbon
Lesser Malay mouse deer
Malayan colugo
Malayan moonrat
Malayan tapir
Northern minke whale
Pileated gibbon
Pygmy sperm whale
Red fox
Rhesus macaque
Serow
Sperm whale

Spinner dolphin
Water buffalo

TOGO
Aardvark
African civet
Blue whale
Common bottlenosed dolphin
Common genet
Forest hog
Gambian rat
Humpback whale
Lord Derby's anomalure
Northern minke whale
Pygmy sperm whale
Rock hyrax
Senegal bushbaby
South African porcupine
Sperm whale
Spinner dolphin

TRINIDAD AND TOBAGO
Pallas's long-tongued bat
Prehensile-tailed porcupine
Silky anteater
Smoky bat
Vampire bat

TUNISIA
Blue whale
Common bentwing bat
Common bottlenosed dolphin
Common genet
Dromedary camel
Eurasian wild pig
European otter
Greater horseshoe bat
Humpback whale
Killer whale
Northern minke whale
Pygmy sperm whale
Red deer
Red fox
Sperm whale
Trident leaf-nosed bat

TURKEY
Blue whale
Common bentwing bat
Common bottlenosed dolphin
Edible dormouse
Egyptian rousette
Eurasian wild pig
European badger
Gray wolf
Greater horseshoe bat
Harbor porpoise
Humpback whale
Northern minke whale
Pygmy sperm whale
Red deer
Sperm whale

TURKMENISTAN
Common bentwing bat
Edible dormouse
Eurasian wild pig
European badger
Gray wolf
Greater horseshoe bat
Hairy-footed jerboa
Red deer
Red fox

UGANDA
Aardvark
African civet
Checkered sengi
Chimpanzee
Common bentwing bat
Common genet
Dwarf epauletted fruit bat
Egyptian rousette
Egyptian slit-faced bat
Forest hog
Gambian rat
Giraffe
Greater cane rat
Ground pangolin
Lord Derby's anomalure
Potto

Senegal bushbaby
South African porcupine
White rhinoceros

UKRAINE
Alpine marmot
Black-bellied hamster
Common bentwing bat
Edible dormouse
Ermine
Eurasian wild pig
European badger
Gray wolf
Greater horseshoe bat
Harbor porpoise
Moose
Red deer
Red fox

UNITED ARAB EMIRATES
Dromedary camel
Egyptian spiny mouse
Gray wolf
Trident leaf-nosed bat

UNITED KINGDOM
Blue whale
Common bottlenosed dolphin
Ermine
Eurasian wild pig
European badger
European otter
Greater horseshoe bat
Harbor porpoise
Humpback whale
Killer whale
Mountain hare
North Atlantic right whale
Northern bottlenosed whale
Northern minke whale
Pygmy sperm whale
Red deer
Red fox
Sperm whale

Western barbastelle
Western European hedgehog

UNITED STATES
American bison
American black bear
American least shrew
American pika
American water shrew
Beluga
Bighorn sheep
Black-tailed prairie dog
Blue whale
Bobcat
Brazilian free-tailed bat
California leaf-nosed bat
California sea lion
Collared peccary
Common bottlenosed dolphin
Desert cottontail
Eastern chipmunk
Eastern mole
Ermine
Giant kangaroo rat
Gray squirrel
Gray whale
Gray wolf
Harbor porpoise
Hawaiian monk seal
Hispid cotton rat
Humpback whale
Killer whale
Little brown bat
Moose
Mountain beaver
Muskrat
Narwhal
Nine-banded armadillo
North American beaver
North American porcupine
North Atlantic right whale
Northern bottlenosed whale
Northern elephant seal
Northern minke whale
Northern raccoon
Pallid bat

Polar bear
Pronghorn
Puma
Pygmy sperm whale
Red deer
Red fox
Reindeer
San Joaquin pocket mouse
Snowshoe hare
Southern flying squirrel
Sperm whale
Spinner dolphin
Star-nosed mole
Steller's sea cow
Striped skunk
Valley pocket gopher
Virginia opossum
Walrus
West Indian manatee
White-tailed deer

URUGUAY
Blue whale
Brazilian free-tailed bat
Burmeister's porpoise
Capybara
Collared peccary
Common bottlenosed dolphin
Coypu
Franciscana dolphin
Giant anteater
Humpback whale
Killer whale
Maned wolf
Northern minke whale
Pearson's tuco-tuco
Prehensile-tailed porcupine
Pygmy right whale
Red deer
Sperm whale
Vampire bat

UZBEKISTAN
Common bentwing bat
Edible dormouse

Eurasian wild pig
European badger
Gray wolf
Hairy-footed jerboa
Red deer
Red fox
Snow leopard

VENEZUELA
Blue whale
Boto
Brazilian free-tailed bat
Capybara
Collared peccary
Colombian woolly monkey
Common bottlenosed dolphin
Common squirrel monkey
Funnel-eared bat
Giant anteater
Greater bulldog bat
Greater dog-faced bat
Greater sac-winged bat
Hispid cotton rat
Hoffman's two-toed sloth
Humpback whale
Lowland tapir
Northern minke whale
Paca
Pacarana
Pallas's long-tongued bat
Parnell's moustached bat
Prehensile-tailed porcupine
Puma
Pygmy sperm whale
Silky anteater
Silky shrew opossum
Smoky bat
Sperm whale
Spinner dolphin
Spix's disk-winged bat
Three-striped night monkey
Three-toed tree sloths
Vampire bat
Venezuelan red howler
  monkey
Water opossum

Weeper capuchin
White-tailed deer

VIETNAM
Asian elephant
Blue whale
Common bentwing bat
Common bottlenosed dolphin
Dugong
Eurasian wild pig
Greater horseshoe bat
Humpback whale
Indian muntjac
Malayan tapir
Northern minke whale
Pygmy slow loris
Pygmy sperm whale
Red fox
Red-shanked douc langur
Rhesus macaque
Serow
Sperm whale
Spinner dolphin

YEMEN
Blue whale
Common bottlenosed dolphin
Dromedary camel
Dugong
Egyptian rousette

Egyptian slit-faced bat
Egyptian spiny mouse
Gray wolf
Hardwicke's lesser mouse-
    tailed bat
Humpback whale
Northern minke whale
Pygmy sperm whale
Rock hyrax
Sperm whale
Spinner dolphin
Trident leaf-nosed bat

YUGOSLAVIA
Alpine marmot
Blue whale
Common bentwing bat
Common bottlenosed dolphin
Edible dormouse
Ermine
Gray wolf
Greater horseshoe bat
Humpback whale
Northern minke whale
Pygmy sperm whale
Red deer
Sperm whale

ZAMBIA
Aardvark

Aardwolf
African civet
Checkered sengi
Common bentwing bat
Common genet
Common hippopotamus
Egyptian rousette
Egyptian slit-faced bat
Gambian rat
Giraffe
Ground pangolin
Lord Derby's anomalure
South African porcupine
Spotted hyena
Springhare

ZIMBABWE
Aardvark
African civet
Common bentwing bat
Common genet
Damaraland mole-rat
Egyptian rousette
Egyptian slit-faced bat
Gambian rat
Ground pangolin
Savanna elephant
South African porcupine
Spotted hyena
Springhare

Index

Italic type indicates volume number; **boldface** type indicates entries and their pages; (ill.) indicates illustrations.

Cougars. *See* Pumas

Cows, mountain. *See* Tapirs

Cows, sea, *4:* 828–32, **833–40**

Coyotes, *1:* 72, *3:* **583–92**

Coypus, *5:* **1194–99,** 1195 (ill.), 1196 (ill.)

Crab-eater seals, *3:* 580

Craseonycteridae. See Kitti's hog-nosed bats

Craseonycteris thonglongyai. See Kitti's hog-nosed bats

Crested capuchins, *3:* 488

Crested genets, *3:* 629

Crested porcupines
    Indian, *5:* 1115–16, 1115 (ill.), 1116 (ill.)
    North African, *5:* 1114

Cricetomys gambianus. See Gambian rats

Cricetus cricetus. See Black-bellied hamsters

Crocuta crocuta. See Spotted hyenas

Crowned lemurs, *3:* 455–57, 455 (ill.), 456 (ill.)

Cryptomys damarensis. See Damaraland mole-rats

Cryptoprocta ferox. See Fossa

Cryptoprocta spelea, 3: 646

Cryptotis parva. See American least shrews

Ctenodactylidae. See Gundis

Ctenomyidae. See Tuco-tucos

Ctenomys pearsoni. See Pearson's tuco-tucos

Cuban hutias, *5:* 1188, 1189, 1191–93, 1191 (ill.), 1192 (ill.)

Cuban solenodons, *2:* 240, 242

Cuniculus brisson. See Pacas

Cuscomys ashaninki, 5: 1178

Cuscomys oblativa, 5: 1178

Cuscuses, *1:* 99, **116–23**

Cuvier's whales, *4:* 751

Cyclopes didactylus. See Silky anteaters

Cynocephalidae. See Colugos

Cynocephalus variegatus. See Malayan colugos

Cynomys ludovicianus. See Black-tailed prairie dogs

D

Dactylopsilinae. See Striped possums

d'Albertis's ringtail possums, *1:* 156

Dall's porpoises, *4:* 729–30

Damaraland mole-rats, *5:* 1106–7, 1106 (ill.), 1107 (ill.)

Dance of death, *3:* 615

Dassie rats, *5:* **1093–96,** 1094 (ill.), 1095 (ill.)

Dasypodidae. See Armadillos

Dasyprocta punctata. See Central American agoutis

Dasyprocta species, *5:* 1153

Dasyproctidae. See Agoutis

Dasypus novemcinctus. See Nine-banded armadillos

Dasyuridae. See Marsupial cats; Marsupial mice; Tasmanian devils

Dasyuromorphia. See Australasian carnivorous marsupials

Daubentonia madagascariensis. See Aye-ayes

Daubentoniidae. See Aye-ayes

Davis Mountains cottontails, *5:* 1215

De-stressing behavior, *3:* 517

De Winton's golden moles, *2:* 227

Death, dance of, *3:* 615

Decompression sickness, *3:* 691

Deer, *4:* 889–90, **933–53**
    See also Mouse deer

Degus, *5:* 1172, 1173, 1174–75, 1174 (ill.), 1175 (ill.)

Delacour langurs, *3:* 537

Delphinapterus leucas. See Belugas

Delphinidae. See Dolphins

Demidoff's bushbabies, *3:* 436

Dendrohyrax arboreus. See Southern tree hyraxes

Dendrolagus bennettianus. See Bennett's tree kangaroos

Dermoptera. See Colugos

Desert bandicoots, *1:* 77, 82

Desert cottontails, *5:* 1220–21, 1220 (ill.), 1221 (ill.)

Desert golden moles, Grant's, *2:* 226, 229–31, 229 (ill.), 230 (ill.)

Desert rat-kangaroos, *1:* 131–32

Desmans, *2:* **255–62**

Desmarest's hutias. *See* Cuban hutias

Desmodus rotundus. See Vampire bats

Devil fish. *See* Gray whales

Dian's tarsiers, *3:* 481

Dibblers, southern, *1:* 54

Dicerorhinus sumatrensis. See Sumatran rhinoceroses

Diclidurus species, *2:* 304

Didelphidae. See New World opossums

Didelphimorphia. See New World opossums

Didelphis virginiana. See Virginia opossums

Digestive recycling, *1:* 156
    See also specific species

Dikdiks, Kirk's, *4:* 981–82, 981 (ill.), 982 (ill.)

Dingoes, *1:* 63

Dinomyidae. See Pacaranas

Dinomys branickii. See Pacaranas

Dipodidae. *See* Birch mice; Jerboas; Jumping mice

Dipodomys ingens. See Giant kangaroo rats

Diprotodontia, *1:* **99–104**

Dipus sagitta. See Hairy-footed jerboas

Disk-winged bats, *2:* 384, **388–94,** 396

Greater dog-faced bats,
2: 309–10, 309 (ill.), 310 (ill.)
Greater dog-like bats. *See*
Greater dog-faced bats
Greater gliders, *1:* 157–58, 157
(ill.), 158 (ill.)
Greater gliding possums,
1: **154–60**
Greater horseshoe bats, 2: 331,
333–35, 333 (ill.), 334 (ill.)
Greater marsupial moles. *See*
Southern marsupial moles
Greater New Zealand short-
tailed bats, 2: 372, 373
Greater sac-winged bats,
2: 307–8, 307 (ill.), 308 (ill.)
Green ringtails, *1:* 154
Grevy's zebras, *4:* 857–59, 857
(ill.), 858 (ill.)
Grieving elephants, *4:* 811
Grooming, mutual, *3:* 517
Ground cuscuses, *1:* 119–20,
119 (ill.), 120 (ill.)
Ground pangolins, *5:* 993–95,
993 (ill.), 994 (ill.)
Ground sloths, lesser Haitian,
1: 183
Ground squirrels, *5:* 998,
1008, 1009, 1010
Guadalupe fur seals, *3:* 674
Guanacos, *4:* **916–26**
Guano, 2: 401
Guardatinajas. *See* Pacas
Guatemalan black howler
monkeys, *3:* 527
Guenons, *3:* 424, 425
Guinea pigs. *See* Cavies
Gundis, *5:* **1081–86**
Gunn's bandicoots. *See* Eastern
barred bandicoots
Gymnures, 2: 214, **218–24**

H

Hairless bats, 2: 399
Hairy-footed jerboas,
5: 1048–49, 1048 (ill.), 1049
(ill.)

Hairy-nosed wombats, *1:* 102,
103, 111, 112, 113, 115 (ill.)
Haitian solenodons. *See*
Hispaniolan solenodons
Hamsters, *5:* 996, 997, 1051,
1058–59, 1058 (ill.), 1059 (ill.)
Harbor Branch Oceanographic
Institution, *4:* 831
Harbor porpoises, *4:* 730, 731,
732–33, 732 (ill.), 733 (ill.)
Hardwicke's lesser mouse-
tailed bats, 2: 301–3, 301
(ill.), 302 (ill.)
Hares, *5:* 1200–1204, **1213–22**
See also Springhares
Harp seals, *3:* 692–94, 692
(ill.), 693 (ill.)
Hawaiian monk seals, *3:* 582,
691, 698–700, 698 (ill.), 699
(ill.)
Heart-nosed bats, 2: 280, 323
Heart-winged bats, 2: 325
Hector's dolphins, *4:* 737–38,
740
Hedgehog tenrecs, 2: 233–34
Hedgehogs, 2: 213, 215, 216,
218–24
Hees. *See* Pacas
Hemicentetes semispinosus. See
Yellow-streaked tenrecs
Herpestidae. *See* Fossa;
Mongooses
Herpestinae, *3:* 637
Heterocephalus glaber. See
Naked mole-rats
Heteromyidae. *See* Kangaroo
mice; Kangaroo rats; Pocket
mice
Hexaprotodon liberiensis. See
Pygmy hippopotamuses
Highland tuco-tucos, *5:* 1167,
1168
Hildebrandt's horseshoe bats,
2: 330
Hippopotamidae. *See*
Hippopotamuses
Hippopotamus amphibius. See
Common hippopotamuses

Hippopotamuses, *4:* 703, 821,
887, **907–15**
Hippos. *See* Hippopotamuses
Hipposideridae. *See* Old World
leaf-nosed bats
Hispaniolan solenodons,
2: 240, 242, 243–44, 243
(ill.), 244 (ill.)
Hispid cotton rats, *5:* 1064–65,
1064 (ill.), 1065 (ill.)
Hoffmann's two-toed sloths,
1: 183, 186–87, 186 (ill.),
187 (ill.)
Hog-nosed bats, Kitti's,
2: 276, **312–15,** 313 (ill.),
314 (ill.)
Hogs
    forest, *4:* 895–96, 895
        (ill.), 896 (ill.)
    Philippine warty, *4:* 894
    pygmy, *4:* 892, 894
    See also Nine-banded
        armadillos
Hollow-faced bats. *See* Slit-
faced bats
Hominidae. *See* Great apes;
Humans
Homo sapiens. See Humans
Honey badgers, *3:* 614
Honey possums, *1:* 101, 102,
167–71, 168 (ill.), 169 (ill.)
Hoofed mammals. *See* Ungulates
Hooker's sea lions, *3:* 674
Hoolock gibbons, *3:* 552
Hoover hogs. *See* Nine-banded
armadillos
Hopping mice, *5:* 997
Hornbills
    eastern yellow-billed,
        3: 638
    red-billed, *3:* 638
Horses, *4:* 821, 848, 849–53,
854–64
Horseshoe bats, 2: 330–38,
339, 340
Hose's palm civets, *3:* 630
Howler monkeys, *3:* 425,
526–35

Lama pacos. See Alpacas

Land carnivores, *3:* **578–82**

Langurs, *3:* 536
  Delacour, *3:* 537
  golden, *3:* 423
  red-shanked douc, *3:* 537,
    544–45, 544 (ill.), 545
    (ill.)
  white-headed, *3:* 537

Lapas. *See* Pacas

Lar gibbons, *3:* 556–58, 556
  (ill.), 557 (ill.)

Large-eared tenrecs, *2:* 233

Large-footed tree shrews,
  2: 265

Large golden moles, *2:* 227

Laughing hyenas. *See* Spotted
  hyenas

Laurasia, *1:* 26

Leadbeater's possums, *1:* 163

Leaf monkeys, *3:* 424, 536, 537

Leaf-nosed bats
  American, *2:* **345–57**
  Old World, *2:* **339–44**

Least shrews, American,
  2: 250–51, 250 (ill.), 251 (ill.)

Least weasels, *3:* 578, 614

Lemmings, *5:* 996, 1051,
  1056–57, 1056 (ill.), 1057
  (ill.)

Lemmus lemmus. See Norway
  lemmings

Lemur catta. See Ringtailed
  lemurs

Lemur coronatus. See Crowned
  lemurs

Lemuridae. *See* Lemurs

Lemuroid ringtail possums,
  1: 156

Lemurs, *3:* 423, 424, 426,
  450–57
  baboon, *3:* 459
  black, *3:* 424
  dwarf, *3:* **444–49**
  mouse, *3:* 423, **444–49**
  sloth, *3:* 459
  sportive, *3:* **466–71**

woolly, *3:* 459
  See also Colugos

Leopards, snow, *3:* 668–69,
  668 (ill.), 669 (ill.)

Lepilemur leucopus. See White-
  footed sportive lemurs

Lepilemur ruficaudatus. See
  Red-tailed sportive lemurs

Lepilemuridae. *See* Sportive
  lemurs

Leporidae. *See* Hares; Rabbits

Lepus americanus. See
  Snowshoe hares

Lepus timidus. See Mountain
  hares

Lesser anteaters. *See* Tamanduas

Lesser bilbies, *1:* 77, 82, 85

Lesser bulldog bats, *2:* 365

Lesser bushbabies. *See* Senegal
  bushbabies

Lesser cane rats, *5:* 1097–98

Lesser galagos. *See* Senegal
  bushbabies

Lesser gymnures, *2:* 219

Lesser Haitian ground sloths,
  1: 183

Lesser Malay mouse deer,
  4: 928, 930–32, 930 (ill.),
  931 (ill.)

Lesser mouse-tailed bats,
  Hardwicke's, *2:* 301–3, 301
  (ill.), 302 (ill.)

Lesser New Zealand short-
  tailed bats, *2:* 373, 374–76,
  374 (ill.), 375 (ill.)

Lesser weasel lemurs. *See* Red-
  tailed sportive lemurs

Lewis, Meriwether, *4:* 964

Lice, *5:* 1031

Linné's two-toed sloths,
  1: 183, 185

Linsangs, *3:* 582, **628–36**

Lion tamarins, *3:* 426
  black, *3:* 497
  black-faced, *3:* 497
  golden, *3:* 423, 498
  golden-headed, *3:* 498

Lions, *3:* 579, 580, 658,
  659–61, 659 (ill.), 660 (ill.),
  4: 855
    See also Pumas

Lipotes vexillifer. See Baijis

Lipotidae. *See* Baijis

Little brown bats, *2:* 417–18,
  417 (ill.), 418 (ill.)

Livestock, domestic, *4:* 890

Llamas, *4:* **916–26,** 924 (ill.),
  925 (ill.)

Long-beaked echidnas, *1:* 2, 3,
  5, 7, 8, 10

Long-eared bats, *2:* 278
    See also Lesser New
      Zealand short-tailed bats

Long-faced potoroos, *1:* 132

Long-haired spider monkeys,
  3: 425

Long-nosed echidnas. *See*
  Long-beaked echidnas

Long-nosed echymiperas. *See*
  Rufous spiny bandicoots

Long-snouted dolphins. *See*
  Spinner dolphins

Long-tailed bats. *See*
  Hardwicke's lesser mouse-
  tailed bats; Mouse-tailed bats

Long-tailed chinchillas,
  5: 1131, 1132–34, 1132 (ill.),
  1133 (ill.)

Long-tailed pygmy possums,
  1: 150

Long-tailed shrews, *2:* 214, 247

Long-tongued bats, Pallas's,
  2: 353–54, 353 (ill.), 354 (ill.)

Lops, *5:* 1200, 1213

Lord Derby's anomalures,
  5: 1072–74, 1072 (ill.), 1073
  (ill.)

Lorises, *3:* 423, 424, **428–35**

Lorisidae. *See* Lorises; Pottos

Louisiana Department of
  Wildlife and Fisheries, *5:* 1197

Lowland tapirs, *4:* 865–66, 868
  (ill.), 869 (ill.)

Loxodonta africana. See
  Savanna elephants

Pteropodidae. *See* Old World fruit bats

Pteropus giganteus. See Indian flying foxes

Pteropus mariannus. See Marianas fruit bats

Pudu pudu. See Southern pudus

Pudus, southern, *4*: 946–47, 946 (ill.), 947 (ill.)

Puma concolor. See Pumas

Pumas, *3*: 658, 665–67, 665 (ill.), 666 (ill.)

Punarés, *5*: 1182

Pygathrix nemaeus. See Red-shanked douc langurs

Pygmy anteaters. *See* Silky anteaters

Pygmy fruit bats, *2*: 282

Pygmy gliders, *1*: 172–74, 175–77, 175 (ill.), 176 (ill.)

Pygmy hippopotamuses, *4*: 908, 909, 913–14, 913 (ill.), 914 (ill.)

Pygmy hogs, *4*: 892, 894

Pygmy marmosets, *3*: 423, 496, 505–7, 505 (ill.), 506 (ill.)

Pygmy mice, *5*: 996

Pygmy mouse lemurs, *3*: 423, 444

Pygmy possums, *1*: 101, 102, **149–53**

Pygmy rabbits, *5*: 1215

Pygmy right whales, *4*: **783–86,** 785 (ill.), 786 (ill.)

Pygmy shrews, Savi's, *2*: 246

Pygmy sloths. *See* Monk sloths

Pygmy slow lorises, *3*: 428, 431–32, 431 (ill.), 432 (ill.)

Pygmy sperm whales, *4*: 765–66, 765 (ill.), 766 (ill.)

Pygmy squirrels, *5*: 1008

Q

Queensland tube-nosed bats, *2*: 295–97, 295 (ill.), 296 (ill.)

Querétaro pocket gophers, *5*: 1032

Quill pigs. *See* Old World porcupines

Quills, throwing, *5*: 1113

Quolls, spotted-tailed, *1*: 52

R

Rabbit-eared bandicoots. *See* Greater bilbies

Rabbits, *1*: 82, *5*: 1200–1204, **1213–22**

Raccoon dogs, *3*: 583, 629

Raccoons, *3*: 578, 579–80, 581, **605–13**

Rainforest bandicoots. *See* Spiny bandicoots

Rangifer tarandus. See Reindeer

Rat-kangaroos, *1*: **129–34**
    See also Musky rat-kangaroos

Rat opossums. *See* Shrew opossums

Rato de Taquara, *5*: 1183

Rats, *5*: 996–1000, **1051–68**
    cane, *5*: **1097–1102**
    chinchilla, *5*: **1177–81**
    dassie, *5*: **1093–96,** 1094 (ill.), 1095 (ill.)
    kangaroo, *5*: 997, 998, **1036–43**
    plains viscacha, *5*: 1173
    Polynesian, *2*: 373
    rock, *5*: 1173
    spiny, *5*: **1182–87,** 1185 (ill.), 1186 (ill.)
    water, *5*: 998
    See also Mole-rats; Moonrats

Red-backed squirrel monkeys, *3*: 488

Red-billed hornbills, *3*: 638

Red colobus
    eastern, *3*: 537
    western, *3*: 537, 538–40, 538 (ill.), 539 (ill.)

Red deer, *4*: 940–42, 940 (ill.), 941 (ill.)

Red foxes, *1*: 54, 65, 68, 134, *3*: 584, 588–89, 588 (ill.), 589 (ill.)

Red howler monkeys, Venezuelan, *3*: 528–30, 528 (ill.), 529 (ill.)

Red kangaroos, *1*: 101, 140–41, 140 (ill.), 141 (ill.)

Red List of Threatened Species. *See* World Conservation Union (IUCN) Red List of Threatened Species

Red mouse lemurs, *3*: 446, 447–48, 447 (ill.), 448 (ill.)

Red pandas, *3*: 579–80, 605, 606, 610–12, 610 (ill.), 611 (ill.)

Red ruffed lemurs, *3*: 450

Red-shanked douc langurs, *3*: 537, 544–45, 544 (ill.), 545 (ill.)

Red-tailed sportive lemurs, *3*: 469–71, 469 (ill.), 470 (ill.)

Red-toothed shrews, *2*: 248

Red wolves, *3*: 581, 584

Reindeer, *4*: 951–52, 951 (ill.), 952 (ill.)

Rhesus macaques, *3*: 426, 546–47, 546 (ill.), 547 (ill.)

Rhesus monkeys. *See* Rhesus macaques

Rhinoceros unicornis. See Indian rhinoceroses

Rhinoceroses, *4*: 821, 848–50, 852, 853, **874–86**

Rhinocerotidae. *See* Rhinoceroses

Rhinolophidae. *See* Horseshoe bats

Rhinolophus capensis. See Cape horseshoe bats

Rhinolophus ferrumequinum. See Greater horseshoe bats

Rhinopoma hardwickei. See Hardwicke's lesser mouse-tailed bats

Rhinopomatidae. *See* Mouse-tailed bats

Rhinos. *See* Rhinoceroses

Rhynchocyon cirnei. See
Checkered sengis

Right whales, 4: 783, **787–94**
See also Pygmy right
whales

"Rikki-tikki-tavi" (Kipling),
3: 639

Ring-tailed mongooses,
3: 641–43, 641 (ill.), 642 (ill.)

Ringed seals, 3: 594

Ringtail possums, 1: **154–60**

Ringtailed lemurs, 3: 451,
453–54, 453 (ill.), 454 (ill.)

Ringtails, 3: 579, 605, 606
common, 1: 159–60, 159
(ill.), 160 (ill.)
golden, 1: 156
green, 1: 154
See also Ringtail possums

River dolphins. *See* Baijis;
Botos; Franciscana dolphins;
Ganges dolphins; Indus
dolphins

River horses. *See*
Hippopotamuses

River otters, 3: 614, 622

Rock cavies, 5: 1139, 1142–43,
1142 (ill.), 1143 (ill.)

Rock hyraxes, 4: 820, 821,
825–26, 825 (ill.), 826 (ill.)

Rock possums, 1: 155

Rock rats, 5: 1173

Rock wallabies
brush-tailed, 1: 142–43,
142 (ill.), 143 (ill.)
yellow-footed, 1: 101

Rodentia. *See* Rodents

Rodents, 4: 821, 5: **996–1002,**
5: 1202

Rorquals, 4: **795–803**

Rough-haired golden moles,
2: 227

Rough-legged jerboas. *See*
Hairy-footed jerboas

Roundleaf bats. *See* Old World
leaf-nosed bats

Rousette bats, 2: 283

Rousettes, Egyptian, 2: 290–91,
290 (ill.), 291 (ill.)

Rousettus aegyptiacus. See
Egyptian rousettes

Ruatan Island agoutis, 5: 1155

Ruedas, Luis, 5: 1215

Rufescent bandicoots. *See*
Rufous spiny bandicoots

Ruffed lemurs, 3: 450

Rufous sengis, 5: 1223

Rufous spiny bandicoots,
1: 91–93, 91 (ill.), 92 (ill.)

Russet mouse lemurs. *See* Red
mouse lemurs

Russian desmans, 2: 256, 257

Ruwenzori otter shrews, 2: 233

S

Sac-winged bats, 2: **304–11**

Saccopteryx bilineata. See
Greater sac-winged bats

Saccopteryx species, 2: 304,
306

Saguinus oedipus. See Cotton-
top tamarins

Saimiri sciureus. See Common
squirrel monkeys

Sakis, 3: **516–25**

Salim Ali's fruit bats, 2: 315

Salt-desert cavies, 5: 1139,
1140

San Diego Zoo, 5: 1136

San Joaquin pocket mice,
5: 1039–40, 1039 (ill.), 1040
(ill.)

Sand puppies. *See* Naked
mole-rats

Sand swimmers. *See* Yellow
golden moles

Sandhill dunnarts, 1: 54

Sandshoes, 5: 1046

Sarcophilus laniarius. See
Tasmanian devils

Sardinian pikas, 2: 1203,
5: 1207

Sauer, Martin, 4: 835

Savanna baboons, 3: 425

Savanna elephants, 4: 815–16,
815 (ill.), 816 (ill.), 817,
818–19

Save the Bilby Fund, 1: 82, 86

Savi's pygmy shrews, 2: 246

Scalopus aquaticus. See Eastern
moles

Scaly anteaters. *See* Pangolins

Scaly-tailed squirrels,
5: **1069–75**

Scandentia. *See* Tree shrews

Scatterhoarding food, 1: 125

Sciuridae, 5: **1008–21**

Sciurus carolinensis. See Gray
squirrels

Sclater's golden moles, 2: 227

Sea cows, 4: **828–32, 833–40**

Sea lions, 3: 581, 582,
673–83, 4: 707

Sea minks, 3: 581

Sea otters, 3: 579, 582, 614,
4: 707

Seals, 4: 707
crab-eater, 3: 580
eared, 3: 579, 582,
673–83, 690
elephant, 3: 578, 684, 691,
695–97, 695 (ill.), 696
(ill.)
fur, 3: **673–83**
monk, 3: 581, 582, 691,
698–700, 698 (ill.), 699
(ill.)
ringed, 3: 594
true, 3: 579, 582, **690–701**

Sei whales, 4: 797

Self-anointing behavior, 2: 220

Senegal bushbabies, 3: 424,
437, 439–40, 439 (ill.), 440
(ill.)

Sengis, 5: **1223–28**

Serows, 4: 983–84, 983 (ill.),
984 (ill.)

Sewellels. *See* Mountain
beavers

Shakespeare, William, 2: 248

Shark Bay, Australia, 4: 834

Sharks, tiger, 4: 834

Sheath-tailed bats, 2: 304–11

Sheep, 4: 888, 890, 969–87

Shepherd's beaked whales, 4: 749, 755–56, 755 (ill.), 756 (ill.)

Short-beaked echidnas, 1: 2–3, 5, 7–8, 9, 11–13, 11 (ill.), 12 (ill.)

Short-nosed echidnas. See Short-beaked echidnas

Short-tailed bats, New Zealand, 2: 371–77

Short-tailed chinchillas, 5: 1131

Short-tailed opossums, gray, 1: 28

Short-tailed shrews, 2: 247, 248

Shrew moles, 2: 255–62

Shrew opossums, 1: 37–43

Shrews, 2: 213–14, 215, 216, 246–54
    otter, 2: 232, 233, 234
    tree, 2: 263–68, 1202, 5: 1224
    true, 1: 37, 5: 1224
    See also Sengis

Siamangs, 3: 552, 559–61, 559 (ill.), 560 (ill.)

Siberian musk deer, 4: 935–36, 935 (ill.), 936 (ill.)

Siberian pikas. See Northern pikas

Sifakas, 3: 425, 458–65

Sigmodon hispidus. See Hispid cotton rats

Silky anteaters, 1: 179, 180, 195, 196, 198–99, 198 (ill.), 199 (ill.)

Silky shrew opossums, 1: 38–39, 40, 41–42, 41 (ill.), 42 (ill.)

Silky tuco-tucos, 5: 1167

Silverbacks, 3: 564, 568

Sirenia, 4: 828–32

Skunks, 3: 578, 579, 614–27, 637

Sleep, dolphins, 4: 720

Slender gray lorises, 3: 428

Slender lorises, 3: 428–29

Slit-faced bats, 2: 316–22

Sloth bears, 3: 593, 594, 595

Sloth lemurs, 3: 459

Sloths, 1: 178–82
    three-toed tree, 1: 178, 181, 189–94
    two-toed tree, 1: 178, 180, 183–88
    West Indian, 1: 183–88

Slow lorises, 3: 428

Small-eared galagos. See Northern greater bushbabies

Small-eared shrews, 2: 247

Small mouse-tailed bats, 2: 299

Small Sulawesi cuscuses, 1: 116

Smoky bats, 2: 383–87, 385 (ill.), 386 (ill.)

Smooth-tailed tree shrews, Bornean, 2: 265

Smooth-toothed pocket gophers. See Valley pocket gophers

Snow leopards, 3: 668–69, 668 (ill.), 669 (ill.)

Snowshoe hares, 5: 1214, 1216–17, 1216 (ill.), 1217 (ill.)

Snub-nosed monkeys, 3: 426, 537

Social tuco-tucos, 5: 1167, 1168

Solenodon paradoxus. See Hispaniolan solenodons

Solenodons, 2: 215, 240–45

Solenodontidae. See Solenodons

Somali sengis, 5: 1225

Sorex palustris. See American water shrews

Soricidae. See Shrews

South African porcupines, 5: 1117–19, 1117 (ill.), 1118 (ill.)

South American beavers. See Coypus

South American mice, 5: 1051, 1052

South American rats, 5: 1051, 1052

Southern brown bandicoots, 1: 76, 80

Southern dibblers, 1: 54

Southern elephant seals, 3: 578

Southern flying squirrels, 5: 1011–12, 1011 (ill.), 1012 (ill.)

Southern hairy-nosed wombats, 1: 103, 111, 112

Southern marsupial moles, 1: 96, 97–98, 97 (ill.), 98 (ill.)

Southern muriquis, 3: 527

Southern opossums, 1: 28

Southern pudus, 4: 946–47, 946 (ill.), 947 (ill.)

Southern tamanduas, 1: 179, 195

Southern tree hyraxes, 4: 823–24, 823 (ill.), 824 (ill.)

Southern two-toed sloths. See Linné's two-toed sloths

Species, introduced, 1: 65
    See also specific species

Spectacled bears, 3: 593, 594, 595

Spectacled porpoises, 4: 729–30, 731

Spectral vampire bats, 2: 345, 347

Sperm whales, 4: 758–66, 761 (ill.), 762 (ill.)

Spermaceti, 4: 759

Spider monkeys, 3: 425, 526–35

Spinner dolphins, 4: 706, 746–47, 746 (ill.), 747 (ill.)

Spiny anteaters. See Echidnas

Spiny bandicoots, 1: 74, 75, 88–93

Spiny mice, Egyptian, 5: 1060–61, 1060 (ill.), 1061 (ill.)

Spiny rats, 5: 1182–87, 1185 (ill.), 1186 (ill.)

on western barbastelles,
2: 416
on western gorillas, 3: 570
on white bats, 2: 356
on woolly monkeys,
3: 534
on Xenarthra, 1: 181
World Wildlife Fund, 4: 797
Wroughton free-tailed bats,
2: 402

X

Xenarthra, *1:* **178–82**

Y

Yapoks. *See* Water opossums
Yellow-bellied gliders, *1:* 163
Yellow-breasted capuchins,
3: 488
Yellow-footed rock wallabies,
1: 101
Yellow golden moles, 2: 226
Yellow-streaked tenrecs,
2: 237–38, 237 (ill.), 238 (ill.)
Yellow-tailed woolly monkeys,
3: 527
Yellow-winged bats, 2: 324,
325

Yellowstone National Park,
3: 587
Yerbua capensis. See Springhares

Z

Zalophus californianus. See
California sea lions
Zalophus wollebaeki. See
Galápagos sea lions
Zebras, 4: 848–50, 852,
854–64
Zenkerella species, 5: 1069
Ziphiidae. See Beaked whales